The Quran With Tafsir Ibn Kathir Part 15 of 30: Al Israa 001 To Al Kahf 074

The Quran With Tafsir Ibn Kathir
Part 15 of 30:
Al Israa 001 To
Al Kahf 074

With
Arabic Script, Transliteration of Arabic, Meaning in English
and Ibn Kathir's Abridged Tafsir (Explanation)

Muhammad Saed Abdul-Rahman

BSc, DipHE

© Muhammad Saed Abdul-Rahman, 2012
ISBN 978-1-86179-870-1

All Rights reserved

British Library Cataloguing in Publication Data. A Catalogue record for this book is available from the British Library

Designed, Typeset and produced by:
MSA Publication Limited, 4 Bello Close, Herne Hill,
London SE24 9BW
United Kingdom

Cover design: Houriyah Abdul-Rahman

TABLE OF CONTENTS

TABLE OF CONTENTS V

PRELUDE XV

   OPENING SERMAN XV
   OUR MISSION XVI
   BIOGRAPHY OF HAFIZ IBN KATHIR (701 H - 774 H) XVI
      Ibn Kathir's Teachers xvi
      Ibn Kathir's Students xvii
      Ibn Kathir's Books xvii
      Ibn Kathir's Death xviii

PREFACE XIX

   ABOUT THIS BOOK XIX
   PERFORMING PROSTRATION WHILE READING THE QUR'AN XIX

PART 15 FULL ARABIC TEXT 1

INTRODUCTION TO CHAPTER (SURAH) 17: AL-ISRAA (THE NIGHT JOURNEY, OR BANI ISRA'IL, OR THE CILDREN OF ISRAEL) 13

   IBN KATHIR'S INTRODUCTION 13
      The Virtues of Surat Al-Isra' 13

CHAPTER (SURAH) 17: AL-ISRAA (THE NIGHT JOURNEY, OR BANI ISRAIL, OR THE CILDREN OF ISRAEL), VERSES 001–111 13

   Surah: 17 Ayah: 1 13
      Tafsir Ibn Kathir 13
         The Isra' (Night Journey) 13
         The Report of Anas bin Malik 14
         The Report of Anas bin Malik from Malik bin Sa`sa`ah 16
         The Report of Anas from Abu Dharr 20
         The Report of Jabir bin `Abdullah 23
         The Report of `Abdullah bin `Abbas 24
         The Report of `Abdullah bin Mas`ud 27
         The Report of Abu Hurayrah 27
         The Time that Isra' took place, and the Fact that it included both Body and Soul, when the Prophet was awake, not in a Dream 29
         An Interesting Story 30
   Surah: 17 Ayah: 2 & Ayah: 3 31
      Tafsir Ibn Kathir 32
         Musa and how He was given the Tawrah 32
   Surah: 17 Ayah: 4, Ayah: 5, Ayah: 6, Ayah: 7 & Ayah: 8 33
      Tafsir Ibn Kathir 34
         It was mentioned in the Tawrah that the Jews would spread Mischief twice 34

- The First Episode of Mischief caused by the Jews, and their Punishment for it 34
- The Second Episode of Mischief 35

Surah: 17 Ayah: 9 & Ayah: 10 36
- Tafsir Ibn Kathir 36
  - Praising the Qur'an 36

Surah: 17 Ayah: 11 37
- Tafsir Ibn Kathir 37
  - Man's Haste and Prayers against Himself 37

Surah: 17 Ayah: 12 38
- Tafsir Ibn Kathir 38
  - The Night and Day are Signs of the Great Power of Allah 38

Surah: 17 Ayah: 13 & Ayah: 14 39
- Tafsir Ibn Kathir 40
  - Every Person will have the Book of his Deeds with Him 40

Surah: 17 Ayah: 15 41
- Tafsir Ibn Kathir 42
  - No One will have to bear the Sins of Another 42
  - No Punishment until a Messenger has been sent 42
  - The Issue of Small Children who die 43
  - The Second Hadith from Abu Hurayrah 44
  - The Third Hadith from Samurah 44
  - The Fourth Hadith from the Paternal Uncle of Hasna 45
  - It is Makruh to discuss this Matter 45

Surah: 17 Ayah: 16 46
- Tafsir Ibn Kathir 46
  - Meanings of Amarna 46

Surah: 17 Ayah: 17 47
- Tafsir Ibn Kathir 47
  - A Threat to Quraysh 47

Surah: 17 Ayah: 18 & Ayah: 19 47
- Tafsir Ibn Kathir 48
  - The Reward of Those who desire this World and Those who desire the Hereafter 48

Surah: 17 Ayah: 20 & Ayah: 21 48
- Tafsir Ibn Kathir 49

Surah: 17 Ayah: 22 50
- Tafsir Ibn Kathir 50
  - Do not associate Anything in Worship with Allah 50

Surah: 17 Ayah: 23 & Ayah: 24 50
- Tafsir Ibn Kathir 51
  - The Command to Worship Allah Alone and to be Dutiful to One's Parents 51
  - Another Hadith Imam Ahmad reported from Abu Hurayrah that the Prophet said: 52
  - Another Hadith 52
  - Another Hadith 53
  - Another Hadith 53

Surah: 17 Ayah: 25 53

Table of Contents

Tafsir Ibn Kathir 54
    Omissions comitted against Parents are pardoned with Good Relations and Repentance
    54
Surah: 17 Ayah: 26, Ayah: 27 & Ayah: 28 54
    Tafsir Ibn Kathir 55
    The Command to maintain the Ties of Kinship and the Prohibition of Extravagance 55
Surah: 17 Ayah: 29 & Ayah: 30 57
    Tafsir Ibn Kathir 57
    Moderation in Spending 57
Surah: 17 Ayah: 31 59
    Tafsir Ibn Kathir 59
    Prohibition of killing Children 59
    Surah: 17 Ayah: 32 60
    Tafsir Ibn Kathir 60
    The Command to avoid Zina (Unlawful Sex) and Everything that leads to it 60
Surah: 17 Ayah: 33 62
    Tafsir Ibn Kathir 62
    Prohibition of Unlawful Killing. Allah forbids killing with no legitimate reason 62
Surah: 17 Ayah: 34 & Ayah: 35 63
    Tafsir Ibn Kathir 64
    The Command to handle the Orphan's Wealth properly and to be Honest in Weights and
    Measures 64
Surah: 17 Ayah: 36 65
    Tafsir Ibn Kathir 65
    Do not speak without Knowledge 65
Surah: 17 Ayah: 37 & Ayah: 38 66
    Tafsir Ibn Kathir 66
    Condemnation of strutting 66
Surah: 17 Ayah: 39 67
    Tafsir Ibn Kathir 67
    Everything previously mentioned is Revelation and Wisdom 67
Surah: 17 Ayah: 40 67
    Tafsir Ibn Kathir 68
    Refutation of Those Who claim that the Angels are Daughters of Allah 68
Surah: 17 Ayah: 41 68
    Tafsir Ibn Kathir 68
Surah: 17 Ayah: 42 & Ayah: 43 69
    Tafsir Ibn Kathir 69
Surah: 17 Ayah: 44 69
    Tafsir Ibn Kathir 70
    Everything glorifies Allah 70
Surah: 17 Ayah: 45 & Ayah: 46 71
    Tafsir Ibn Kathir 72
    The Veil over the Hearts of the Idolators 72

- Surah: 17 Ayah: 47 & Ayah: 48 ... 73
  - Tafsir Ibn Kathir ... 74
    - The Secret Counsel of Quraysh after hearing the Qur'an ... 74
- Surah: 17 Ayah: 49, Ayah: 50, Ayah: 51 & Ayah: 52 ... 75
  - Tafsir Ibn Kathir ... 75
    - Refutation of Those Who do not believe in Life after Death ... 75
- Surah: 17 Ayah: 53 ... 78
  - Tafsir Ibn Kathir ... 78
    - People should speak Good Words with Politeness ... 78
- Surah: 17 Ayah: 54 & Ayah: 55 ... 78
  - Tafsir Ibn Kathir ... 79
    - The Preference of some Prophets above Others ... 79
- Surah: 17 Ayah: 56 & Ayah: 57 ... 80
  - Tafsir Ibn Kathir ... 81
    - The gods of the Idolators can neither benefit nor harm; rather they themselves seek to draw close to Allah ... 81
- Surah: 17 Ayah: 58 ... 82
  - Tafsir Ibn Kathir ... 82
    - The Destruction or Torment of all Disbelieving Towns before the Hour begins ... 82
- Surah: 17 Ayah: 59 ... 82
  - Tafsir Ibn Kathir ... 83
    - The Reason why Allah did not send Signs or Miracles ... 83
- Surah: 17 Ayah: 60 ... 84
  - Tafsir Ibn Kathir ... 85
    - Allah has encompassed Mankind and made the Vision of His Prophet a Trial for Them ... 85
- Surah: 17 Ayah: 61 & Ayah: 62 ... 86
  - Tafsir Ibn Kathir ... 86
    - The Story of Adam and Iblis ... 86
- Surah: 17 Ayah: 63, Ayah: 64 & Ayah: 65 ... 87
  - Tafsir Ibn Kathir ... 87
- Surah: 17 Ayah: 66 ... 89
  - Tafsir Ibn Kathir ... 90
    - Ships are a Sign of the Mercy of Allah ... 90
- Surah: 17 Ayah: 67 ... 90
  - Tafsir Ibn Kathir ... 90
    - When Harm befalls Them, the Disbelievers do not remember anyone except Allah ... 90
- Surah: 17 Ayah: 68 ... 91
  - Tafsir Ibn Kathir ... 91
    - Does not the Punishment of Allah come on Land too ... 91
- Surah: 17 Ayah: 69 ... 91
  - Tafsir Ibn Kathir ... 92
    - Perhaps He will send You back to the Sea ... 92
- Surah: 17 Ayah: 70 ... 92
  - Tafsir Ibn Kathir ... 92

Table of Contents

The Honor and noble Nature of Man 92
Surah: 17 Ayah: 71 & Ayah: 72 93
Tafsir Ibn Kathir 93
Everyone will be called by his Imam on the Day of Resurrection 93
Surah: 17 Ayah: 73, Ayah: 74 & Ayah: 75 95
Tafsir Ibn Kathir 96
How the Prophet would have been punished if He had given in at all to the Disbelievers' Demands that He change some of the Revelation 96
Surah: 17 Ayah: 76 & Ayah: 77 96
Tafsir Ibn Kathir 97
The Reason why these Ayat were revealed 97
Surah: 17 Ayah: 78 & Ayah: 79 97
Tafsir Ibn Kathir 98
The Command to offer the Prayers at their appointed Times 98
The Meeting of the Angels at the Times of Fajr and `Asr Prayers 98
The Command to pray Tahajjud 99
The Hadith of Abu Hurayrah 102
Surah: 17 Ayah: 80 & Ayah: 81 105
Tafsir Ibn Kathir 106
The Command to emigrate 106
A Threat to the Disbelievers of the Quraysh 106
Surah: 17 Ayah: 82 107
Tafsir Ibn Kathir 107
The Qur'an is a Cure and a Mercy 107
Surah: 17 Ayah: 83 & Ayah: 84 108
Tafsir Ibn Kathir 108
Turning away from Allah at Times of Ease and despairing at Times of Calamity 108
Surah: 17 Ayah: 85 109
Tafsir Ibn Kathir 109
The Ruh (spirit) 109
The Ruh and the Nafs 110
Surah: 17 Ayah: 86, Ayah: 87, Ayah: 88 & Ayah: 89 111
Tafsir Ibn Kathir 112
If Allah willed, He could take away the Qur'an 112
Challenging by the Qur'an 112
Surah: 17 Ayah: 90, Ayah: 91, Ayah: 92 & Ayah: 93 112
Tafsir Ibn Kathir 113
The Demand of Quraysh for a specific Sign, and the Rejection of that 113
Untitled 113
Untitled 114
The Reason why the Idolators' Demands were refused 116
Surah: 17 Ayah: 94 & Ayah: 95 118
Tafsir Ibn Kathir 118
The refusal of the Idolators to believe because the Messenger was a Human -- and its refutation 118

Surah: 17 Ayah: 96 119
    Tafsir Ibn Kathir 119
Surah: 17 Ayah: 97 120
    Tafsir Ibn Kathir 120
        Guidance and Misguidance are in the Hands of Allah 120
        The Punishment of the People of Misguidance 120
Surah: 17 Ayah: 98 & Ayah: 99 121
    Tafsir Ibn Kathir 121
        Allah says: 'This punishment, being resurrected blind, dumb and deaf, is what they deserve, because they disbelieved, ... 121
Surah: 17 Ayah: 100 122
    Tafsir Ibn Kathir 123
        Holding back is Part of Man's Nature 123
Surah: 17 Ayah: 101, Ayah: 102, Ayah: 103 & Ayah: 104 123
    Tafsir Ibn Kathir 124
        The Nine Signs of Musa 124
        The Destruction of Fir`awn and His People 125
Surah: 17 Ayah: 105 & Ayah: 106 126
    Tafsir Ibn Kathir 126
        The Revelation of the Qur'an in Stages 126
Surah: 17 Ayah: 107, Ayah: 108 & Ayah: 109 127
    Tafsir Ibn Kathir 128
        Those Who were given Knowledge before truly admit the Qur'an 128
Surah: 17 Ayah: 110 & Ayah: 111 128
    Tafsir Ibn Kathir 129
        To Allah belong the Most Beautiful Names 129
        The Command to recite neither loudly nor softly 130
        Declaration of Tawhid 130

INTRODUCTION TO CHAPTER (SURAH) 18: AL-KAHF (THE CAVE) 131

    IBN KATHIR'S INTRODUCTION 131
        What has been mentioned about the Virtues of this Surah and the first and last ten Ayat, which provide protection from the Dajjal 131

CHAPTER 18: AL-KAHF (THE CAVE), VERSES 001–074 132

    Surah: 18 Ayah: 1, Ayah: 2, Ayah: 3, Ayah: 4 & Ayah: 5 132
        Tafsir Ibn Kathir 133
        The Revelation of the Qur'an brings both Good News and a Warning 133
        Reason why this Surah was revealed 134
    Surah: 18 Ayah: 6, Ayah: 7 & Ayah: 8 135
        Tafsir Ibn Kathir 136
        Do not feel sorry because the Idolators do not believe. Allah consoles His Messenger for his sorrow over the idolators because they would not believe and keep away from him. He also said: 136

Table of Contents

Surah: 18 Ayah: 9, Ayah: 10, Ayah: 11 & Ayah: 12 .... *137*
    Tafsir Ibn Kathir 137
        The Story of the People of Al-Kahf. Here Allah tells us about the story of the people of Al-Kahf in brief and general terms, then He explains it in more detail. He says: 137

Surah: 18 Ayah: 13, Ayah: 14, Ayah: 15 & Ayah: 16 .... *139*
    Tafsir Ibn Kathir 140
        Their Belief in Allah and their Retreat from their People 140

Surah: 18 Ayah: 17 .... *143*
    Tafsir Ibn Kathir 143
        The Location of the Cave. This indicates that the entrance to the cave faced north, because Allah tells us that when the sun was rising, sunlight entered the cave 143

Surah: 18 Ayah: 18 .... *144*
    Tafsir Ibn Kathir 145
        Their Sleep in the Cave 145

Surah: 18 Ayah: 19 & Ayah: 20 .... *146*
    Tafsir Ibn Kathir 146
        Their awakening and sending One of Themselves to buy Food. Allah says: `just as We caused them to sleep, We resurrected them with their bodies, hair and skin intact, and nothing lacking in their form and appearance.' This was after three hundred and nine years. This is why they asked each other, ... 146

Surah: 18 Ayah: 21 .... *147*
    Tafsir Ibn Kathir 148
        How the People of the City came to know about Them; building a Memorial over the Cave 148

Surah: 18 Ayah: 22 .... *149*
    Tafsir Ibn Kathir 150
        Their Number 150

Surah: 18 Ayah: 23 & Ayah: 24 .... *150*
    Tafsir Ibn Kathir 151
        Saying "If Allah wills" when determining to do Something in the Future 151

Surah: 18 Ayah: 25 & Ayah: 26 .... *152*
    Tafsir Ibn Kathir 153
        The Length of their Stay in the Cave 153

Surah: 18 Ayah: 27 & Ayah: 28 .... *154*
    Tafsir Ibn Kathir 154
        The Command to recite the Qur'an and to patiently keep Company with the Believers 154

Surah: 18 Ayah: 29 .... *156*
    Tafsir Ibn Kathir 156
        The Truth is from Allah, and the Punishment of Those Who do not believe in it 156

Surah: 18 Ayah: 30 & Ayah: 31 .... *157*
    Tafsir Ibn Kathir 158
        The Reward of those Who believe and do Righteous Deeds 158

Surah: 18 Ayah: 32, Ayah: 33, Ayah: 34, Ayah: 35 & Ayah: 36 .... *159*
    Tafsir Ibn Kathir 160

The Example of the Rich Idolators and the Poor Muslims 160
Surah: 18 Ayah: 37, Ayah: 38, Ayah: 39, Ayah: 40 & Ayah: 41 161
    Tafsir Ibn Kathir 162
        The Response of the Poor Believer 162
Surah: 18 Ayah: 42, Ayah: 43 & Ayah: 44 163
    Tafsir Ibn Kathir 164
        The Evil Results of Kufr 164
Surah: 18 Ayah: 45 & Ayah: 46 165
    Tafsir Ibn Kathir 165
        The Parable of the Worldly Life 165
        Between Wealth and Good Deeds 166
Surah: 18 Ayah: 47, Ayah: 48 & Ayah: 49 167
    Tafsir Ibn Kathir 168
        The Major Terrors of the Hour 168
Surah: 18 Ayah: 50 171
    Tafsir Ibn Kathir 172
        The Story of Adam and Iblis 172
Surah: 18 Ayah: 51 173
    Tafsir Ibn Kathir 173
        The gods of the Idolators did not witness the Creation of anything, not even Themselves
        173
Surah: 18 Ayah: 52 & Ayah: 53 174
    Tafsir Ibn Kathir 174
        Their Partners are not able to respond and the Criminals are brought to the Fire 174
Surah: 18 Ayah: 54 175
    Tafsir Ibn Kathir 176
        Examples put forth in the Qur'an 176
Surah: 18 Ayah: 55 & Ayah: 56 176
    Tafsir Ibn Kathir 177
        The Rebellion of the Disbelievers 177
Surah: 18 Ayah: 57, Ayah: 58 & Ayah: 59 178
    Tafsir Ibn Kathir 178
        The Worst People are Those Who turn away after being reminded 178
Surah: 18 Ayah: 60, Ayah: 61, Ayah: 62, Ayah: 63, Ayah: 64 & Ayah: 65 179
    Tafsir Ibn Kathir 180
        The Story of Musa and Al-Khidr 180
Surah: 18 Ayah: 66, Ayah: 67, Ayah: 68, Ayah: 69 & Ayah: 70 183
    Tafsir Ibn Kathir 184
        Musa meeting with Al-Khidr and accompanying Him 184
Surah: 18 Ayah: 71, Ayah: 72 & Ayah: 73 185
    Tafsir Ibn Kathir 186
        Damaging the Boat 186
Surah: 18 Ayah: 74 (end of Part 15), Ayah: 75 & Ayah: 76 (beginning of Part 16; included here for completing the tafsir that follows) 186

Table of Contents

Tafsir Ibn Kathir 187
    The Story of killing the Boy 187

PRELUDE

Opening Serman

Indeed, all praise is due to Allah. We praise Him and seek His help and forgiveness. We seek refuge with Allah from our soul's evil and our wrong doings. He whom Allah guides, no one can misguide; and he whom He misguides, no one can guide

I bear witness that there is no (true) god except Allah – alone without a partner, and I bear witness that Muhammad (peace and blessings of Allah be upon him) is His 'abd (servant) and messenger.

$$\text{يَٰٓأَيُّهَا ٱلَّذِينَ ءَامَنُواْ ٱتَّقُواْ ٱللَّهَ حَقَّ تُقَاتِهِۦ وَلَا تَمُوتُنَّ إِلَّا وَأَنتُم مُّسۡلِمُونَ}$$

O you who believe! Fear Allâh (by doing all that He has ordered and by abstaining from all that He has forbidden) as He should be feared. (Obey Him, be thankful to Him, and remember Him always), and die not except in a state of Islâm (as Muslims (with complete submission to Allâh)).

$$\text{يَٰٓأَيُّهَا ٱلنَّاسُ ٱتَّقُواْ رَبَّكُمُ ٱلَّذِى خَلَقَكُم مِّن نَّفۡسٖ وَٰحِدَةٖ وَخَلَقَ مِنۡهَا زَوۡجَهَا وَبَثَّ مِنۡهُمَا رِجَالٗا كَثِيرٗا وَنِسَآءٗۚ وَٱتَّقُواْ ٱللَّهَ ٱلَّذِى تَسَآءَلُونَ بِهِۦ وَٱلۡأَرۡحَامَۚ إِنَّ ٱللَّهَ كَانَ عَلَيۡكُمۡ رَقِيبٗا}$$

O mankind! Be dutiful to your Lord, Who created you from a single person (Adam), and from him (Adam) He created his wife (Hawwâ (Eve)) and from them both He created many men and women; and fear Allâh through Whom you demand (your mutual rights), and (do not cut the relations of) the wombs (kinship). Surely, Allâh is Ever an All-Watcher over you.

$$\text{يُصۡلِحۡ لَكُمۡ أَعۡمَٰلَكُمۡ وَيَغۡفِرۡ لَكُمۡ ذُنُوبَكُمۡۗ وَمَن يُطِعِ ٱللَّهَ وَرَسُولَهُۥ فَقَدۡ فَازَ فَوۡزًا عَظِيمًا}$$

He will direct you to do righteous good deeds and will forgive you your sins. And whosoever obeys Allâh and His Messenger (peace be upon him), he has indeed achieved a great achievement (i.e. he will be saved from the Hell-fire and will be admitted to Paradise).

Indeed, the best speech is Allah's Book and the best guidance is Muhammad's () guidance. The worst affairs (of religion) are those innovated (by people), for every such innovation is an act of misguidance leading to the Fire

Our Mission

Our mission is to gather in one place, for the English-speaking public, all relevant information needed to make the Qur'an more understandable and easier to study. This book tries to do this by providing the following:

1. The Arabic Text for those who are able to read Arabic
2. Transliteration of the Arabic text for those who are unable to read the Arabic script. This will give them a sample of the sound of the Qur'an, which they could not otherwise comprehend from reading the English meaning.
3. The meaning of the qur'an (translated by Dr. Muhammad Taqi-ud-Din Al-Hilali, Ph.D. and Dr. Muhammad Muhsin Khan)
4. Explanation (abridged Tafsir) by Ibn Kathir (translated by Safi-ur-Rahman al-Mubarakpuri)

We hope that by doing this an ordinary English-speaker will be able to pick up a copy of this book and study and comprehend The Glorious Qur'an in a way that is acceptable to the understanding of the Rightly-guided Muslim Ummah (Community).

Biography of Hafiz Ibn Kathir (701 H - 774 H)

By the Honored Shaykh `Abdul-Qadir Al-Arna'ut, may Allah protect him.

He is the respected Imam, Abu Al-Fida', `Imad Ad-Din Isma il bin 'Umar bin Kathir Al-Qurashi Al-Busrawi - Busraian in origin; Dimashqi in training, learning and residence.

Ibn Kathir was born in the city of Busra in 701 H. His father was the Friday speaker of the village, but he died while Ibn Kathir was only four years old. Ibn Kathir's brother, Shaykh Abdul-Wahhab, reared him and taught him until he moved to Damascus in 706 H., when he was five years old.

Ibn Kathir's Teachers

Ibn Kathir studied Fiqh - Islamic jurisprudence - with Burhan Ad-Din, Ibrahim bin `Abdur-Rahman Al-Fizari, known as Ibn Al-Firkah (who died in 729 H). Ibn Kathir heard Hadiths from `Isa bin Al-Mutim, Ahmad bin Abi Talib, (Ibn Ash-Shahnah) (who died in 730 H), Ibn Al-Hajjar, (who died in 730 H), and the Hadith narrator of Ash-Sham (modern day Syria and surrounding areas); Baha Ad-Din Al-Qasim bin Muzaffar bin `Asakir (who died in 723 H), and Ibn Ash-Shirdzi, Ishaq bin Yahya Al-Ammuddi, also known as `Afif Ad-Din, the Zahiriyyah Shaykh who died in 725 H, and Muhammad bin Zarrad. He remained with Jamal Ad-Din, Yusuf bin Az-Zaki AlMizzi who died in 724 H, he benefited from his knowledge and also married his daughter. He also read with Shaykh Al-Islam, Taqi Ad-Din Ahmad bin `Abdul-Halim bin `Abdus-Salam bin Taymiyyah who died in 728 H. He also read with the Imam Hafiz and historian Shams Ad-Din, Muhammad bin Ahmad bin Uthman bin Qaymaz Adh-Dhahabi, who died in 748 H. Also, Abu Musa Al-Qarafai, Abu Al-Fath Ad-Dabbusi and

'Ali bin `Umar As-Suwani and others who gave him permission to transmit the knowledge he learned with them in Egypt.

In his book, Al-Mu jam Al-Mukhtas, Al-Hafiz Adh-Dhaliabi wrote that Ibn Kathir was, "The Imam, scholar of jurisprudence, skillful scholar of Hadith, renowned Faqih and scholar of Tafsir who wrote several beneficial books."

Further, in Ad-Durar Al-Kdminah, Al-Hafiz Ibn Hajar AlAsqalani said, "Ibn Kathir worked on the subject of the Hadith in the areas of texts and chains of narrators. He had a good memory, his books became popular during his lifetime, and people benefited from them after his death."

Also, the renowned historian Abu Al-Mahasin, Jamal Ad-Din Yusuf bin Sayf Ad-Din (Ibn Taghri Bardi), said in his book, AlManhal As-Safi, "He is the Shaykh, the Imam, the great scholar `Imad Ad-Din Abu Al-Fida'. He learned extensively and was very active in collecting knowledge and writing. He was excellent in the areas of Fiqh, Tafsir and Hadith. He collected knowledge, authored (books), taught, narrated Hadith and wrote. He had immense knowledge in the fields of Hadith, Tafsir, Fiqh, the Arabic language, and so forth. He gave Fatawa (religious verdicts) and taught until he died, may Allah grant him mercy. He was known for his precision and vast knowledge, and as a scholar of history, Hadith and Tafsir."

Ibn Kathir's Students

Ibn Hajji was one of Ibn Kathir's students, and he described Ibn Kathir: "He had the best memory of the Hadith texts. He also had the most knowledge concerning the narrators and authenticity, his contemporaries and teachers admitted to these qualities. Every time I met him I gained some benefit from him."

Also, Ibn Al-`Imad Al-Hanbali said in his book, Shadhardt Adh-Dhahab, "He is the renowned Hafiz `Imad Ad-Din, whose memory was excellent, whose forgetfulness was miniscule, whose understanding was adequate, and who had good knowledge in the Arabic language." Also, Ibn Habib said about Ibn Kathir, "He heard knowledge and collected it and wrote various books. He brought comfort to the ears with his Fatwas and narrated Hadith and brought benefit to other people. The papers that contained his Fatwas were transmitted to the various (Islamic) provinces. Further, he was known for his precision and encompassing knowledge."

Ibn Kathir's Books

1 - One of the greatest books that Ibn Kathir wrote was his Tafsir of the Noble Qur'an, which is one of the best Tafsir that rely on narrations [of Ahadith, the Tafsir of the Companions, etc.]. The Tafsir by Ibn Kathir was printed many times and several scholars have summarized it.

2- The History Collection known as Al-Biddyah, which was printed in 14 volumes under the name Al-Bidayah wanNihdyah, and contained the stories of the Prophets and previous nations, the Prophet's Seerah (life story) and Islamic history until his time. He also added a book Al-Fitan, about the Signs of the Last Hour.

3- At-Takmil ft Ma`rifat Ath-Thiqat wa Ad-Du'afa wal Majdhil which Ibn Kathir collected from the books of his two Shaykhs Al-Mizzi and Adh-Dhahabi; Al-Kdmal and Mizan Al-Ftiddl. He added several benefits regarding the subject of Al-Jarh and AtT'adil.

4- Al-Hadi was-Sunan ft Ahadith Al-Masdnfd was-Sunan which is also known by, Jami` Al-Masdnfd. In this book, Ibn Kathir collected the narrations of Imams Ahmad bin Hanbal, Al-Bazzar, Abu Ya`la Al-Mawsili, Ibn Abi Shaybah and from the six collections of Hadith: the Two Sahihs [Al-Bukhari and Muslim] and the Four Sunan [Abu Dawud, At-Tirmidhi, AnNasa and Ibn Majah]. Ibn Kathir divided this book according to areas of Fiqh.

5-Tabaqat Ash-Shaf iyah which also contains the virtues of Imam Ash-Shafi.

6- Ibn Kathir wrote references for the Ahadith of Adillat AtTanbfh, from the Shafi school of Fiqh.

7- Ibn Kathir began an explanation of Sahih Al-Bukhari, but he did not finish it.

8- He started writing a large volume on the Ahkam (Laws), but finished only up to the Hajj rituals.

9- He summarized Al-Bayhaqi's 'Al-Madkhal. Many of these books were not printed.

10- He summarized `Ulum Al-Hadith, by Abu `Amr bin AsSalah and called it Mukhtasar `Ulum Al-Hadith. Shaykh Ahmad Shakir, the Egyptian Muhaddith, printed this book along with his commentary on it and called it Al-Ba'th Al-Hathfth fi Sharh Mukhtasar `Ulum Al-Hadith.

11- As-Sfrah An-Nabawiyyah, which is contained in his book Al-Biddyah, and both of these books are in print.

12- A research on Jihad called Al-Ijtihad ft Talabi Al-Jihad, which was printed several times.

Ibn Kathir's Death

Al-Hafiz Ibn Hajar Al-Asgalani said, "Ibn Kathir lost his sight just before his life ended. He died in Damascus in 774 H." May Allah grant mercy upon Ibn Kathir and make him among the residents of His Paradise.

PREFACE

In the name of Allah, Most Gracious, Most Merciful.

About this book

The previous publication of this book included some background information to the chapters of the Qur'an by an Islamic scholar known as Abul Ala Maududi. This information was used to shed more light on the chapters by giving a summery of why each chapter was given its name, It's period of revelation and the circumstances surrounding its revelatiom. However, some Muslims objected to the inclusion of the contributions of Maududi.

In this new publication of Tafsir Ibn Kathir, we have removed all traces of the contribution of Abul Ala Maududi. Personally, I do not know the reasons for the objections to Maududi, but this work concerns only the tafsir of Ibn Kathir, so we have not included anything from Maududi in it. We have also corrected all the typing and formatting errors found in the previous publication. We have not alter the structure of the book. The reader is still able to read the full Arabic Text of the thirty Parts of the Qur'an and follow its meanings in the English language. The transliteration of the Arabic text should also give the reader a taste of the sound of the original Arabic.

May Almighty Allah accept this effort from us, and make it a source of blessings for us in this world and in the next. I bear witness that there is none worthy of worship but Allah and I bear witness that Muhammad (may the peace and blessings of Allah be upon him) is the slave and messenger of Allah.

Performing Prostration While Reading the Qur'an

Question:

Could you please give a list of the Qur'anic verses when a prostration is recommended? What happens if we read these verses and not perform a prostration?

A. Jalil

Answer:

There are 15 verses in the Qur'an that mention prostration before God Almighty as a good action by God-fearing believers. Therefore, it is strongly recommended to perform such a prostration when we read or listen to any of these verses, whether during prayer or in any situation.

Some scholars are of the view that even if one has not performed ablution, one should prostrate oneself. These verses are given here, starting with the Arabic title of the surah which is followed by two numbers, the first indicating the surah, and the second indicating the verse,: Al-Araf 7: 206; Al-Raad 13: 15; Al-Nahl 16: 50; Al-Isra 17: 109; Maryam 19: 58; Al-Hajj 22: 18 & 22: 77; Al-Furqan 25: 60; Al-Naml 27: 26;

Al-Sajdah 32: 15; Saad 38: 25; Fussilat 41: 38; Al-Najm 53: 62; Al-Inshiqaq 84: 21 and Al-Alaq 96: 19.

If you do not perform a prostration when you read or listen to any of these verses, you have done badly because you miss out on the reward of performing a prostration for God. You incur no sin and violate no divine order.

Reference:
http://archive.arabnews.com/?page=5&section=0&article=97811&d=1&m=7&y=2007

The Glorious Qur'an Juz' 15 (Part 15): Chapter (Surah) 17: Al-Israa (The Night Journey, Or Bani Isra'il, Or The Children of Israel) 001 To Chapter (Surah) 18: Al-Kahf (The Cave) 074

PART 15 FULL ARABIC TEXT

Chapter (Surah) 17: Al-Israa 001-111

﴿ سُبْحَٰنَ ٱلَّذِىٓ أَسْرَىٰ بِعَبْدِهِۦ لَيْلًا مِّنَ ٱلْمَسْجِدِ ٱلْحَرَامِ إِلَى ٱلْمَسْجِدِ ٱلْأَقْصَا ٱلَّذِى بَٰرَكْنَا حَوْلَهُۥ لِنُرِيَهُۥ مِنْ ءَايَٰتِنَآ ۚ إِنَّهُۥ هُوَ ٱلسَّمِيعُ ٱلْبَصِيرُ ۝ وَءَاتَيْنَا مُوسَى ٱلْكِتَٰبَ وَجَعَلْنَٰهُ هُدًى لِّبَنِىٓ إِسْرَٰٓءِيلَ أَلَّا تَتَّخِذُوا۟ مِن دُونِى وَكِيلًا ۝ ذُرِّيَّةَ مَنْ حَمَلْنَا مَعَ نُوحٍ ۚ إِنَّهُۥ كَانَ عَبْدًا شَكُورًا ۝ وَقَضَيْنَآ إِلَىٰ بَنِىٓ إِسْرَٰٓءِيلَ فِى ٱلْكِتَٰبِ لَتُفْسِدُنَّ فِى ٱلْأَرْضِ مَرَّتَيْنِ وَلَتَعْلُنَّ عُلُوًّا كَبِيرًا ۝ فَإِذَا جَآءَ وَعْدُ أُولَىٰهُمَا بَعَثْنَا عَلَيْكُمْ عِبَادًا لَّنَآ أُو۟لِى بَأْسٍ شَدِيدٍ فَجَاسُوا۟ خِلَٰلَ ٱلدِّيَارِ ۚ وَكَانَ وَعْدًا مَّفْعُولًا ۝ ثُمَّ رَدَدْنَا لَكُمُ ٱلْكَرَّةَ عَلَيْهِمْ وَأَمْدَدْنَٰكُم بِأَمْوَٰلٍ وَبَنِينَ وَجَعَلْنَٰكُمْ أَكْثَرَ نَفِيرًا ۝ إِنْ أَحْسَنتُمْ أَحْسَنتُمْ لِأَنفُسِكُمْ ۖ وَإِنْ أَسَأْتُمْ فَلَهَا ۚ فَإِذَا جَآءَ وَعْدُ ٱلْءَاخِرَةِ لِيَسُۥٓـُٔوا۟ وُجُوهَكُمْ وَلِيَدْخُلُوا۟ ٱلْمَسْجِدَ كَمَا دَخَلُوهُ أَوَّلَ مَرَّةٍ وَلِيُتَبِّرُوا۟ مَا عَلَوْا۟ تَتْبِيرًا ۝ عَسَىٰ رَبُّكُمْ أَن يَرْحَمَكُمْ ۚ وَإِنْ عُدتُّمْ عُدْنَا ۘ وَجَعَلْنَا جَهَنَّمَ لِلْكَٰفِرِينَ حَصِيرًا ۝ إِنَّ هَٰذَا ٱلْقُرْءَانَ يَهْدِى لِلَّتِى هِىَ أَقْوَمُ وَيُبَشِّرُ ٱلْمُؤْمِنِينَ ٱلَّذِينَ يَعْمَلُونَ ٱلصَّٰلِحَٰتِ أَنَّ لَهُمْ أَجْرًا كَبِيرًا ۝ وَأَنَّ ٱلَّذِينَ لَا

يُؤْمِنُونَ بِٱلْءَاخِرَةِ أَعْتَدْنَا لَهُمْ عَذَابًا أَلِيمًا ۝ وَيَدْعُ ٱلْإِنسَـٰنُ بِٱلشَّرِّ دُعَاءَهُۥ بِٱلْخَيْرِ ۖ وَكَانَ ٱلْإِنسَـٰنُ عَجُولًا ۝ وَجَعَلْنَا ٱلَّيْلَ وَٱلنَّهَارَ ءَايَتَيْنِ ۖ فَمَحَوْنَا ءَايَةَ ٱلَّيْلِ وَجَعَلْنَا ءَايَةَ ٱلنَّهَارِ مُبْصِرَةً لِّتَبْتَغُوا۟ فَضْلًا مِّن رَّبِّكُمْ وَلِتَعْلَمُوا۟ عَدَدَ ٱلسِّنِينَ وَٱلْحِسَابَ ۚ وَكُلَّ شَىْءٍ فَصَّلْنَـٰهُ تَفْصِيلًا ۝ وَكُلَّ إِنسَـٰنٍ أَلْزَمْنَـٰهُ طَـٰٓئِرَهُۥ فِى عُنُقِهِۦ ۖ وَنُخْرِجُ لَهُۥ يَوْمَ ٱلْقِيَـٰمَةِ كِتَـٰبًا يَلْقَىٰهُ مَنشُورًا ۝ ٱقْرَأْ كِتَـٰبَكَ كَفَىٰ بِنَفْسِكَ ٱلْيَوْمَ عَلَيْكَ حَسِيبًا ۝ مَّنِ ٱهْتَدَىٰ فَإِنَّمَا يَهْتَدِى لِنَفْسِهِۦ ۖ وَمَن ضَلَّ فَإِنَّمَا يَضِلُّ عَلَيْهَا ۚ وَلَا تَزِرُ وَازِرَةٌ وِزْرَ أُخْرَىٰ ۗ وَمَا كُنَّا مُعَذِّبِينَ حَتَّىٰ نَبْعَثَ رَسُولًا ۝ وَإِذَآ أَرَدْنَآ أَن نُّهْلِكَ قَرْيَةً أَمَرْنَا مُتْرَفِيهَا فَفَسَقُوا۟ فِيهَا فَحَقَّ عَلَيْهَا ٱلْقَوْلُ فَدَمَّرْنَـٰهَا تَدْمِيرًا ۝ وَكَمْ أَهْلَكْنَا مِنَ ٱلْقُرُونِ مِنۢ بَعْدِ نُوحٍ ۗ وَكَفَىٰ بِرَبِّكَ بِذُنُوبِ عِبَادِهِۦ خَبِيرًۢا بَصِيرًا ۝ مَّن كَانَ يُرِيدُ ٱلْعَاجِلَةَ عَجَّلْنَا لَهُۥ فِيهَا مَا نَشَآءُ لِمَن نُّرِيدُ ثُمَّ جَعَلْنَا لَهُۥ جَهَنَّمَ يَصْلَىٰهَا مَذْمُومًا مَّدْحُورًا ۝ وَمَنْ أَرَادَ ٱلْءَاخِرَةَ وَسَعَىٰ لَهَا سَعْيَهَا وَهُوَ مُؤْمِنٌ فَأُو۟لَـٰٓئِكَ كَانَ سَعْيُهُم مَّشْكُورًا ۝ كُلًّا نُّمِدُّ هَـٰٓؤُلَآءِ وَهَـٰٓؤُلَآءِ مِنْ عَطَآءِ رَبِّكَ ۚ وَمَا كَانَ عَطَآءُ رَبِّكَ مَحْظُورًا ۝ ٱنظُرْ كَيْفَ فَضَّلْنَا بَعْضَهُمْ عَلَىٰ بَعْضٍ ۚ وَلَلْءَاخِرَةُ أَكْبَرُ دَرَجَـٰتٍ وَأَكْبَرُ تَفْضِيلًا ۝ لَّا تَجْعَلْ مَعَ ٱللَّهِ إِلَـٰهًا ءَاخَرَ فَتَقْعُدَ مَذْمُومًا مَّخْذُولًا ۝ ۞ وَقَضَىٰ رَبُّكَ أَلَّا تَعْبُدُوٓا۟ إِلَّآ إِيَّاهُ وَبِٱلْوَٰلِدَيْنِ إِحْسَـٰنًا ۚ إِمَّا يَبْلُغَنَّ عِندَكَ ٱلْكِبَرَ أَحَدُهُمَآ أَوْ كِلَاهُمَا فَلَا تَقُل لَّهُمَآ أُفٍّ وَلَا تَنْهَرْهُمَا وَقُل لَّهُمَا قَوْلًا كَرِيمًا ۝ وَٱخْفِضْ لَهُمَا جَنَاحَ ٱلذُّلِّ مِنَ ٱلرَّحْمَةِ وَقُل رَّبِّ ٱرْحَمْهُمَا كَمَا رَبَّيَانِى صَغِيرًا ۝ رَّبُّكُمْ أَعْلَمُ بِمَا فِى نُفُوسِكُمْ ۚ إِن تَكُونُوا۟ صَـٰلِحِينَ فَإِنَّهُۥ كَانَ لِلْأَوَّٰبِينَ غَفُورًا ۝ وَءَاتِ ذَا ٱلْقُرْبَىٰ حَقَّهُۥ وَٱلْمِسْكِينَ وَٱبْنَ ٱلسَّبِيلِ وَلَا تُبَذِّرْ تَبْذِيرًا ۝ إِنَّ ٱلْمُبَذِّرِينَ

كَانُوٓاْ إِخْوَٰنَ ٱلشَّيَٰطِينِ ۖ وَكَانَ ٱلشَّيْطَٰنُ لِرَبِّهِۦ كَفُورًا ۝ وَإِمَّا تُعْرِضَنَّ عَنْهُمُ ٱبْتِغَآءَ رَحْمَةٍ مِّن رَّبِّكَ تَرْجُوهَا فَقُل لَّهُمْ قَوْلًا مَّيْسُورًا ۝ وَلَا تَجْعَلْ يَدَكَ مَغْلُولَةً إِلَىٰ عُنُقِكَ وَلَا تَبْسُطْهَا كُلَّ ٱلْبَسْطِ فَتَقْعُدَ مَلُومًا مَّحْسُورًا ۝ إِنَّ رَبَّكَ يَبْسُطُ ٱلرِّزْقَ لِمَن يَشَآءُ وَيَقْدِرُ ۚ إِنَّهُۥ كَانَ بِعِبَادِهِۦ خَبِيرًۢا بَصِيرًا ۝ وَلَا تَقْتُلُوٓاْ أَوْلَٰدَكُمْ خَشْيَةَ إِمْلَٰقٍ ۖ نَّحْنُ نَرْزُقُهُمْ وَإِيَّاكُمْ ۚ إِنَّ قَتْلَهُمْ كَانَ خِطْـًٔا كَبِيرًا ۝ وَلَا تَقْرَبُواْ ٱلزِّنَىٰٓ ۖ إِنَّهُۥ كَانَ فَٰحِشَةً وَسَآءَ سَبِيلًا ۝ وَلَا تَقْتُلُواْ ٱلنَّفْسَ ٱلَّتِى حَرَّمَ ٱللَّهُ إِلَّا بِٱلْحَقِّ ۗ وَمَن قُتِلَ مَظْلُومًا فَقَدْ جَعَلْنَا لِوَلِيِّهِۦ سُلْطَٰنًا فَلَا يُسْرِف فِّى ٱلْقَتْلِ ۖ إِنَّهُۥ كَانَ مَنصُورًا ۝ وَلَا تَقْرَبُواْ مَالَ ٱلْيَتِيمِ إِلَّا بِٱلَّتِى هِىَ أَحْسَنُ حَتَّىٰ يَبْلُغَ أَشُدَّهُۥ ۚ وَأَوْفُواْ بِٱلْعَهْدِ ۖ إِنَّ ٱلْعَهْدَ كَانَ مَسْـُٔولًا ۝ وَأَوْفُواْ ٱلْكَيْلَ إِذَا كِلْتُمْ وَزِنُواْ بِٱلْقِسْطَاسِ ٱلْمُسْتَقِيمِ ۚ ذَٰلِكَ خَيْرٌ وَأَحْسَنُ تَأْوِيلًا ۝ وَلَا تَقْفُ مَا لَيْسَ لَكَ بِهِۦ عِلْمٌ ۚ إِنَّ ٱلسَّمْعَ وَٱلْبَصَرَ وَٱلْفُؤَادَ كُلُّ أُوْلَٰٓئِكَ كَانَ عَنْهُ مَسْـُٔولًا ۝ وَلَا تَمْشِ فِى ٱلْأَرْضِ مَرَحًا ۖ إِنَّكَ لَن تَخْرِقَ ٱلْأَرْضَ وَلَن تَبْلُغَ ٱلْجِبَالَ طُولًا ۝ كُلُّ ذَٰلِكَ كَانَ سَيِّئُهُۥ عِندَ رَبِّكَ مَكْرُوهًا ۝ ذَٰلِكَ مِمَّآ أَوْحَىٰٓ إِلَيْكَ رَبُّكَ مِنَ ٱلْحِكْمَةِ ۗ وَلَا تَجْعَلْ مَعَ ٱللَّهِ إِلَٰهًا ءَاخَرَ فَتُلْقَىٰ فِى جَهَنَّمَ مَلُومًا مَّدْحُورًا ۝ أَفَأَصْفَىٰكُمْ رَبُّكُم بِٱلْبَنِينَ وَٱتَّخَذَ مِنَ ٱلْمَلَٰٓئِكَةِ إِنَٰثًا ۚ إِنَّكُمْ لَتَقُولُونَ قَوْلًا عَظِيمًا ۝ وَلَقَدْ صَرَّفْنَا فِى هَٰذَا ٱلْقُرْءَانِ لِيَذَّكَّرُواْ وَمَا يَزِيدُهُمْ إِلَّا نُفُورًا ۝ قُل لَّوْ كَانَ مَعَهُۥٓ ءَالِهَةٌ كَمَا يَقُولُونَ إِذًا لَّٱبْتَغَوْاْ إِلَىٰ ذِى ٱلْعَرْشِ سَبِيلًا ۝ سُبْحَٰنَهُۥ وَتَعَٰلَىٰ عَمَّا يَقُولُونَ عُلُوًّا كَبِيرًا ۝ تُسَبِّحُ لَهُ ٱلسَّمَٰوَٰتُ ٱلسَّبْعُ وَٱلْأَرْضُ وَمَن فِيهِنَّ ۚ وَإِن مِّن شَىْءٍ إِلَّا يُسَبِّحُ بِحَمْدِهِۦ وَلَٰكِن لَّا تَفْقَهُونَ تَسْبِيحَهُمْ ۗ إِنَّهُۥ كَانَ حَلِيمًا غَفُورًا ۝ وَإِذَا قَرَأْتَ ٱلْقُرْءَانَ جَعَلْنَا بَيْنَكَ

وَبَيْنَ ٱلَّذِينَ لَا يُؤْمِنُونَ بِٱلْأَخِرَةِ حِجَابًا مَّسْتُورًا ۝ وَجَعَلْنَا عَلَىٰ قُلُوبِهِمْ أَكِنَّةً أَن يَفْقَهُوهُ وَفِىٓ ءَاذَانِهِمْ وَقْرًا ۚ وَإِذَا ذَكَرْتَ رَبَّكَ فِى ٱلْقُرْءَانِ وَحْدَهُۥ وَلَّوْا۟ عَلَىٰٓ أَدْبَـٰرِهِمْ نُفُورًا ۝ نَّحْنُ أَعْلَمُ بِمَا يَسْتَمِعُونَ بِهِۦٓ إِذْ يَسْتَمِعُونَ إِلَيْكَ وَإِذْ هُمْ نَجْوَىٰٓ إِذْ يَقُولُ ٱلظَّـٰلِمُونَ إِن تَتَّبِعُونَ إِلَّا رَجُلًا مَّسْحُورًا ۝ ٱنظُرْ كَيْفَ ضَرَبُوا۟ لَكَ ٱلْأَمْثَـٰلَ فَضَلُّوا۟ فَلَا يَسْتَطِيعُونَ سَبِيلًا ۝ وَقَالُوٓا۟ أَءِذَا كُنَّا عِظَـٰمًا وَرُفَـٰتًا أَءِنَّا لَمَبْعُوثُونَ خَلْقًا جَدِيدًا ۝ ۞ قُلْ كُونُوا۟ حِجَارَةً أَوْ حَدِيدًا ۝ أَوْ خَلْقًا مِّمَّا يَكْبُرُ فِى صُدُورِكُمْ ۚ فَسَيَقُولُونَ مَن يُعِيدُنَا ۖ قُلِ ٱلَّذِى فَطَرَكُمْ أَوَّلَ مَرَّةٍ ۚ فَسَيُنْغِضُونَ إِلَيْكَ رُءُوسَهُمْ وَيَقُولُونَ مَتَىٰ هُوَ ۖ قُلْ عَسَىٰٓ أَن يَكُونَ قَرِيبًا ۝ يَوْمَ يَدْعُوكُمْ فَتَسْتَجِيبُونَ بِحَمْدِهِۦ وَتَظُنُّونَ إِن لَّبِثْتُمْ إِلَّا قَلِيلًا ۝ وَقُل لِّعِبَادِى يَقُولُوا۟ ٱلَّتِى هِىَ أَحْسَنُ ۚ إِنَّ ٱلشَّيْطَـٰنَ يَنزَغُ بَيْنَهُمْ ۚ إِنَّ ٱلشَّيْطَـٰنَ كَانَ لِلْإِنسَـٰنِ عَدُوًّا مُّبِينًا ۝ رَّبُّكُمْ أَعْلَمُ بِكُمْ ۖ إِن يَشَأْ يَرْحَمْكُمْ أَوْ إِن يَشَأْ يُعَذِّبْكُمْ ۚ وَمَآ أَرْسَلْنَـٰكَ عَلَيْهِمْ وَكِيلًا ۝ وَرَبُّكَ أَعْلَمُ بِمَن فِى ٱلسَّمَـٰوَٰتِ وَٱلْأَرْضِ ۗ وَلَقَدْ فَضَّلْنَا بَعْضَ ٱلنَّبِيِّـۧنَ عَلَىٰ بَعْضٍ ۖ وَءَاتَيْنَا دَاوُۥدَ زَبُورًا ۝ قُلِ ٱدْعُوا۟ ٱلَّذِينَ زَعَمْتُم مِّن دُونِهِۦ فَلَا يَمْلِكُونَ كَشْفَ ٱلضُّرِّ عَنكُمْ وَلَا تَحْوِيلًا ۝ أُو۟لَـٰٓئِكَ ٱلَّذِينَ يَدْعُونَ يَبْتَغُونَ إِلَىٰ رَبِّهِمُ ٱلْوَسِيلَةَ أَيُّهُمْ أَقْرَبُ وَيَرْجُونَ رَحْمَتَهُۥ وَيَخَافُونَ عَذَابَهُۥٓ ۚ إِنَّ عَذَابَ رَبِّكَ كَانَ مَحْذُورًا ۝ وَإِن مِّن قَرْيَةٍ إِلَّا نَحْنُ مُهْلِكُوهَا قَبْلَ يَوْمِ ٱلْقِيَـٰمَةِ أَوْ مُعَذِّبُوهَا عَذَابًا شَدِيدًا ۚ كَانَ ذَٰلِكَ فِى ٱلْكِتَـٰبِ مَسْطُورًا ۝ وَمَا مَنَعَنَآ أَن نُّرْسِلَ بِٱلْأَيَـٰتِ إِلَّآ أَن كَذَّبَ بِهَا ٱلْأَوَّلُونَ ۚ وَءَاتَيْنَا ثَمُودَ ٱلنَّاقَةَ مُبْصِرَةً فَظَلَمُوا۟ بِهَا ۚ وَمَا نُرْسِلُ بِٱلْأَيَـٰتِ إِلَّا تَخْوِيفًا ۝ وَإِذْ قُلْنَا لَكَ إِنَّ رَبَّكَ أَحَاطَ بِٱلنَّاسِ ۚ وَمَا جَعَلْنَا ٱلرُّءْيَا ٱلَّتِىٓ أَرَيْنَـٰكَ إِلَّا

فِتْنَةً لِّلنَّاسِ وَالشَّجَرَةَ الْمَلْعُونَةَ فِى الْقُرْءَانِ ۚ وَنُخَوِّفُهُمْ فَمَا يَزِيدُهُمْ إِلَّا طُغْيَـٰنًا كَبِيرًا ۝٦٠ وَإِذْ قُلْنَا لِلْمَلَـٰٓئِكَةِ اسْجُدُوا۟ لِـَٔادَمَ فَسَجَدُوٓا۟ إِلَّآ إِبْلِيسَ قَالَ ءَأَسْجُدُ لِمَنْ خَلَقْتَ طِينًا ۝٦١ قَالَ أَرَءَيْتَكَ هَـٰذَا الَّذِى كَرَّمْتَ عَلَىَّ لَئِنْ أَخَّرْتَنِ إِلَىٰ يَوْمِ الْقِيَـٰمَةِ لَأَحْتَنِكَنَّ ذُرِّيَّتَهُۥٓ إِلَّا قَلِيلًا ۝٦٢ قَالَ اذْهَبْ فَمَن تَبِعَكَ مِنْهُمْ فَإِنَّ جَهَنَّمَ جَزَآؤُكُمْ جَزَآءً مَّوْفُورًا ۝٦٣ وَاسْتَفْزِزْ مَنِ اسْتَطَعْتَ مِنْهُم بِصَوْتِكَ وَأَجْلِبْ عَلَيْهِم بِخَيْلِكَ وَرَجِلِكَ وَشَارِكْهُمْ فِى الْأَمْوَٰلِ وَالْأَوْلَـٰدِ وَعِدْهُمْ ۚ وَمَا يَعِدُهُمُ الشَّيْطَـٰنُ إِلَّا غُرُورًا ۝٦٤ إِنَّ عِبَادِى لَيْسَ لَكَ عَلَيْهِمْ سُلْطَـٰنٌ ۚ وَكَفَىٰ بِرَبِّكَ وَكِيلًا ۝٦٥ رَّبُّكُمُ الَّذِى يُزْجِى لَكُمُ الْفُلْكَ فِى الْبَحْرِ لِتَبْتَغُوا۟ مِن فَضْلِهِۦٓ ۚ إِنَّهُۥ كَانَ بِكُمْ رَحِيمًا ۝٦٦ وَإِذَا مَسَّكُمُ الضُّرُّ فِى الْبَحْرِ ضَلَّ مَن تَدْعُونَ إِلَّآ إِيَّاهُ ۖ فَلَمَّا نَجَّىٰكُمْ إِلَى الْبَرِّ أَعْرَضْتُمْ ۚ وَكَانَ الْإِنسَـٰنُ كَفُورًا ۝٦٧ أَفَأَمِنتُمْ أَن يَخْسِفَ بِكُمْ جَانِبَ الْبَرِّ أَوْ يُرْسِلَ عَلَيْكُمْ حَاصِبًا ثُمَّ لَا تَجِدُوا۟ لَكُمْ وَكِيلًا ۝٦٨ أَمْ أَمِنتُمْ أَن يُعِيدَكُمْ فِيهِ تَارَةً أُخْرَىٰ فَيُرْسِلَ عَلَيْكُمْ قَاصِفًا مِّنَ الرِّيحِ فَيُغْرِقَكُم بِمَا كَفَرْتُمْ ۙ ثُمَّ لَا تَجِدُوا۟ لَكُمْ عَلَيْنَا بِهِۦ تَبِيعًا ۝٦٩ ۞ وَلَقَدْ كَرَّمْنَا بَنِىٓ ءَادَمَ وَحَمَلْنَـٰهُمْ فِى الْبَرِّ وَالْبَحْرِ وَرَزَقْنَـٰهُم مِّنَ الطَّيِّبَـٰتِ وَفَضَّلْنَـٰهُمْ عَلَىٰ كَثِيرٍ مِّمَّنْ خَلَقْنَا تَفْضِيلًا ۝٧٠ يَوْمَ نَدْعُوا۟ كُلَّ أُنَاسٍۭ بِإِمَـٰمِهِمْ ۖ فَمَنْ أُوتِىَ كِتَـٰبَهُۥ بِيَمِينِهِۦ فَأُو۟لَـٰٓئِكَ يَقْرَءُونَ كِتَـٰبَهُمْ وَلَا يُظْلَمُونَ فَتِيلًا ۝٧١ وَمَن كَانَ فِى هَـٰذِهِۦٓ أَعْمَىٰ فَهُوَ فِى الْـَٔاخِرَةِ أَعْمَىٰ وَأَضَلُّ سَبِيلًا ۝٧٢ وَإِن كَادُوا۟ لَيَفْتِنُونَكَ عَنِ الَّذِىٓ أَوْحَيْنَآ إِلَيْكَ لِتَفْتَرِىَ عَلَيْنَا غَيْرَهُۥ ۖ وَإِذًا لَّاتَّخَذُوكَ خَلِيلًا ۝٧٣ وَلَوْلَآ أَن ثَبَّتْنَـٰكَ لَقَدْ كِدتَّ تَرْكَنُ إِلَيْهِمْ شَيْـًٔا قَلِيلًا ۝٧٤ إِذًا لَّأَذَقْنَـٰكَ ضِعْفَ الْحَيَوٰةِ وَضِعْفَ الْمَمَاتِ ثُمَّ لَا تَجِدُ لَكَ عَلَيْنَا

نَصِيرًا ۝ وَإِن كَادُوا۟ لَيَسْتَفِزُّونَكَ مِنَ ٱلْأَرْضِ لِيُخْرِجُوكَ مِنْهَا ۖ وَإِذًا لَّا يَلْبَثُونَ خِلَٰفَكَ إِلَّا قَلِيلًا ۝ سُنَّةَ مَن قَدْ أَرْسَلْنَا قَبْلَكَ مِن رُّسُلِنَا ۖ وَلَا تَجِدُ لِسُنَّتِنَا تَحْوِيلًا ۝ أَقِمِ ٱلصَّلَوٰةَ لِدُلُوكِ ٱلشَّمْسِ إِلَىٰ غَسَقِ ٱلَّيْلِ وَقُرْءَانَ ٱلْفَجْرِ ۖ إِنَّ قُرْءَانَ ٱلْفَجْرِ كَانَ مَشْهُودًا ۝ وَمِنَ ٱلَّيْلِ فَتَهَجَّدْ بِهِ نَافِلَةً لَّكَ عَسَىٰ أَن يَبْعَثَكَ رَبُّكَ مَقَامًا مَّحْمُودًا ۝ وَقُل رَّبِّ أَدْخِلْنِى مُدْخَلَ صِدْقٍ وَأَخْرِجْنِى مُخْرَجَ صِدْقٍ وَٱجْعَل لِّى مِن لَّدُنكَ سُلْطَٰنًا نَّصِيرًا ۝ وَقُلْ جَآءَ ٱلْحَقُّ وَزَهَقَ ٱلْبَٰطِلُ ۚ إِنَّ ٱلْبَٰطِلَ كَانَ زَهُوقًا ۝ وَنُنَزِّلُ مِنَ ٱلْقُرْءَانِ مَا هُوَ شِفَآءٌ وَرَحْمَةٌ لِّلْمُؤْمِنِينَ ۙ وَلَا يَزِيدُ ٱلظَّٰلِمِينَ إِلَّا خَسَارًا ۝ وَإِذَآ أَنْعَمْنَا عَلَى ٱلْإِنسَٰنِ أَعْرَضَ وَنَـَٔا بِجَانِبِهِۦ ۖ وَإِذَا مَسَّهُ ٱلشَّرُّ كَانَ يَـُٔوسًا ۝ قُلْ كُلٌّ يَعْمَلُ عَلَىٰ شَاكِلَتِهِۦ فَرَبُّكُمْ أَعْلَمُ بِمَنْ هُوَ أَهْدَىٰ سَبِيلًا ۝ وَيَسْـَٔلُونَكَ عَنِ ٱلرُّوحِ ۖ قُلِ ٱلرُّوحُ مِنْ أَمْرِ رَبِّى وَمَآ أُوتِيتُم مِّنَ ٱلْعِلْمِ إِلَّا قَلِيلًا ۝ وَلَئِن شِئْنَا لَنَذْهَبَنَّ بِٱلَّذِىٓ أَوْحَيْنَآ إِلَيْكَ ثُمَّ لَا تَجِدُ لَكَ بِهِۦ عَلَيْنَا وَكِيلًا ۝ إِلَّا رَحْمَةً مِّن رَّبِّكَ ۚ إِنَّ فَضْلَهُۥ كَانَ عَلَيْكَ كَبِيرًا ۝ قُل لَّئِنِ ٱجْتَمَعَتِ ٱلْإِنسُ وَٱلْجِنُّ عَلَىٰٓ أَن يَأْتُوا۟ بِمِثْلِ هَٰذَا ٱلْقُرْءَانِ لَا يَأْتُونَ بِمِثْلِهِۦ وَلَوْ كَانَ بَعْضُهُمْ لِبَعْضٍ ظَهِيرًا ۝ وَلَقَدْ صَرَّفْنَا لِلنَّاسِ فِى هَٰذَا ٱلْقُرْءَانِ مِن كُلِّ مَثَلٍ فَأَبَىٰٓ أَكْثَرُ ٱلنَّاسِ إِلَّا كُفُورًا ۝ وَقَالُوا۟ لَن نُّؤْمِنَ لَكَ حَتَّىٰ تَفْجُرَ لَنَا مِنَ ٱلْأَرْضِ يَنۢبُوعًا ۝ أَوْ تَكُونَ لَكَ جَنَّةٌ مِّن نَّخِيلٍ وَعِنَبٍ فَتُفَجِّرَ ٱلْأَنْهَٰرَ خِلَٰلَهَا تَفْجِيرًا ۝ أَوْ تُسْقِطَ ٱلسَّمَآءَ كَمَا زَعَمْتَ عَلَيْنَا كِسَفًا أَوْ تَأْتِىَ بِٱللَّهِ وَٱلْمَلَٰٓئِكَةِ قَبِيلًا ۝ أَوْ يَكُونَ لَكَ بَيْتٌ مِّن زُخْرُفٍ أَوْ تَرْقَىٰ فِى ٱلسَّمَآءِ وَلَن نُّؤْمِنَ لِرُقِيِّكَ حَتَّىٰ تُنَزِّلَ عَلَيْنَا كِتَٰبًا نَّقْرَؤُهُۥ ۗ قُلْ سُبْحَانَ رَبِّى هَلْ كُنتُ إِلَّا بَشَرًا رَّسُولًا ۝ وَمَا مَنَعَ ٱلنَّاسَ أَن

يُؤْمِنُوٓا۟ إِذْ جَآءَهُمُ ٱلْهُدَىٰٓ إِلَّآ أَن قَالُوٓا۟ أَبَعَثَ ٱللَّهُ بَشَرًۭا رَّسُولًۭا ۝ قُل لَّوْ كَانَ فِى ٱلْأَرْضِ مَلَـٰٓئِكَةٌۭ يَمْشُونَ مُطْمَئِنِّينَ لَنَزَّلْنَا عَلَيْهِم مِّنَ ٱلسَّمَآءِ مَلَكًۭا رَّسُولًۭا ۝ قُلْ كَفَىٰ بِٱللَّهِ شَهِيدًۢا بَيْنِى وَبَيْنَكُمْ ۚ إِنَّهُۥ كَانَ بِعِبَادِهِۦ خَبِيرًۢا بَصِيرًۭا ۝ وَمَن يَهْدِ ٱللَّهُ فَهُوَ ٱلْمُهْتَدِ ۖ وَمَن يُضْلِلْ فَلَن تَجِدَ لَهُمْ أَوْلِيَآءَ مِن دُونِهِۦ ۖ وَنَحْشُرُهُمْ يَوْمَ ٱلْقِيَـٰمَةِ عَلَىٰ وُجُوهِهِمْ عُمْيًۭا وَبُكْمًۭا وَصُمًّۭا ۖ مَّأْوَىٰهُمْ جَهَنَّمُ ۖ كُلَّمَا خَبَتْ زِدْنَـٰهُمْ سَعِيرًۭا ۝ ذَٰلِكَ جَزَآؤُهُم بِأَنَّهُمْ كَفَرُوا۟ بِـَٔايَـٰتِنَا وَقَالُوٓا۟ أَءِذَا كُنَّا عِظَـٰمًۭا وَرُفَـٰتًا أَءِنَّا لَمَبْعُوثُونَ خَلْقًۭا جَدِيدًا ۝ ۞ أَوَلَمْ يَرَوْا۟ أَنَّ ٱللَّهَ ٱلَّذِى خَلَقَ ٱلسَّمَـٰوَٰتِ وَٱلْأَرْضَ قَادِرٌ عَلَىٰٓ أَن يَخْلُقَ مِثْلَهُمْ وَجَعَلَ لَهُمْ أَجَلًۭا لَّا رَيْبَ فِيهِ فَأَبَى ٱلظَّـٰلِمُونَ إِلَّا كُفُورًۭا ۝ قُل لَّوْ أَنتُمْ تَمْلِكُونَ خَزَآئِنَ رَحْمَةِ رَبِّىٓ إِذًۭا لَّأَمْسَكْتُمْ خَشْيَةَ ٱلْإِنفَاقِ ۚ وَكَانَ ٱلْإِنسَـٰنُ قَتُورًۭا ۝ وَلَقَدْ ءَاتَيْنَا مُوسَىٰ تِسْعَ ءَايَـٰتٍۭ بَيِّنَـٰتٍۢ ۖ فَسْـَٔلْ بَنِىٓ إِسْرَٰٓءِيلَ إِذْ جَآءَهُمْ فَقَالَ لَهُۥ فِرْعَوْنُ إِنِّى لَأَظُنُّكَ يَـٰمُوسَىٰ مَسْحُورًۭا ۝ قَالَ لَقَدْ عَلِمْتَ مَآ أَنزَلَ هَـٰٓؤُلَآءِ إِلَّا رَبُّ ٱلسَّمَـٰوَٰتِ وَٱلْأَرْضِ بَصَآئِرَ وَإِنِّى لَأَظُنُّكَ يَـٰفِرْعَوْنُ مَثْبُورًۭا ۝ فَأَرَادَ أَن يَسْتَفِزَّهُم مِّنَ ٱلْأَرْضِ فَأَغْرَقْنَـٰهُ وَمَن مَّعَهُۥ جَمِيعًۭا ۝ وَقُلْنَا مِنۢ بَعْدِهِۦ لِبَنِىٓ إِسْرَٰٓءِيلَ ٱسْكُنُوا۟ ٱلْأَرْضَ فَإِذَا جَآءَ وَعْدُ ٱلْـَٔاخِرَةِ جِئْنَا بِكُمْ لَفِيفًۭا ۝ وَبِٱلْحَقِّ أَنزَلْنَـٰهُ وَبِٱلْحَقِّ نَزَلَ ۗ وَمَآ أَرْسَلْنَـٰكَ إِلَّا مُبَشِّرًۭا وَنَذِيرًۭا ۝ وَقُرْءَانًۭا فَرَقْنَـٰهُ لِتَقْرَأَهُۥ عَلَى ٱلنَّاسِ عَلَىٰ مُكْثٍۢ وَنَزَّلْنَـٰهُ تَنزِيلًۭا ۝ قُلْ ءَامِنُوا۟ بِهِۦٓ أَوْ لَا تُؤْمِنُوٓا۟ ۚ إِنَّ ٱلَّذِينَ أُوتُوا۟ ٱلْعِلْمَ مِن قَبْلِهِۦٓ إِذَا يُتْلَىٰ عَلَيْهِمْ يَخِرُّونَ لِلْأَذْقَانِ سُجَّدًۭا ۝ وَيَقُولُونَ سُبْحَـٰنَ رَبِّنَآ إِن كَانَ وَعْدُ رَبِّنَا لَمَفْعُولًۭا ۝ وَيَخِرُّونَ لِلْأَذْقَانِ يَبْكُونَ وَيَزِيدُهُمْ خُشُوعًۭا ۩ ۝ قُلِ ٱدْعُوا۟ ٱللَّهَ أَوِ ٱدْعُوا۟ ٱلرَّحْمَـٰنَ ۖ أَيًّۭا مَّا تَدْعُوا۟ فَلَهُ ٱلْأَسْمَآءُ

ٱلْحُسْنَىٰ ۚ وَلَا تَجْهَرْ بِصَلَاتِكَ وَلَا تُخَافِتْ بِهَا وَٱبْتَغِ بَيْنَ ذَٰلِكَ سَبِيلًا ۝ وَقُلِ ٱلْحَمْدُ لِلَّهِ ٱلَّذِى لَمْ يَتَّخِذْ وَلَدًا وَلَمْ يَكُن لَّهُ شَرِيكٌ فِى ٱلْمُلْكِ وَلَمْ يَكُن لَّهُ وَلِىٌّ مِّنَ ٱلذُّلِّ ۖ وَكَبِّرْهُ تَكْبِيرًا ۝

(Al-Israa 001-111)

Chapter (Surah) 18: Al-Kahf 001-074

بِسْمِ ٱللَّهِ ٱلرَّحْمَٰنِ ٱلرَّحِيمِ

﴿ ٱلْحَمْدُ لِلَّهِ ٱلَّذِىٓ أَنزَلَ عَلَىٰ عَبْدِهِ ٱلْكِتَٰبَ وَلَمْ يَجْعَل لَّهُۥ عِوَجَا ۝ قَيِّمًا لِّيُنذِرَ بَأْسًا شَدِيدًا مِّن لَّدُنْهُ وَيُبَشِّرَ ٱلْمُؤْمِنِينَ ٱلَّذِينَ يَعْمَلُونَ ٱلصَّٰلِحَٰتِ أَنَّ لَهُمْ أَجْرًا حَسَنًا ۝ مَّٰكِثِينَ فِيهِ أَبَدًا ۝ وَيُنذِرَ ٱلَّذِينَ قَالُوا۟ ٱتَّخَذَ ٱللَّهُ وَلَدًا ۝ مَّا لَهُم بِهِۦ مِنْ عِلْمٍ وَلَا لِءَابَآئِهِمْ ۚ كَبُرَتْ كَلِمَةً تَخْرُجُ مِنْ أَفْوَٰهِهِمْ ۚ إِن يَقُولُونَ إِلَّا كَذِبًا ۝ فَلَعَلَّكَ بَٰخِعٌ نَّفْسَكَ عَلَىٰٓ ءَاثَٰرِهِمْ إِن لَّمْ يُؤْمِنُوا۟ بِهَٰذَا ٱلْحَدِيثِ أَسَفًا ۝ إِنَّا جَعَلْنَا مَا عَلَى ٱلْأَرْضِ زِينَةً لَّهَا لِنَبْلُوَهُمْ أَيُّهُمْ أَحْسَنُ عَمَلًا ۝ وَإِنَّا لَجَٰعِلُونَ مَا عَلَيْهَا صَعِيدًا جُرُزًا ۝ أَمْ حَسِبْتَ أَنَّ أَصْحَٰبَ ٱلْكَهْفِ وَٱلرَّقِيمِ كَانُوا۟ مِنْ ءَايَٰتِنَا عَجَبًا ۝ إِذْ أَوَى ٱلْفِتْيَةُ إِلَى ٱلْكَهْفِ فَقَالُوا۟ رَبَّنَآ ءَاتِنَا مِن لَّدُنكَ رَحْمَةً وَهَيِّئْ لَنَا مِنْ أَمْرِنَا رَشَدًا ۝ فَضَرَبْنَا عَلَىٰٓ ءَاذَانِهِمْ فِى ٱلْكَهْفِ سِنِينَ عَدَدًا ۝ ثُمَّ بَعَثْنَٰهُمْ لِنَعْلَمَ أَىُّ ٱلْحِزْبَيْنِ أَحْصَىٰ لِمَا لَبِثُوٓا۟ أَمَدًا ۝ نَّحْنُ نَقُصُّ عَلَيْكَ نَبَأَهُم بِٱلْحَقِّ ۚ إِنَّهُمْ فِتْيَةٌ ءَامَنُوا۟ بِرَبِّهِمْ وَزِدْنَٰهُمْ هُدًى ۝ وَرَبَطْنَا عَلَىٰ قُلُوبِهِمْ إِذْ قَامُوا۟ فَقَالُوا۟ رَبُّنَا رَبُّ ٱلسَّمَٰوَٰتِ وَٱلْأَرْضِ لَن نَّدْعُوَا۟ مِن دُونِهِۦٓ إِلَٰهًا ۖ لَّقَدْ قُلْنَآ إِذًا شَطَطًا ۝ هَٰٓؤُلَآءِ قَوْمُنَا ٱتَّخَذُوا۟ مِن دُونِهِۦٓ ءَالِهَةً ۖ لَّوْلَا يَأْتُونَ عَلَيْهِم بِسُلْطَٰنٍۭ بَيِّنٍ ۖ فَمَنْ أَظْلَمُ مِمَّنِ ٱفْتَرَىٰ عَلَى ٱللَّهِ كَذِبًا ۝ وَإِذِ ٱعْتَزَلْتُمُوهُمْ وَمَا يَعْبُدُونَ إِلَّا ٱللَّهَ فَأْوُۥٓا۟ إِلَى ٱلْكَهْفِ يَنشُرْ لَكُمْ رَبُّكُم مِّن رَّحْمَتِهِۦ وَيُهَيِّئْ لَكُم مِّنْ أَمْرِكُم مِّرْفَقًا

۞ وَتَرَى ٱلشَّمْسَ إِذَا طَلَعَت تَّزَٰوَرُ عَن كَهْفِهِمْ ذَاتَ ٱلْيَمِينِ وَإِذَا غَرَبَت تَّقْرِضُهُمْ ذَاتَ ٱلشِّمَالِ وَهُمْ فِى فَجْوَةٍ مِّنْهُ ۚ ذَٰلِكَ مِنْ ءَايَٰتِ ٱللَّهِ ۗ مَن يَهْدِ ٱللَّهُ فَهُوَ ٱلْمُهْتَدِ ۖ وَمَن يُضْلِلْ فَلَن تَجِدَ لَهُۥ وَلِيًّا مُّرْشِدًا ۞ وَتَحْسَبُهُمْ أَيْقَاظًا وَهُمْ رُقُودٌ ۚ وَنُقَلِّبُهُمْ ذَاتَ ٱلْيَمِينِ وَذَاتَ ٱلشِّمَالِ ۖ وَكَلْبُهُم بَٰسِطٌ ذِرَاعَيْهِ بِٱلْوَصِيدِ ۚ لَوِ ٱطَّلَعْتَ عَلَيْهِمْ لَوَلَّيْتَ مِنْهُمْ فِرَارًا وَلَمُلِئْتَ مِنْهُمْ رُعْبًا ۞ وَكَذَٰلِكَ بَعَثْنَٰهُمْ لِيَتَسَآءَلُوا۟ بَيْنَهُمْ ۚ قَالَ قَآئِلٌ مِّنْهُمْ كَمْ لَبِثْتُمْ ۖ قَالُوا۟ لَبِثْنَا يَوْمًا أَوْ بَعْضَ يَوْمٍ ۚ قَالُوا۟ رَبُّكُمْ أَعْلَمُ بِمَا لَبِثْتُمْ فَٱبْعَثُوٓا۟ أَحَدَكُم بِوَرِقِكُمْ هَٰذِهِۦٓ إِلَى ٱلْمَدِينَةِ فَلْيَنظُرْ أَيُّهَآ أَزْكَىٰ طَعَامًا فَلْيَأْتِكُم بِرِزْقٍ مِّنْهُ وَلْيَتَلَطَّفْ وَلَا يُشْعِرَنَّ بِكُمْ أَحَدًا ۞ إِنَّهُمْ إِن يَظْهَرُوا۟ عَلَيْكُمْ يَرْجُمُوكُمْ أَوْ يُعِيدُوكُمْ فِى مِلَّتِهِمْ وَلَن تُفْلِحُوٓا۟ إِذًا أَبَدًا ۞ وَكَذَٰلِكَ أَعْثَرْنَا عَلَيْهِمْ لِيَعْلَمُوٓا۟ أَنَّ وَعْدَ ٱللَّهِ حَقٌّ وَأَنَّ ٱلسَّاعَةَ لَا رَيْبَ فِيهَآ إِذْ يَتَنَٰزَعُونَ بَيْنَهُمْ أَمْرَهُمْ ۖ فَقَالُوا۟ ٱبْنُوا۟ عَلَيْهِم بُنْيَٰنًا ۖ رَّبُّهُمْ أَعْلَمُ بِهِمْ ۚ قَالَ ٱلَّذِينَ غَلَبُوا۟ عَلَىٰٓ أَمْرِهِمْ لَنَتَّخِذَنَّ عَلَيْهِم مَّسْجِدًا ۞ سَيَقُولُونَ ثَلَٰثَةٌ رَّابِعُهُمْ كَلْبُهُمْ وَيَقُولُونَ خَمْسَةٌ سَادِسُهُمْ كَلْبُهُمْ رَجْمًۢا بِٱلْغَيْبِ ۖ وَيَقُولُونَ سَبْعَةٌ وَثَامِنُهُمْ كَلْبُهُمْ ۚ قُل رَّبِّىٓ أَعْلَمُ بِعِدَّتِهِم مَّا يَعْلَمُهُمْ إِلَّا قَلِيلٌ ۗ فَلَا تُمَارِ فِيهِمْ إِلَّا مِرَآءً ظَٰهِرًا وَلَا تَسْتَفْتِ فِيهِم مِّنْهُمْ أَحَدًا ۞ وَلَا تَقُولَنَّ لِشَا۟ىْءٍ إِنِّى فَاعِلٌ ذَٰلِكَ غَدًا ۞ إِلَّآ أَن يَشَآءَ ٱللَّهُ ۚ وَٱذْكُر رَّبَّكَ إِذَا نَسِيتَ وَقُلْ عَسَىٰٓ أَن يَهْدِيَنِ رَبِّى لِأَقْرَبَ مِنْ هَٰذَا رَشَدًا ۞ وَلَبِثُوا۟ فِى كَهْفِهِمْ ثَلَٰثَ مِا۟ئَةٍ سِنِينَ وَٱزْدَادُوا۟ تِسْعًا ۞ قُلِ ٱللَّهُ أَعْلَمُ بِمَا لَبِثُوا۟ ۖ لَهُۥ غَيْبُ ٱلسَّمَٰوَٰتِ وَٱلْأَرْضِ ۖ أَبْصِرْ بِهِۦ وَأَسْمِعْ ۚ مَا لَهُم مِّن دُونِهِۦ مِن وَلِىٍّ وَلَا يُشْرِكُ فِى حُكْمِهِۦٓ أَحَدًا ۞ وَٱتْلُ مَآ أُوحِىَ إِلَيْكَ مِن كِتَابِ رَبِّكَ ۖ لَا مُبَدِّلَ لِكَلِمَٰتِهِۦ وَلَن تَجِدَ مِن دُونِهِۦ مُلْتَحَدًا ۞ وَٱصْبِرْ نَفْسَكَ

مَعَ ٱلَّذِينَ يَدْعُونَ رَبَّهُم بِٱلْغَدَوٰةِ وَٱلْعَشِيِّ يُرِيدُونَ وَجْهَهُۥ ۖ وَلَا تَعْدُ عَيْنَاكَ عَنْهُمْ تُرِيدُ زِينَةَ ٱلْحَيَوٰةِ ٱلدُّنْيَا ۖ وَلَا تُطِعْ مَنْ أَغْفَلْنَا قَلْبَهُۥ عَن ذِكْرِنَا وَٱتَّبَعَ هَوَىٰهُ وَكَانَ أَمْرُهُۥ فُرُطًا ۝ وَقُلِ ٱلْحَقُّ مِن رَّبِّكُمْ ۖ فَمَن شَآءَ فَلْيُؤْمِن وَمَن شَآءَ فَلْيَكْفُرْ ۚ إِنَّآ أَعْتَدْنَا لِلظَّٰلِمِينَ نَارًا أَحَاطَ بِهِمْ سُرَادِقُهَا ۚ وَإِن يَسْتَغِيثُوا۟ يُغَاثُوا۟ بِمَآءٍ كَٱلْمُهْلِ يَشْوِى ٱلْوُجُوهَ ۚ بِئْسَ ٱلشَّرَابُ وَسَآءَتْ مُرْتَفَقًا ۝ إِنَّ ٱلَّذِينَ ءَامَنُوا۟ وَعَمِلُوا۟ ٱلصَّٰلِحَٰتِ إِنَّا لَا نُضِيعُ أَجْرَ مَنْ أَحْسَنَ عَمَلًا ۝ أُو۟لَٰٓئِكَ لَهُمْ جَنَّٰتُ عَدْنٍ تَجْرِى مِن تَحْتِهِمُ ٱلْأَنْهَٰرُ يُحَلَّوْنَ فِيهَا مِنْ أَسَاوِرَ مِن ذَهَبٍ وَيَلْبَسُونَ ثِيَابًا خُضْرًا مِّن سُندُسٍ وَإِسْتَبْرَقٍ مُّتَّكِـِٔينَ فِيهَا عَلَى ٱلْأَرَآئِكِ ۚ نِعْمَ ٱلثَّوَابُ وَحَسُنَتْ مُرْتَفَقًا ۝ ۞ وَٱضْرِبْ لَهُم مَّثَلًا رَّجُلَيْنِ جَعَلْنَا لِأَحَدِهِمَا جَنَّتَيْنِ مِنْ أَعْنَٰبٍ وَحَفَفْنَٰهُمَا بِنَخْلٍ وَجَعَلْنَا بَيْنَهُمَا زَرْعًا ۝ كِلْتَا ٱلْجَنَّتَيْنِ ءَاتَتْ أُكُلَهَا وَلَمْ تَظْلِم مِّنْهُ شَيْـًٔا ۚ وَفَجَّرْنَا خِلَٰلَهُمَا نَهَرًا ۝ وَكَانَ لَهُۥ ثَمَرٌ فَقَالَ لِصَٰحِبِهِۦ وَهُوَ يُحَاوِرُهُۥٓ أَنَا۠ أَكْثَرُ مِنكَ مَالًا وَأَعَزُّ نَفَرًا ۝ وَدَخَلَ جَنَّتَهُۥ وَهُوَ ظَالِمٌ لِّنَفْسِهِۦ قَالَ مَآ أَظُنُّ أَن تَبِيدَ هَٰذِهِۦٓ أَبَدًا ۝ وَمَآ أَظُنُّ ٱلسَّاعَةَ قَآئِمَةً وَلَئِن رُّدِدتُّ إِلَىٰ رَبِّى لَأَجِدَنَّ خَيْرًا مِّنْهَا مُنقَلَبًا ۝ قَالَ لَهُۥ صَاحِبُهُۥ وَهُوَ يُحَاوِرُهُۥٓ أَكَفَرْتَ بِٱلَّذِى خَلَقَكَ مِن تُرَابٍ ثُمَّ مِن نُّطْفَةٍ ثُمَّ سَوَّىٰكَ رَجُلًا ۝ لَّٰكِنَّا۠ هُوَ ٱللَّهُ رَبِّى وَلَآ أُشْرِكُ بِرَبِّىٓ أَحَدًا ۝ وَلَوْلَآ إِذْ دَخَلْتَ جَنَّتَكَ قُلْتَ مَا شَآءَ ٱللَّهُ لَا قُوَّةَ إِلَّا بِٱللَّهِ ۚ إِن تَرَنِ أَنَا۠ أَقَلَّ مِنكَ مَالًا وَوَلَدًا ۝ فَعَسَىٰ رَبِّىٓ أَن يُؤْتِيَنِ خَيْرًا مِّن جَنَّتِكَ وَيُرْسِلَ عَلَيْهَا حُسْبَانًا مِّنَ ٱلسَّمَآءِ فَتُصْبِحَ صَعِيدًا زَلَقًا ۝ أَوْ يُصْبِحَ مَآؤُهَا غَوْرًا فَلَن تَسْتَطِيعَ لَهُۥ طَلَبًا ۝ وَأُحِيطَ بِثَمَرِهِۦ فَأَصْبَحَ يُقَلِّبُ كَفَّيْهِ عَلَىٰ مَآ أَنفَقَ فِيهَا وَهِىَ خَاوِيَةٌ عَلَىٰ عُرُوشِهَا وَيَقُولُ يَٰلَيْتَنِى لَمْ أُشْرِكْ بِرَبِّىٓ أَحَدًا ۝ وَلَمْ تَكُن لَّهُۥ فِئَةٌ يَنصُرُونَهُۥ

مِن دُونِ ٱللَّهِ وَمَا كَانَ مُنتَصِرًا ۝ هُنَالِكَ ٱلْوَلَٰيَةُ لِلَّهِ ٱلْحَقِّ ۚ هُوَ خَيْرٌ ثَوَابًا وَخَيْرٌ عُقْبًا ۝ وَٱضْرِبْ لَهُم مَّثَلَ ٱلْحَيَوٰةِ ٱلدُّنْيَا كَمَآءٍ أَنزَلْنَٰهُ مِنَ ٱلسَّمَآءِ فَٱخْتَلَطَ بِهِۦ نَبَاتُ ٱلْأَرْضِ فَأَصْبَحَ هَشِيمًا تَذْرُوهُ ٱلرِّيَٰحُ ۗ وَكَانَ ٱللَّهُ عَلَىٰ كُلِّ شَىْءٍ مُّقْتَدِرًا ۝ ٱلْمَالُ وَٱلْبَنُونَ زِينَةُ ٱلْحَيَوٰةِ ٱلدُّنْيَا ۖ وَٱلْبَٰقِيَٰتُ ٱلصَّٰلِحَٰتُ خَيْرٌ عِندَ رَبِّكَ ثَوَابًا وَخَيْرٌ أَمَلًا ۝ وَيَوْمَ نُسَيِّرُ ٱلْجِبَالَ وَتَرَى ٱلْأَرْضَ بَارِزَةً وَحَشَرْنَٰهُمْ فَلَمْ نُغَادِرْ مِنْهُمْ أَحَدًا ۝ وَعُرِضُوا۟ عَلَىٰ رَبِّكَ صَفًّا لَّقَدْ جِئْتُمُونَا كَمَا خَلَقْنَٰكُمْ أَوَّلَ مَرَّةٍ ۚ بَلْ زَعَمْتُمْ أَلَّن نَّجْعَلَ لَكُم مَّوْعِدًا ۝ وَوُضِعَ ٱلْكِتَٰبُ فَتَرَى ٱلْمُجْرِمِينَ مُشْفِقِينَ مِمَّا فِيهِ وَيَقُولُونَ يَٰوَيْلَتَنَا مَالِ هَٰذَا ٱلْكِتَٰبِ لَا يُغَادِرُ صَغِيرَةً وَلَا كَبِيرَةً إِلَّآ أَحْصَىٰهَا ۚ وَوَجَدُوا۟ مَا عَمِلُوا۟ حَاضِرًا ۗ وَلَا يَظْلِمُ رَبُّكَ أَحَدًا ۝ وَإِذْ قُلْنَا لِلْمَلَٰٓئِكَةِ ٱسْجُدُوا۟ لِءَادَمَ فَسَجَدُوٓا۟ إِلَّآ إِبْلِيسَ كَانَ مِنَ ٱلْجِنِّ فَفَسَقَ عَنْ أَمْرِ رَبِّهِۦٓ ۗ أَفَتَتَّخِذُونَهُۥ وَذُرِّيَّتَهُۥٓ أَوْلِيَآءَ مِن دُونِى وَهُمْ لَكُمْ عَدُوٌّۢ ۚ بِئْسَ لِلظَّٰلِمِينَ بَدَلًا ۝ ۞ مَّآ أَشْهَدتُّهُمْ خَلْقَ ٱلسَّمَٰوَٰتِ وَٱلْأَرْضِ وَلَا خَلْقَ أَنفُسِهِمْ وَمَا كُنتُ مُتَّخِذَ ٱلْمُضِلِّينَ عَضُدًا ۝ وَيَوْمَ يَقُولُ نَادُوا۟ شُرَكَآءِىَ ٱلَّذِينَ زَعَمْتُمْ فَدَعَوْهُمْ فَلَمْ يَسْتَجِيبُوا۟ لَهُمْ وَجَعَلْنَا بَيْنَهُم مَّوْبِقًا ۝ وَرَءَا ٱلْمُجْرِمُونَ ٱلنَّارَ فَظَنُّوٓا۟ أَنَّهُم مُّوَاقِعُوهَا وَلَمْ يَجِدُوا۟ عَنْهَا مَصْرِفًا ۝ وَلَقَدْ صَرَّفْنَا فِى هَٰذَا ٱلْقُرْءَانِ لِلنَّاسِ مِن كُلِّ مَثَلٍ ۚ وَكَانَ ٱلْإِنسَٰنُ أَكْثَرَ شَىْءٍ جَدَلًا ۝ وَمَا مَنَعَ ٱلنَّاسَ أَن يُؤْمِنُوٓا۟ إِذْ جَآءَهُمُ ٱلْهُدَىٰ وَيَسْتَغْفِرُوا۟ رَبَّهُمْ إِلَّآ أَن تَأْتِيَهُمْ سُنَّةُ ٱلْأَوَّلِينَ أَوْ يَأْتِيَهُمُ ٱلْعَذَابُ قُبُلًا ۝ وَمَا نُرْسِلُ ٱلْمُرْسَلِينَ إِلَّا مُبَشِّرِينَ وَمُنذِرِينَ ۚ وَيُجَٰدِلُ ٱلَّذِينَ كَفَرُوا۟ بِٱلْبَٰطِلِ لِيُدْحِضُوا۟ بِهِ ٱلْحَقَّ ۖ وَٱتَّخَذُوٓا۟ ءَايَٰتِى وَمَآ أُنذِرُوا۟ هُزُوًا ۝ وَمَنْ أَظْلَمُ مِمَّن ذُكِّرَ بِـَٔايَٰتِ رَبِّهِۦ فَأَعْرَضَ عَنْهَا وَنَسِىَ مَا قَدَّمَتْ يَدَاهُ ۚ إِنَّا جَعَلْنَا عَلَىٰ قُلُوبِهِمْ أَكِنَّةً أَن

يَفْقَهُوهُ وَفِى ءَاذَانِهِمْ وَقْرًا ۖ وَإِن تَدْعُهُمْ إِلَى ٱلْهُدَىٰ فَلَن يَهْتَدُوٓاْ إِذًا أَبَدًا ۝ وَرَبُّكَ ٱلْغَفُورُ ذُو ٱلرَّحْمَةِ ۖ لَوْ يُؤَاخِذُهُم بِمَا كَسَبُواْ لَعَجَّلَ لَهُمُ ٱلْعَذَابَ ۚ بَل لَّهُم مَّوْعِدٌ لَّن يَجِدُواْ مِن دُونِهِۦ مَوْئِلًا ۝ وَتِلْكَ ٱلْقُرَىٰٓ أَهْلَكْنَـٰهُمْ لَمَّا ظَلَمُواْ وَجَعَلْنَا لِمَهْلِكِهِم مَّوْعِدًا ۝ وَإِذْ قَالَ مُوسَىٰ لِفَتَىٰهُ لَآ أَبْرَحُ حَتَّىٰٓ أَبْلُغَ مَجْمَعَ ٱلْبَحْرَيْنِ أَوْ أَمْضِىَ حُقُبًا ۝ فَلَمَّا بَلَغَا مَجْمَعَ بَيْنِهِمَا نَسِيَا حُوتَهُمَا فَٱتَّخَذَ سَبِيلَهُۥ فِى ٱلْبَحْرِ سَرَبًا ۝ فَلَمَّا جَاوَزَا قَالَ لِفَتَىٰهُ ءَاتِنَا غَدَآءَنَا لَقَدْ لَقِينَا مِن سَفَرِنَا هَـٰذَا نَصَبًا ۝ قَالَ أَرَءَيْتَ إِذْ أَوَيْنَآ إِلَى ٱلصَّخْرَةِ فَإِنِّى نَسِيتُ ٱلْحُوتَ وَمَآ أَنسَىٰنِيهُ إِلَّا ٱلشَّيْطَـٰنُ أَنْ أَذْكُرَهُۥ ۚ وَٱتَّخَذَ سَبِيلَهُۥ فِى ٱلْبَحْرِ عَجَبًا ۝ قَالَ ذَٰلِكَ مَا كُنَّا نَبْغِ ۚ فَٱرْتَدَّا عَلَىٰٓ ءَاثَارِهِمَا قَصَصًا ۝ فَوَجَدَا عَبْدًا مِّنْ عِبَادِنَآ ءَاتَيْنَـٰهُ رَحْمَةً مِّنْ عِندِنَا وَعَلَّمْنَـٰهُ مِن لَّدُنَّا عِلْمًا ۝ قَالَ لَهُۥ مُوسَىٰ هَلْ أَتَّبِعُكَ عَلَىٰٓ أَن تُعَلِّمَنِ مِمَّا عُلِّمْتَ رُشْدًا ۝ قَالَ إِنَّكَ لَن تَسْتَطِيعَ مَعِىَ صَبْرًا ۝ وَكَيْفَ تَصْبِرُ عَلَىٰ مَا لَمْ تُحِطْ بِهِۦ خُبْرًا ۝ قَالَ سَتَجِدُنِىٓ إِن شَآءَ ٱللَّهُ صَابِرًا وَلَآ أَعْصِى لَكَ أَمْرًا ۝ قَالَ فَإِنِ ٱتَّبَعْتَنِى فَلَا تَسْـَٔلْنِى عَن شَىْءٍ حَتَّىٰٓ أُحْدِثَ لَكَ مِنْهُ ذِكْرًا ۝ فَٱنطَلَقَا حَتَّىٰٓ إِذَا رَكِبَا فِى ٱلسَّفِينَةِ خَرَقَهَا ۖ قَالَ أَخَرَقْتَهَا لِتُغْرِقَ أَهْلَهَا لَقَدْ جِئْتَ شَيْـًٔا إِمْرًا ۝ قَالَ أَلَمْ أَقُلْ إِنَّكَ لَن تَسْتَطِيعَ مَعِىَ صَبْرًا ۝ قَالَ لَا تُؤَاخِذْنِى بِمَا نَسِيتُ وَلَا تُرْهِقْنِى مِنْ أَمْرِى عُسْرًا ۝ فَٱنطَلَقَا حَتَّىٰٓ إِذَا لَقِيَا غُلَـٰمًا فَقَتَلَهُۥ قَالَ أَقَتَلْتَ نَفْسًا زَكِيَّةً بِغَيْرِ نَفْسٍ لَّقَدْ جِئْتَ شَيْـًٔا نُّكْرًا ۝

(Al-Kahf 001-074)

INTRODUCTION TO CHAPTER (SURAH) 17: AL-ISRAA (THE NIGHT JOURNEY, OR BANI ISRA'IL, OR THE CILDREN OF ISRAEL)

Ibn kathir's Introduction

The Virtues of Surat Al-Isra'

Imam Al-Hafiz Abu `Abdullah Muhammad bin Isma`il Al-Bukhari recorded that Ibn Mas`ud said concerning Surah Bani Isra`il (i.e., Surat Al-Isra'), Al-Kahf and Maryam: "They are among the earliest and most beautiful Surahs and they are my treasure." Imam Ahmad recorded that `A'ishah said: "The Messenger of Allah used to fast until we would say, he does not want to break his fast, then he would not fast until we would say, he does not want to fast, and he used to recite Bani Isra'il and Az-Zumar every night."

CHAPTER (SURAH) 17: AL-ISRAA (THE NIGHT JOURNEY, OR BANI ISRAIL, OR THE CILDREN OF ISRAEL), VERSES 001–111

(بِسْمِ اللَّهِ الرَّحْمَـنِ الرَّحِيمِ)

In the Name of Allah, the Most Gracious, the Most Merciful.

Surah: 17 Ayah: 1

سُبْحَـنَ ٱلَّذِىۤ أَسْرَىٰ بِعَبْدِهِۦ لَيْلاً مِّنَ ٱلْمَسْجِدِ ٱلْحَرَامِ إِلَى ٱلْمَسْجِدِ ٱلأَقْصَا ٱلَّذِى بَـٰرَكْنَا حَوْلَهُۥ لِنُرِيَهُۥ مِنْ ءَايَـٰتِنَآ إِنَّهُۥ هُوَ ٱلسَّمِيعُ ٱلْبَصِيرُ

1. Glorified be He Who took His servant for a Journey by Night from Al-Masjid Al-Haram to Al-Masjid Al-Aqsa, the neighborhood whereof We have blessed, in order that We might show him of Our Ayat. Verily, He is the All-Hearer, the All-Seer.

Transliteration

1. Subhana allathee asra biAAabdihi laylan mina almasjidi alharami ila almasjidi al-aqsa allathee barakna hawlahu linuriyahu min ayatina innahu huwa alssameeAAu albaseeru

Tafsir Ibn Kathir

The Isra' (Night Journey)

Allah glorifies Himself, for His ability to do that which none but He can do, for there is no God but He and no Lord besides Him.

(Who took His servant for a Journey) refers to Muhammad

(by Night) means, in the depths of the night.

(from Al-Masjid Al-Haram) means the Masjid in Makkah.

(to Al-Masjid Al-Aqsa,) means the Sacred House which is in Jerusalem, the origin of the Prophets from the time of Ibrahim Al-Khalil. The Prophets all gathered there, and he (Muhammad) led them in prayer in their own homeland. This indicates that he is the greatest leader of all, may the peace and blessings of Allah be upon him and upon them.

(the neighborhood whereof We have blessed) means, its agricultural produce and fruits are blessed

(in order that We might show him), i.e., Muhammad

(of Our Ayat.) i.e., great signs. As Allah says:

(Indeed he did see of the greatest signs, of his Lord (Allah).) (53:18) We will mention below what was narrated in the Sunnah concerning this.

(Verily, He is the All-Hearer, the All-Seer.) means, He hears all the words of His servants, believers and disbelievers, faithful and infidel, and He sees them and gives each of them what he deserves in this world and the Hereafter. Hadiths about Al-Isra'

The Report of Anas bin Malik

Imam Ahmad reported from Anas bin Malik that the Messenger of Allah said:

(Al-Buraq was brought to me, and it was a white animal bigger than a donkey and smaller than a mule. One stride of this creature covered a distance as far as it could see. I rode on it and it took me to Bayt Al-Maqdis (Jerusalem), where I tethered it at the hitching post of the Prophets. Then I entered and prayed two Rak`ahs there, and came out. Jibril brought me a vessel of wine and a vessel of milk, and I chose the milk. Jibril said: `You have chosen the Fitrah (natural instinct).' Then I was taken up to the first heaven and Jibril asked for it to be opened. It was said, `Who are you' He said, `Jibril.' It was said, `Who is with you' He said, `Muhammad.' It was asked, `Has his Mission started' He said, `His Mission has started.' So it was opened for us, and there I saw Adam, who welcomed me and prayed for good for me. Then I was taken up to the second heaven and Jibril asked for it to be opened. It was said, `Who are you' He said, `Jibril.' It was said, `Who is with you' He said, `Muhammad.' It was asked, `Has his Mission started' He said, `His Mission has started.' So it was opened for us, and there I saw the two maternal cousins, Yahya and `Isa, who welcomed me and prayed for good for me. Then I was taken up to the third heaven and Jibril asked for it to be opened. It was said, `Who are you' He said, `Jibril.' It was said, `Who is with you' He said, `Muhammad.' It was asked, `Has his Mission started' He said, `His Mission has started.' So it was opened for us, and there I saw Yusuf, who had been given the beautiful half. He welcomed me and prayed for good for me. Then I was taken up to the fourth heaven and Jibril asked for it to be opened. It was said, `Who are you' He said, `Jibril.' It was said, `Who is with you' He said, `Muhammad.' It was asked, `Has his Mission started' He said, `His Mission has started.' So it was opened

Chapter 17: Al-Israa (The Night Journey or Bani Isra'il), Verses 001-111

for us, and there I saw Idris, who welcomed me and prayed for good for me. - then (the Prophet) said: Allah says:

(And We raised him to a high station) (19:57).

(Then he resumed his narrative:) (Then I was taken up to the fifth heaven and Jibril asked for it to be opened. It was said, `Who are you' He said, `Jibril.' It was said, `Who is with you' He said, `Muhammad.' It was asked, `Has his Mission started' He said, `His Mission has started.' So it was opened for us, and there I saw Harun, who welcomed me and prayed for good for me. Then I was taken up to the sixth heaven and Jibril asked for it to be opened. It was said, `Who are you' He said, `Jibril. It was said, `Who is with you' He said, `Muhammad.' It was asked, `Has his Mission started' He said, `His Mission has started.' So it was opened for us, and there I saw Musa, who welcomed me and prayed for good for me. Then I was taken up to the seventh heaven and Jibril asked for it to be opened. It was said, `Who are you' He said, `Jibril.' It was said, `Who is with you' He said, `Muhammad.' It was asked, `Has his Mission started' He said, `His Mission has started.' So it was opened for us, and there I saw Ibrahim, who was leaning back against the Much-Frequented House (Al-Bayt Al-Ma`mur). Every day seventy thousand angels enter it, then they never come back to it again. Then I was taken to Sidrat Al-Muntaha (the Lote tree beyond which none may pass), and its leaves were like the leaves (ears) of elephants and its fruits were like jugs, and when it was veiled with whatever it was veiled with by the command of Allah, it changed, and none of the creatures of Allah can describe it because it is so beautiful. Then Allah revealed that which He revealed to me. He enjoined on me fifty prayers every day and night. I came down until I reached Musa, and he said, `What did your Lord enjoin on your Ummah' I said, `Fifty prayers everyday and night.' He said, `Go back to your Lord and ask Him to reduce (the burden) for your Ummah, for your Ummah will not be able to do that. I tested the Children of Israel and found out how they were.' So I went back to my Lord and said, `O Lord, reduce (the burden) for my Ummah for they will never be able to do that.' So He reduced it by five. I came back down until I met Musa and he asked me, `What did you do' I said, `(My Lord) reduced (my burden) by five.' He said, `Go back to your Lord and ask Him to reduce (the burden) for your Ummah.' I kept going back between my Lord and Musa, and (my Lord) reduced it by five each time, until He said, `O Muhammad, these are five prayers every day and night, and for every prayer there is (the reward of) ten, so they are (like) fifty prayers. Whoever wants to do something good then does not do it, one good deed will be recorded for him, and if he does it, ten good deeds will be recorded for him. Whoever wants to do something evil and does not do it, no evil deed will be recorded for him, and if he does it, one evil deed will be recorded for him.' I came down until I reached Musa, and told him about this. He said: `Go back to your Lord and ask him to reduce (the burden) for your Ummah, for they will never be able to do that.' I had kept going back to my Lord until I felt too shy.) This version was also recorded by Muslim. Imam Ahmad recorded Anas saying that Al-Buraq was brought to the Prophet on the Night of the Isra' with his saddle and reins ready for riding. The animal shied, and Jibril said to him: "Why are you doing this By Allah, no one has ever ridden you who is more honored by Allah than him." At this, Al-Buraq started to sweat. This was also recorded by At-Tirmidhi, who said it is Gharib. Ahmad also recorded that Anas said: "The Messenger of Allah said:

«لَمَّا عَرَجَ بِي رَبِّي عَزَّ وَجَلَّ مَرَرْتُ بِقَوْمٍ لَهُمْ أَظْفَارٌ مِنْ نُحَاسٍ يَخْمِشُونَ بِهَا وُجُوهَهُمْ وَصُدُورَهُمْ، فَقُلْتُ: مَنْ هَؤُلَاءِ يَا جِبْرِيلُ؟ قَالَ: هَؤُلَاءِ الَّذِينَ يَأْكُلُونَ لُحُومَ النَّاسِ وَيَقَعُونَ فِي أَعْرَاضِهِم»

(When I was taken up to my Lord (during Al-Mi'raj), I passed by people who had nails of copper with which they were scratching their faces and chests. I asked, `Who are these, O Jibril' He said, `These are those who ate the flesh of the people (i.e., backbiting) and slandered their honor.') This was also recorded by Abu Dawud. Anas also said that the Messenger of Allah said:

«مَرَرْتُ لَيْلَةَ أُسْرِيَ بِي عَلَى مُوسَى عَلَيْهِ السَّلَامُ قَائِمًا يُصَلِّي فِي قَبْرِه»

(On the night when I was taken on my Night Journey (Al-Isra'), I passed by Musa, who was standing, praying in his grave.) This was also recorded by Muslim.

The Report of Anas bin Malik from Malik bin Sa`sa`ah

Imam Ahmad recorded that Anas bin Malik said that Malik bin Sa`sa`ah told him that the Prophet of Allah told them about the night in which he was taken on the Night Journey (Al-Isra'). He said:

«بَيْنَمَا أَنَا فِي الْحَطِيمِ وَرُبَّمَا قَالَ قَتَادَةُ: فِي الْحِجْرِ مُضْطَجِعًا إِذْ أَتَانِي آتٍ، فَجَعَلَ يَقُولُ لِصَاحِبِهِ الْأَوْسَطِ بَيْنَ الثَّلَاثَةِ قَالَ فَأَتَانِي فَقَدَّ سَمِعْتُ قَتَادَةَ يَقُولُ: فَشَقَّ مَا بَيْنَ هَذِهِ إِلَى هَذِه»

(While I was lying down in Al-Hatim (or maybe, Qatadah said, in Al-Hijr) 'someone came to me and said to his companion, `The one who is in the middle of these three.' He came to me and opened me.) I (one of the narrators) heard Qatadah say, `split me - from here to here.' Qatadah said: "I said to Al-Jarud, who was beside me, `What does that mean' He said, `From the top of his chest to below his navel', and I heard him say, `from his throat to below his navel'. The Prophet said:

«فَاسْتُخْرِجَ قَلْبِي قَالَ فَأُتِيتُ بِطَسْتٍ مِنْ ذَهَبٍ مَمْلُوءَةٍ إِيمَانًا وَحِكْمَةً فَغُسِلَ قَلْبِي ثُمَّ حُشِيَ ثُمَّ أُعِيدَ ثُمَّ أُتِيتُ بِدَابَّةٍ دُونَ الْبَغْلِ وَفَوْقَ الْحِمَارِ أَبْيَض»

(He took out my heart and brought a golden vessel filled with faith and wisdom. He washed my heart then filled it up and put it back, then a white animal was brought to me that was smaller than a mule and larger than a donkey.) Al-Jarud said, `Was this Al-Buraq, O Abu Hamzah' He said, `Yes, and its stride covered a distance as far as it could see.' The Prophet said:

«فَحُمِلْتُ عَلَيْهِ فَانْطَلَقَ بِي جِبْرِيلُ عَلَيْهِ السَّلَامُ حَتَّى أَتَى بِي إِلَى السَّمَاءِ الدُّنْيَا فَاسْتَفْتَحَ، فَقِيلَ: مَنْ هَذَا؟ قَالَ: جِبْرِيلُ، قِيلَ: وَمَنْ مَعَكَ؟ قَالَ: مُحَمَّدٌ، قِيلَ: أَوَ قَدْ أُرْسِلَ إِلَيْهِ؟ قَالَ: نَعَمْ فَقِيلَ: مَرْحَبًا بِهِ وَلَنِعْمَ الْمَجِيءُ جَاءَ قَالَ فَفُتِحَ لَنَا فَلَمَّا خَلَصْتُ فَإِذَا فِيهَا آدَمُ عَلَيْهِ السَّلَامُ، قَالَ: هَذَا أَبُوكَ آدَمُ فَسَلِّمْ عَلَيْهِ، فَسَلَّمْتُ عَلَيْهِ فَرَدَّ السَّلَامَ ثُمَّ قَالَ: مَرْحَبًا بِالْابْنِ الصَّالِحِ وَالنَّبِيِّ الصَّالِحِ، قَالَ: فَلَمَّا تَجَاوَزْتُهُ بَكَى قِيلَ لَهُ: مَا يُبْكِيكَ؟ قَالَ: أَبْكِي لِأَنَّ غُلَامًا بُعِثَ بَعْدِي يَدْخُلُ الْجَنَّةَ مِنْ أُمَّتِهِ أَكْثَرُ مِمَّا يَدْخُلُهَا مِنْ أُمَّتِي. قَالَ: ثُمَّ صَعِدَ حَتَّى أَتَى السَّمَاءَ السَّابِعَةَ فَاسْتَفْتَحَ قِيلَ: مَنْ هَذَا؟ قَالَ: جِبْرِيلُ، قِيلَ: وَمَنْ مَعَكَ؟ قَالَ: مُحَمَّدٌ، قِيلَ: أَوَ قَدْ بُعِثَ إِلَيْهِ؟ قَالَ: نَعَمْ، قِيلَ: مَرْحَبًا بِهِ وَلَنِعْمَ الْمَجِيءُ جَاءَ، قَالَ: فَفُتِحَ لَنَا فَلَمَّا خَلَصْتُ فَإِذَا إِبْرَاهِيمُ عَلَيْهِ السَّلَامُ فَقَالَ: هَذَا إِبْرَاهِيمُ فَسَلِّمْ عَلَيْهِ قَالَ: فَسَلَّمْتُ عَلَيْهِ فَرَدَّ السَّلَامَ، ثُمَّ قَالَ: مَرْحَبًا بِالْابْنِ الصَّالِحِ وَالنَّبِيِّ الصَّالِحِ قَالَ ثُمَّ رُفِعَتْ إِلَيَّ سِدْرَةُ الْمُنْتَهَى فَإِذَا نَبْقُهَا مِثْلُ قِلَالِ هَجَرَ، وَإِذَا وَرَقُهَا مِثْلُ آذَانِ الْفِيلَةِ، فَقَالَ: هَذِهِ سِدْرَةُ الْمُنْتَهَى، قَالَ: وَإِذَا أَرْبَعَةُ أَنْهَارٍ: نَهْرَانِ بَاطِنَانِ وَنَهْرَانِ ظَاهِرَانِ، فَقُلْتُ: مَا هَذَا يَا جِبْرِيلُ؟ قَالَ: أَمَّا الْبَاطِنَانِ فَنَهْرَانِ فِي الْجَنَّةِ، وَأَمَّا الظَّاهِرَانِ فَالنِّيلُ وَالْفُرَاتُ قَالَ ثُمَّ رُفِعَ إِلَيَّ الْبَيْتُ الْمَعْمُورُ»

(I was mounted upon it and Jibril brought me to the first heaven, and asked for it to be opened. It was said, `Who is this' He said, `Jibril.' It was said, `Who is with you'

He said, 'Muhammad.' It was said, 'Has his Mission started' He said, 'Yes.' It was said, 'Welcome to him, blessed is the one who comes.' So it was opened for us and when I entered, I saw Adam. (Jibril) said, 'This is your father Adam, greet him.' So I greeted him, and he returned the greeting then said, 'Welcome to the righteous son and righteous Prophet.' Then I was taken up to the fifth heaven, and (Jibril) asked for it to be opened. It was said, 'Who is this' He said, 'Jibril.' It was said, 'Who is with you' He said, 'Muhammad.' It was said, 'Has his Mission started' He said, 'Yes.' It was said, 'Welcome to him, blessed is the one who comes.' So it was opened for us and when I entered, I saw Harun. (Jibril) said, 'This is Harun, greet him.' So I greeted him, and he returned the greeting then said, 'Welcome to the righteous brother and righteous Prophet.' Then I was taken up to the sixth heaven, and (Jibril) asked for it to be opened. It was said, 'Who is this' He said, 'Jibril.' It was said, 'Who is with you' He said, 'Muhammad.' It was said, 'Has his Mission started' He said, 'Yes.' It was said, 'Welcome to him, blessed is the one who comes.' So it was opened for us and when I entered, I saw Musa. (Jibril) said, 'This is Musa, greet him.' So I greeted him, and he returned the greeting then said, 'Welcome to the righteous brother and righteous Prophet.' When I passed by him, he wept, and it was said to him, 'Why are you weeping' He said, 'I am weeping because a young man was sent after me and more people from his Ummah than from mine will enter Paradise.' Then I was taken up to the seventh heaven, and (Jibril) asked for it to be opened. It was said, 'Who is this' He said, 'Jibril.' It was said, 'Who is with you' He said, 'Muhammad'. It was said, 'Has his Mission started' He said, 'Yes.' It was said, 'Welcome to him, blessed is the one who comes.' So it was opened for us and when I entered, I saw Ibrahim. (Jibril) said, 'This is Ibrahim, greet him.' So I greeted him, and he returned the greeting then said, 'Welcome to the righteous son and righteous Prophet.' Then I was taken up to Sidrat Al-Muntaha, whose fruits like the clay jugs of Hajar (a region in Arabia) and its leaves were like the ears of elephants. (Jibril) said: 'This is Sidrat Al-Muntaha.' And there were four rivers, two hidden and two visible. I said, 'What is this, O Jibril' He said, 'The two hidden rivers are rivers in Paradise, and the two visible rivers are the Nile and the Euphrates.' Then I was shown Al-Bayt Al-Ma`mur.) Qatadah said: Al-Hasan told us narrating from Abu Hurayrah that the Prophet saw Al-Bayt Al-Ma`mur. Each day seventy thousand angels enter it, then they never return from it. Then he continued to narrate the Hadith of Anas;

«ثُمَّ أُتِيتُ بِإِنَاءٍ مِنْ خَمْرٍ وَإِنَاءٍ مِنْ لَبَنٍ وَإِنَاءٍ مِنْ عَسَلٍ. قَالَ فَأَخَذْتُ اللَّبَنَ قَالَ: هَذِهِ الْفِطْرَةُ أَنْتَ عَلَيْهَا وَأُمَّتُكَ قَالَ ثُمَّ فُرِضَتْ عَلَيَّ الصَّلَاةُ خَمْسِينَ صَلَاةً كُلَّ يَوْمٍ قَالَ فَنَزَلْتُ حَتَّى أَتَيْتُ مُوسَى، فَقَالَ: مَا فَرَضَ رَبُّكَ عَلَى أُمَّتِكَ؟ قَالَ: فَقُلْتُ: خَمْسِينَ صَلَاةً كُلَّ يَوْمٍ، قَالَ: إِنَّ أُمَّتَكَ لَا تَسْتَطِيعُ خَمْسِينَ صَلَاةً وَإِنِّي قَدْ خَبَرْتُ النَّاسَ قَبْلَكَ، وَعَالَجْتُ بَنِي إِسْرَائِيلَ أَشَدَّ

الْمُعَالَجَةِ، فَارْجِعْ إِلَى رَبِّكَ فَاسْأَلْهُ التَّخْفِيفَ لِأُمَّتِكَ قَالَ فَرَجَعْتُ فَوَضَعَ عَنِّي عَشْرًا قَالَ فَرَجَعْتُ إِلَى مُوسَى فَقَالَ: بِمَ أُمِرْتَ؟ قُلْتُ: بِأَرْبَعِينَ صَلَاةً كُلَّ يَوْمٍ، قَالَ: إِنَّ أُمَّتَكَ لَا تَسْتَطِيعُ أَرْبَعِينَ صَلَاةً كُلَّ يَوْمٍ، وَإِنِّي قَدْ خَبَرْتُ النَّاسَ قَبْلَكَ وَعَالَجْتُ بَنِي إِسْرَائِيلَ أَشَدَّ الْمُعَالَجَةِ، فَارْجِعْ إِلَى رَبِّكَ فَاسْأَلْهُ التَّخْفِيفَ لِأُمَّتِكَ قَالَ فَرَجَعْتُ فَوَضَعَ عَنِّي عَشْرًا أُخَرَ، فَرَجَعْتُ إِلَى مُوسَى فَقَالَ: بِمَ أُمِرْتَ؟ قُلْتُ: بِثَلَاثِينَ صَلَاةً، قَالَ: إِنَّ أُمَّتَكَ لَا تَسْتَطِيعُ ثَلَاثِينَ صَلَاةً كُلَّ يَوْمٍ، وَإِنِّي قَدْ خَبَرْتُ النَّاسَ قَبْلَكَ وَعَالَجْتُ بَنِي إِسْرَائِيلَ أَشَدَّ الْمُعَالَجَةِ، فَارْجِعْ إِلَى رَبِّكَ فَاسْأَلْهُ التَّخْفِيفَ لِأُمَّتِكَ قَالَ فَرَجَعْتُ فَوَضَعَ عَنِّي عَشْرًا أُخَرَ، فَرَجَعْتُ إِلَى مُوسَى فَقَالَ: بِمَ أُمِرْتَ؟ قُلْتُ: أُمِرْتُ بِعِشْرِينَ صَلَاةً كُلَّ يَوْمٍ، قَالَ: إِنَّ أُمَّتَكَ لَا تَسْتَطِيعُ عِشْرِينَ صَلَاةً كُلَّ يَوْمٍ، وَإِنِّي قَدْ خَبَرْتُ النَّاسَ قَبْلَكَ وَعَالَجْتُ بَنِي إِسْرَائِيلَ أَشَدَّ الْمُعَالَجَةِ، فَارْجِعْ إِلَى رَبِّكَ فَاسْأَلْهُ التَّخْفِيفَ لِأُمَّتِكَ قَالَ فَرَجَعْتُ فَوَضَعَ عَنِّي عَشْرًا أُخَرَ، فَرَجَعْتُ إِلَى مُوسَى فَقَالَ: بِمَ أُمِرْتَ؟ فَقُلْتُ: أُمِرْتُ بِعَشْرِ صَلَوَاتٍ كُلَّ يَوْمٍ، فَقَالَ: إِنَّ أُمَّتَكَ لَا تَسْتَطِيعُ لِعَشْرِ صَلَوَاتٍ كُلَّ يَوْمٍ، وَإِنِّي قَدْ خَبَرْتُ النَّاسَ قَبْلَكَ وَعَالَجْتُ بَنِي إِسْرَائِيلَ أَشَدَّ الْمُعَالَجَةِ، فَارْجِعْ إِلَى رَبِّكَ فَاسْأَلْهُ التَّخْفِيفَ لِأُمَّتِكَ قَالَ فَرَجَعْتُ فَأُمِرْتُ بِخَمْسِ صَلَوَاتٍ كُلَّ يَوْمٍ، فَرَجَعْتُ إِلَى مُوسَى فَقَالَ: بِمَ أُمِرْتَ؟ فَقُلْتُ: أُمِرْتُ بِخَمْسِ صَلَوَاتٍ كُلَّ يَوْمٍ، فَقَالَ: إِنَّ أُمَّتَكَ لَا تَسْتَطِيعُ لِخَمْسِ صَلَوَاتٍ كُلَّ يَوْمٍ، وَإِنِّي قَدْ خَبَرْتُ النَّاسَ قَبْلَكَ وَعَالَجْتُ بَنِي إِسْرَائِيلَ أَشَدَّ الْمُعَالَجَةِ، فَارْجِعْ إِلَى رَبِّكَ فَاسْأَلْهُ التَّخْفِيفَ لِأُمَّتِكَ قَالَ قُلْتُ: قَدْ سَأَلْتُ رَبِّي حَتَّى اسْتَحْيَيْتُ،

وَلَكِنْ أَرْضَى وَأُسَلِّمُ، فَنَفَذْتُ فَنَادَى مُنَادٍ: قَدْ أَمْضَيْتُ فَرِيضَتِي وَخَفَّفْتُ عَنْ عِبَادِي»

(Then I was brought a vessel of wine, a vessel of milk and a vessel of honey. I chose the milk, and he (Jibril) said, `This is the Fitrah (natural instinct) on which you and your Ummah will be. ' Then the prayer was enjoined upon me, fifty prayers each day. I came down until I reached Musa, who said, `What did your Lord enjoin upon your Ummah' I said, `Fifty prayers each day.' He said, `Your Ummah will not be able to do fifty prayers each day. I tried the people before you, I had to deal with the Children of Israel and it was very difficult for me. Go back to your Lord and ask Him to reduce the burden on your Ummah.' So I went back, and the number was reduced by ten. I came back to Musa and he asked, `What were you commanded to do' I said, `Forty prayers each day.' He said, `Your Ummah will not be able to do forty prayers each day. I tried the people before you, I had to deal with the Children of Israel and it was very difficult for me. Go back to your Lord and ask Him to reduce the burden on your Ummah.' So I went back, and the number was reduced by ten. I came back to Musa and he asked, `What were you commanded to do' I said, `I was commanded to do thirty prayers each day.' He said, `Your Ummah will not be able to do thirty prayers each day. I tried the people before you, I had to deal with the Children of Israel and it was very difficult for me. Go back to your Lord and ask Him to reduce the burden on your Ummah.' So I went back, and the number was reduced by ten. I came back to Musa and he asked, `What were you commanded to do' I said, `Twenty prayers each day.' He said, `Your Ummah will not be able to do twenty prayers each day. I tried the people before you, I had to deal with the Children of Israel and it was very difficult for me. Go back to your Lord and ask Him to reduce the burden on your Ummah.' So I went back, and the number was reduced by ten more. I came back to Musa and he asked, `What were you commanded to do' I said, `Ten prayers each day.' He said, `Your Ummah will not be able to do ten prayers each day. I tried the people before you, I had to deal with the Children of Israel and it was very difficult for me. Go back to your Lord and ask Him to reduce the burden on your Ummah.' So I went back, and I was commanded to do five prayers every day. I came back to Musa and he asked, `What were you commanded to do' I said, `Five prayers each day.' He said, `Your Ummah will not be able to do five prayers each day. I tried the people before you, I had to deal with the Children of Israel and it was very difficult for me. Go back to your Lord and ask Him to reduce the burden on your Ummah.' I said, `I have asked my Lord until I feel too shy. I accept this and submit to Him.' Then a voice called out: `My order has been decreed and I have reduced the burden on My servants.') Similar narrations were recorded in the Two Sahihs.

The Report of Anas from Abu Dharr

Al-Bukhari recorded that Anas bin Malik said: Abu Dharr used to tell us that the Messenger of Allah said:

«فُرِجَ عَنْ سَقْفِ بَيْتِي وَأَنَا بِمَكَّةَ، فَنَزَلَ جِبْرِيلُ فَفَرَجَ صَدْرِي ثُمَّ غَسَلَهُ بِمَاءِ زَمْزَمَ، ثُمَّ جَاءَ بِطَسْتٍ مِنْ ذَهَبٍ مُمْتَلِىءٍ حِكْمَةً وَإِيمَانًا، فَأَفْرَغَهُ فِي صَدْرِي، ثُمَّ أَطْبَقَهُ ثُمَّ أَخَذَ بِيَدِي فَعَرَجَ بِي إِلَى السَّمَاءِ الدُّنْيَا، فَلَمَّا جِئْتُ إِلَى السَّمَاءِ قَالَ جِبْرِيلُ لِخَازِنِ السَّمَاءِ: افْتَحْ قَالَ: مَنْ هَذَا؟ قَالَ: جِبْرِيلُ، قَالَ: هَلْ مَعَكَ أَحَدٌ؟ قَالَ: نَعَمْ مَعِيَ مُحَمَّدٌ صلى الله عليه وسلّم، فَقَالَ: أُرْسِلَ إِلَيْهِ؟ قَالَ: نَعَمْ فَلَمَّا فَتَحَ عَلَوْنَا السَّمَاءَ الدُّنْيَا فَإِذَا رَجُلٌ قَاعِدٌ عَلَى يَمِينِهِ أَسْوِدَةٌ وَعَلَى يَسَارِهِ أَسْوِدَةٌ، إِذَا نَظَرَ قِبَلَ يَمِينِهِ ضَحِكَ وَإِذَا نَظَرَ قِبَلَ شِمَالِهِ بَكَى، فَقَالَ: مَرْحَبًا بِالنَّبِيِّ الصَّالِحِ وَالْابْنِ الصَّالِحِ قَالَ قُلْتُ لِجِبْرِيلَ: مَنْ هَذَا؟ قَالَ: هَذَا آدَمُ وَهَذِهِ الْأَسْوِدَةُ عَنْ يَمِينِهِ وَعَنْ شِمَالِهِ نَسَمُ بَنِيهِ، فَأَهْلُ الْيَمِينِ مِنْهُمْ أَهْلُ الْجَنَّةِ، وَالْأَسْوِدَةُ الَّتِي عَنْ شِمَالِهِ أَهْلُ النَّارِ، فَإِذَا نَظَرَ عَنْ يَمِينِهِ ضَحِكَ، وَإِذَا نَظَرَ عَنْ شِمَالِهِ بَكَى، ثُمَّ عَرَجَ بِي إِلَى السَّمَاءِ الثَّانِيَةِ»

«ثُمَّ مَرَرْتُ بِإِبْرَاهِيمَ فَقَالَ: مَرْحَبًا بِالنَّبِيِّ الصَّالِحِ وَالْابْنِ الصَّالِحِ، قُلْتُ: مَنْ هَذَا؟ قَالَ: هَذَا إِبْرَاهِيمُ»

(The roof of my house was opened while I was in Makkah, and Jibril came down and opened my chest, then he washed it with Zamzam water. Then he brought a vessel of gold filled with wisdom and faith, and poured it into my chest, then he closed it up. Then he took me by the hand and took me up to the lowest heaven. When we came to the lowest heaven, Jibril said to its keeper, `Open up!' He said, `Who is this' He said, `Jibril. ' He said, `Is there anyone with you' He said, `Yes, Muhammad is with me.' He said, `Has his Mission started' He said, `Yes.' When it was opened, we went up into the first heaven, where I saw a man sitting with a multitude to his right and another to his left. When he looked to his right he smiled, and when he looked to his left, he wept. He said, `Welcome to the righteous Prophet and the righteous son.' I said to Jibril, `Who is this' He said, `This is Adam, and these multitudes to his right and left are the souls of his descendants. The people on his right include the people of Paradise, and the people on his left include the people of Hell, so when he looks to his right he smiles, and when he looks to his left he weeps.' Then he took me up to the second heaven...Then we passed by Ibrahim, who said, `Welcome to the righteous Prophet and the righteous son.' I said, `Who is this' He said, `This is Ibrahim.') Az-Zuhri said: Ibn Hazm told me that Ibn `Abbas and Abu Habbah Al-Ansari used to say: the Prophet narrated here –

«ثُمَّ عُرِجَ بِي حَتَّى ظَهَرْتُ لِمُسْتَوًى أَسْمَعُ فِيهِ صَرِيفَ الْأَقْلَامِ»

(Then I was taken up until I reached a level where I could hear the sound of the pens.) Ibn Hazm and Anas bin Malik said: the Messenger of Allah said:

«فَفَرَضَ اللهُ عَلَى أُمَّتِي خَمْسِينَ صَلَاةً، فَرَجَعْتُ بِذَلِكَ حَتَّى مَرَرْتُ عَلَى مُوسَى عَلَيْهِ السَّلَامُ، فَقَالَ: مَا فَرَضَ اللهُ عَلَى أُمَّتِكَ؟ قُلْتُ: فَرَضَ خَمْسِينَ صَلَاةً، قَالَ مُوسَى: فَارْجِعْ إِلَى رَبِّكَ فَإِنَّ أُمَّتَكَ لَا تُطِيقُ ذَلِكَ، فَرَجَعْتُ فَوَضَعَ شَطْرَهَا، فَرَجَعْتُ إِلَى مُوسَى، قُلْتُ: وَضَعَ شَطْرَهَا، فَقَالَ: ارْجِعْ إِلَى رَبِّكَ، فَإِنَّ أُمَّتَكَ لَا تُطِيقُ ذَلِكَ، فَرَجَعْتُ فَوَضَعَ شَطْرَهَا، فَرَجَعْتُ إِلَيْهِ فَقَالَ: ارْجِعْ إِلَى رَبِّكَ فَإِنَّ أُمَّتَكَ لَا تُطِيقُ ذَلِكَ، فَرَاجَعْتُهُ فَقَالَ: هِيَ خَمْسٌ وَهِيَ خَمْسُونَ لَا يُبَدَّلُ الْقَوْلُ لَدَيَّ، فَرَجَعْتُ إِلَى مُوسَى فَقَالَ: ارْجِعْ إِلَى رَبِّكَ، قُلْتُ: قَدِ اسْتَحْيَيْتُ مِنْ رَبِّي، ثُمَّ انْطَلَقَ بِي حَتَّى انْتَهَى إِلَى سِدْرَةِ الْمُنْتَهَى فَغَشِيَهَا أَلْوَانٌ لَا أَدْرِي مَا هِيَ، ثُمَّ أُدْخِلْتُ الْجَنَّةَ، فَإِذَا فِيهَا حَبَائِلُ اللُّؤْلُؤِ، وَإِذَا تُرَابُهَا الْمِسْكُ»

(Allah enjoined upon my Ummah fifty prayers. I came back with this (message) until I passed by Musa, who said, `What did your Lord enjoin upon your Ummah' I said, `He enjoined fifty prayers.' Musa said, `Go back to your Lord, for your Ummah will not be able to do that.' So I went back, and He reduced it by half. Then I came back to Musa and said, `It has been reduced by half.' He said, `Go back to your Lord, for your Ummah will not be able to do that.' So I went back, and it was reduced by half. I came back to him, and he said, `Go back to your Lord, for your Ummah will not be able to do that.' So I went back, and He said: `They are five but equal in reward to fifty, for My word does not change.' I came back to Musa and he said, `Go back to your Lord.' I said, `I feel too shy before my Lord.' Then I was taken up until I reached Sidrat Al-Muntaha, which was veiled in indescribable colors. Then I entered Paradise, in which I saw nets of pearls and its soil of musk.) This version was recorded by Al-Bukhari in the Book of Prayer. He also reported in the Book of Tafsir, under the discussion of Bani Isra'il (i.e., Surat Al-Isra'), the Book of Hajj and the Stories of the Prophets, via different chains of narration from Yunus. Muslim recorded similar Hadiths in his Sahih in the Book of Faith. Imam Ahmad recorded that `Abdullah bin Shaqiq said: I said to Abu Dharr, "If I had seen the Messenger of Allah , I would have asked him." He said, "What would you have asked him" He said, "I would have asked him, if he saw his Lord" He said, "I did ask him that, and he said,

«قَدْ رَأَيْتُهُ نُورًا، أَنَّى أَرَاهُ»

(I saw it as light, how could I see Him)" This is how it was narrated in the report of Imam Ahmad. Muslim recorded that `Abdullah bin Shaqiq said that Abu Dharr said: "I asked the Messenger of Allah , `Did you see your Lord' He said,

«نُورٌ أَنَّى أَرَاهُ»

((I saw) a light, how could I see Him)" `Abdullah bin Shaqiq said: I said to Abu Dharr, "If I had seen the Messenger of Allah , I would have asked him." He said, "What would you have asked him" He said, "I would have asked him, `Did you see your Lord" Abu Dharr said, "I asked him that, and he said,

«رَأَيْتُ نُورًا»

(I saw light.)

The Report of Jabir bin `Abdullah

Imam Ahmad recorded that Jabir bin `Abdullah said that he heard the Messenger of Allah say:

«لَمَّا كَذَّبَتْنِي قُرَيْشٌ حِينَ أُسْرِيَ بِي إِلَى بَيْتِ الْمَقْدِسِ، قُمْتُ فِي الْحِجْرِ فَجَلَى اللهُ لِي بَيْتَ الْمَقْدِسِ، فَطَفِقْتُ أُخْبِرُهُمْ عَنْ آيَاتِهِ وَأَنَا أَنْظُرُ إِلَيْهِ»

(When Quraysh did not believe that I had been taken on the Night Journey to Bayt Al-Maqdis, I stood up in Al-Hijr and Allah displayed Bayt Al-Maqdis before me, so I told them about its features while I was looking at it.) This was also reported in the Two Sahihs with different chains of narration. According to Al-Bayhaqi, Ibn Shihab said: Abu Salamah bin `Abdur-Rahman said: Some people from Quraish went to Abu Bakr and said, "Have you heard what your companion is saying He is claiming that he went to Bayt Al-Maqdis and came back to Makkah in one night!" Abu Bakr said, "Did he say that" They said, "Yes." Abu Bakr said, "Then I bear witness that if he said that, he is speaking the truth." They said, "You believe that he went to Ash-Sham (Greater Syria) in one night and came back to Makkah before morning" He said, "Yes, I believe him with regard to something even more than that. I believe him with regard to the revelation that comes to him from heaven." Abu Salamah said, from then on Abu Bakr was known as As-Siddiq (the true believer).

The Report of `Abdullah bin `Abbas

Imam Ahmad recorded that Ibn `Abbas said: "On the night when the Messenger of Allah was taken on his Night Journey, he entered Paradise, in some part of which he heard a sound. He said, `O Jibril, what is this' He said, `This is Bilal, the Mu'adhdhin.' When the Prophet came back to the people, he said,

«قَدْ أَفْلَحَ بِلَالٌ، رَأَيْتُ لَهُ كَذَا وَكَذَا»

(Bilal has succeeded, I saw that he will have such and such.) He (the Prophet) was met by Musa, who welcomed him and said, `Welcome to the Unlettered Prophet.' He was a tall, dark man with lank hair coming down to his ears or above his ears. He said, `Who is this, O Jibril' He said, `This is Musa.' Then he went on and met a venerable, distinguished old man, who welcomed him and greeted him with Salam, and all of them were greeting him. He said, `Who is this, O Jibril' He said, `This is your father Ibrahim.' Then he looked into Hell and saw some people eating rotten meat. He said, `Who are these people, O Jibril' He said, `They are those who used to eat the flesh of the people (i.e., backbiting).' He saw a man who was very red and dark blue, and said, `Who is this, O Jibril' He said, `This is the one who slaughtered the she-camel (of Salih).' When the Messenger of Allah came to Al-Masjid Al-Aqsa, he stood up to pray, and all the Prophets gathered and prayed with him. When he finished, he was brought two cups, one on his right and one on his left, one containing milk and one containing honey. He took the milk and drank it, and the one who was carrying the cup said, `You have chosen the Fitrah (natural instinct).'" The chain of narrators is Sahih, although they (Al-Bukhari and Muslim) did not record it. Imam Ahmad reported that Ibn `Abbas said: "The Messenger of Allah was taken on the Night Journey to Bayt Al-Maqdis, then he came back and told them about his journey and the features of Bayt Al-Maqdis and the caravan (of Quraysh). Some people said, `We do not believe what Muhammad is saying,' and they left Islam and became disbelievers. Allah destroyed them when He destroyed Abu Jahl. Abu Jahl said: `Muhammad is trying to scare us with the tree of Zaqqum; bring some dates and butter and let us have some Zaqqum!' The Prophet also saw the Dajjal in his true form, in real life, not in a dream, and he saw `Isa, Musa and Ibrahim. The Prophet was asked about the Dajjal, and he said:

«رَأَيْتُهُ فَيْلَمَانِيًّا أَقْمَرَ هِجَانًا، إِحْدَى عَيْنَيْهِ قَائِمَةٌ كَأَنَّهَا كَوْكَبٌ دُرِّيٌّ، كَأَنَّ شَعْرَ رَأْسِهِ أَغْصَانُ شَجَرَةٍ، وَرَأَيْتُ عِيسَى عَلَيْهِ السَّلَامُ (شَابًّا) أَبْيَضَ، جَعْدَ

الرَّأْسِ حَدِيدَ الْبَصَرِ، وَمُبَطَّنَ الْخَلْقِ، وَرَأَيْتُ مُوسَى عَلَيْهِ السَّلَامُ أَسْحَمَ آدَمَ، كَثِيرَ الشَّعْرِ، شَدِيدَ الْخَلْقِ، وَنَظَرْتُ إِلَى إِبْرَاهِيمَ عَلَيْهِ السَّلَامُ فَلَمْ أَنْظُرْ إِلَى إِرْبٍ مِنْهُ إِلَّا نَظَرْتُ إِلَيْهِ مِنِّي حَتَّى كَأَنَّهُ صَاحِبُكُمْ، قَالَ جِبْرِيلُ: سَلِّمْ عَلَى أَبِيكَ، فَسَلَّمْتُ عَلَيْهِ»

(I saw him as a tall and huge man, with a whitish complexion. One of his eyes stood out like a shining star. The hair on his head looked like the branches of a tree. And I saw `Isa, white with curly hair and an intense gaze, of average build. I saw Musa, dark-skinned, with a lot of hair and a strong build. I looked at Ibrahim and did not see anything in him that I do not see in myself; it is as if he were your companion (meaning himself). Jibril said: `Greet your father with Salam,' so I greeted him with Salam.) This was also recorded by An-Nasa'i from the Hadith of Abu Zayd Thabit bin Yazid from Hilal, who is Ibn Khabbab, and it is a Sahih chain of narrators. Al-Bayhaqi recorded that Abu Al-`Aliyah said: "The cousin of your Prophet , Ibn `Abbas narrated to us from the Messenger of Allah , he said: Allah's Messenger said,

«رَأَيْتُ لَيْلَةَ أُسْرِيَ بِي مُوسَى بْنَ عِمْرَانَ رَجُلًا طُوَالًا جَعْدًا، كَأَنَّهُ مِنْ رِجَالِ شَنُوءَةَ، وَرَأَيْتُ عِيسَى ابْنَ مَرْيَمَ عَلَيْهِ السَّلَامُ مَرْبُوعَ الْخَلْقِ إِلَى الْحُمْرَةِ وَالْبَيَاضِ سَبْطَ الرَّأْسِ»

(On the night when I was taken on the Night Journey, I saw Musa bin `Imran, a tall, curly-haired man, as if he was from the tribe of Shanu'ah. And I saw `Isa bin Maryam, of medium stature, white with a reddish complexion, with straight hair.) And he was shown Malik, the keeper of Hell, and the Dajjal, with the signs that Allah revealed to him.' He said,

(So be not you in doubt of meeting him.) (32:33) Qatadah used to interpret this to mean that the Prophet of Allah met Musa.

(And We made it (or him) a guide to the Children of Israel) (32:33) Qatadah said: "(This means) Allah made Musa a guide for the Children of Israel. " Muslim reported this in his Sahih, and Al-Bukhari and Muslim recorded a shorter version from Qatadah. Imam Ahmad also recorded that Ibn `Abbas said: "The Messenger of Allah said:

«لَمَّا كَانَ لَيْلَةَ أُسْرِيَ بِي، فَأَصْبَحْتُ بِمَكَّةَ فَظِعْتُ وَعَرَفْتُ أَنَّ النَّاسَ مُكَذِّبِي»

(On the night when I was taken on the Night Journey, I woke up in Makkah the next morning having anxiety that, I knew that the people would not believe me.) He kept away from people, feeling anxious and sad, then the enemy of Allah Abu Jahl passed by him and came to sit with him, saying mockingly, `Is there anything new' The Messenger of Allah said,

«نَعَم»

(Yes). He said, `What is it' He said,

«إِنِّي أُسْرِيَ بِي اللَّيْلَة»

(I was taken on a Journey last night.) He said, `Where to' He said,

«إِلَى بَيْتِ الْمَقْدِس»

(To Bayt Al-Maqdis.) He said, `Then this morning you were among us' He said,

«نَعَم»

(Yes). Abu Jahl did not want to say to his face that he was lying, lest he deny saying it when he called other people to hear him, so he said: `Do you think that if I call your people, you will tell them about what happened' The Messenger of Allah said,

«نَعَم»

(Yes.) Abu Jahl said, `O people of Bani Ka`b bin Lu'ay!' People got up from where they were sitting and came to join them. Abu Jahl said, `Tell your people what you told me.' The Messenger of Allah said:

«إِنِّي أُسْرِيَ بِي اللَّيْلَة»

(I was taken on a Journey last night.) They said, `Where to' He said,

«إِلَى بَيْتِ الْمَقْدِس»

(To Bayt Al-Maqdis.) They said, `Then this morning you were among us' He said,

«نَعَم»

(Yes). They began to clap their hands together and put their hands on their heads in astonishment at this "lie" - as they claimed it to be. They said, `Can you describe the sanctuary to us' Among them were some who had travelled to that land and seen the sanctuary, so the Messenger of Allah said,

»فَمَا زِلْتُ أَنْعَتُ حَتَّى الْتَبَسَ عَلَيَّ بَعْضُ النَّعْتِ قَالَ فَجِيءَ بِالْمَسْجِدِ وَأَنَا أَنْظُرُ إِلَيْهِ حَتَّى وُضِعَ دُونَ دَارِ عُقَيْلٍ أَوْ عِقَالٍ فَنَعَتُّهُ وَأَنَا أَنْظُرُ إِلَيْهِ قَالَ وَكَانَ مَعَ هَذَا نَعْتٌ لَمْ أَحْفَظْهُ قَالَ فَقَالَ الْقَوْمُ: أَمَّا النَّعْتُ فَوَاللهِ لَقَدْ أَصَابَ فِيهِ«

(I started to describe it, until I reached a point where I was not sure about some of the details, but then the sanctuary was brought close and placed near the house of `Uqayl - or `Iqal - so I could look at it and describe the details.) I could not remember those description. The people said, `As for the description, by Allah he has got it right." This was recorded by An-Nasa'i and Al-Bayhaqi.

The Report of `Abdullah bin Mas`ud

Al-Hafiz Abu Bakr Al-Bayhaqi reported that `Abdullah bin Mas`ud said: "When the Messenger of Allah was taken on the Night Journey, he went as far as Sidrat Al-Muntaha, which is in the sixth heaven. Everything that ascends stops there, until it is taken from that point, and everything that comes down stops there, until it is taken from there.

(When that covered As-Sidrat Al-Muntaha which did cover it!) (53:16) Ibn Mas`ud said: "It is covered with gold butterflies. The Messenger of Allah was given the five prayers and the final Ayat of Surat Al-Baqarah, and forgiveness was granted for major sins to those who do not associate anything in worship with Allah." This was recorded by Muslim in his Sahih.

The Report of Abu Hurayrah

Al-Bukhari and Muslim reported in their Sahihs that Abu Hurayrah said: the Messenger of Allah said:

»حِينَ أُسْرِيَ بِي، لَقِيتُ مُوسَى عَلَيْهِ السَّلَامُ فَنَعَتَهُ، فَإِذَا رَجُلٌ حَسِبْتُهُ قَالَ مُضْطَرِبٌ رَجِلُ الرَّأْسِ كَأَنَّهُ مِنْ رِجَالِ شَنُوءَةَ، قَالَ: وَلَقِيتُ عِيسَى فَنَعَتَهُ النَّبِيُّ صلى الله عليه وسلم قَالَ رَبْعَةٌ أَحْمَرُ كَأَنَّمَا خَرَجَ مِنْ دِيمَاسٍ يَعْنِي حَمَّامًا، قَالَ وَلَقِيتُ إِبْرَاهِيمَ وَأَنَا أَشْبَهُ وَلَدِهِ بِهِ، قَالَ: وَأُتِيتُ بِإِنَاءَيْنِ فِي أَحَدِهِمَا لَبَنٌ

وَفِي الْآخَرِ خَمْرٌ، قِيلَ لِي: خُذْ أَيَّهُمَا شِئْتَ، فَأَخَذْتُ اللَّبَنَ فَشَرِبْتُ، فَقِيلَ لِي: هُدِيتَ الْفِطْرَةَ أَوْ أَصَبْتَ الْفِطْرَةَ أَمَا إِنَّكَ لَوْ أَخَذْتَ الْخَمْرَ غَوَتْ أُمَّتُكَ»

(When I was taken on the Night Journey, I met Musa.) He described him as a man - I think he said - a curly-haired man, as if he were from the tribe of Shanu'ah. (And I met `Isa.) And the Prophet described him as being of average height, with a reddish complexion, as if he had just come out of the bath. (And I met Ibrahim, and I am the one who resembles him most among his children. I was brought two vessels, one containing milk and the other containing wine. It was said to me, `Take whichever one you want.' So I took the milk and drank it, and it was said to me, `You have been guided to the Fitrah - or - You have chosen the Fitrah. If you had chosen the wine, your Ummah would have gone astray.')" They also recorded it with another chain of narrators. Muslim recorded that Abu Hurayrah said: "The Messenger of Allah said:

«لَقَدْ رَأَيْتُنِي فِي الْحِجْرِ وَقُرَيْشٌ تَسْأَلُنِي عَنْ مَسْرَايَ،فَسَأَلُونِي عَنْ أَشْيَاءَ مِنْ بَيْتِ الْمَقْدِسِ لَمْ أُثْبِتْهَا، فَكُرِبْتُ (كُرْبَةً) مَا كُرِبْتُ مِثْلَهُ قَطُّ، فَرَفَعَهُ اللهُ إِلَيَّ أَنْظُرُ إِلَيْهِ مَا سَأَلُونِي عَنْ شَيْءٍ إِلَّا أَنْبَأْتُهُمْ بِهِ، وَقَدْ رَأَيْتُنِي فِي جَمَاعَةٍ مِنَ الْأَنْبِيَاءِ، وَإِذَا مُوسَى قَائِمٌ يُصَلِّي، وَإِذَا هُوَ رَجُلٌ جَعْدٌ كَأَنَّهُ مِنْ رِجَالِ شَنُوءَةَ، وَإِذَا عِيسَى ابْنُ مَرْيَمَ قَائِمٌ يُصَلِّي أَقْرَبُ النَّاسِ شَبَهًا بِهِ عَرْوَةُ بْنُ مَسْعُودٍ الثَّقَفِيُّ، وَإِذَا إِبْرَاهِيمُ قَائِمٌ يُصَلِّي أَقْرَبُ النَّاسِ شَبَهًا بِهِ صَاحِبُكُمْ يَعْنِي نَفْسَهُ فَحَانَتِ الصَّلَاةُ فَأَمَمْتُهُمْ، فَلَمَّا فَرَغْتُ قَالَ قَائِلٌ: يَا مُحَمَّدُ هَذَا مَالِكٌ خَازِنُ جَهَنَّمَ، (فَسَلِّمْ عَلَيْهِ) فَالْتَفَتُّ إِلَيْهِ فَبَدَأَنِي بِالسَّلَامِ»

(I remember being in Al-Hijr, and the Quraysh were asking me about my Night Journey. They asked me things about Bayt Al-Maqdis that I was not sure of, and I felt more anxious and stressed then than I have ever felt. Then Allah raised up Bayt Al-Maqdis for me to see, and there was nothing they asked me about but I told them about it. And I remember being in a gathering of the Prophets. Musa was standing there praying, and he was a man with curly hair, as if he were one of the men of Shanu'ah. I saw `Isa bin Maryam standing there praying, and the one who most resembles him is `Urwah bin Mas`ud Ath-Thaqafi. And I saw Ibrahim standing there praying, and the one who most resembles him is your companion (meaning himself). Then the time for prayer came, and I led them in prayer. When I finished, a voice said, `O Muhammad, this is Malik, the keeper of Hell,' so I turned to him, and he greeted me first.)"

The Time that Isra' took place, and the Fact that it included both Body and Soul, when the Prophet was awake, not in a Dream

Musa bin `Uqbah said, narrating from Az-Zuhri: "The Isra' happened one year before the Hijrah." This was also the opinion of `Urwah. As-Suddi said: "It happened sixteen months before the Hijrah." The truth is that the Prophet was taken on the Night Journey when he was awake, not in a dream, and he went from Makkah to Bayt Al-Maqdis riding on Al-Buraq. When he reached the door of the sanctuary, he tied up his animal by the door and entered, where he prayed two Rak`ahs to `greet the Masjid'. Then the Mi`raj was brought to him, which is a ladder with steps which one climbs up. So he went up on it to the first heaven, then he went up to the rest of the seven heavens. In each heaven he was welcomed by the most pious of its inhabitants, and he greeted the Prophets who were in the various heavens according to their positions and status. He passed by Musa, the one who spoke with Allah, in the sixth heaven, and Ibrahim, the close friend (Khalil) of Allah in the seventh heaven. Then he surpassed them and all the Prophets in status and reached a level where he could hear the creaking of the pens, i.e., the pens of destiny which write down what is decreed to happen. He saw Sidrat Al-Muntaha, covered by the command of Allah, and its greatness, its butterflies of gold and various colours, surrounded by the angels. There he saw Jibril in his real form, with six hundred wings. He saw green cushions blocking the horizon. He saw Al-Bayt Al-Ma`mur, and Ibrahim Al-Khalil, the builder of the earthly Ka`bah, leaning back against it, the heavenly Ka`bah; every day, seventy thousand angels enter and worship therein, then they do not return to it until the Day of Resurrection. He saw Paradise and Hell, and Allah enjoined upon him fifty prayers, then reduced it to five, as an act of mercy and kindness towards His servants. In this is a strong indication of the greatness and virtue of the prayers. Then he came back down to Bayt Al-Maqdis, and the Prophets came down with him and he led them in prayer there when the time for prayer came. It may have been the dawn prayer of that day. Some people claim that he led them in prayer in heaven, but the reports seem to say that it was in Bayt Al-Maqdis. In some reports it says that it happened when he first entered (i.e., before ascending into the heavens), but it is more likely that it was after he came back, because when he passed by them in the places in the heavens, he asked Jibril about them, one by one, and Jibril told him about them. This is more appropriate, because he was first required to come before the Divine Presence, so that what Allah willed could be enjoined upon him and his Ummah. When the matter for which he was required had been dealt with, he and his brother-Prophets gathered, and his virtue and high position in relation to them became apparent when he was asked to come forward to lead them, which was when Jibril indicated to him that he should do so. Then he came out of Bayt Al-Maqdis and rode on Al-Buraq back to Makkah in the darkness of the night. And Allah knows best. As for his being presented with the vessels containing milk and honey, or milk and wine, or milk and water, or all of these, some reports say that this happened in Bayt Al-Maqdis, and others say that it happened in the heavens. It is possible that it happened in both places, because it is like offering food or drink to a guest when he arrives, and Allah knows best. The Prophet was taken on the Night Journey with body and soul, he was awake, not asleep. The evidence for this is the Ayah:

(Glorified (and Exalted) be He (Allah) Who took His servant for a Journey by Night from Al-Masjid Al-Haram to Al-Masjid Al-Aqsa, the neighborhood whereof We have blessed,) The words "Subhan Allah" (Glorified and exalted be Allah) are spoken in the case of serious matters. If it had been a dream, it would have been a significant matter and would not have been so astounding; the disbelievers of the Quraysh would not have hastened to label him a liar and the group of people who had become Muslims would not have deserted the faith. The word `Abd (servant) refers to both soul and body. Allah says:

(took His servant for a Journey by Night) and:

(And We made not the vision which we showed you but a trial for mankind) (17:60) Ibn `Abbas said: "This is the vision that the Messenger of Allah saw with his own eyes during the Journey by Night, and the cursed tree is the tree of Zaqqum." This was recorded by Al-Bukhari. Allah said:

(The sight (of Prophet Muhammad) turned not aside (right or left), nor it transgressed beyond the limit (ordained for it))(53:17) Sight (Al-Basr) is a physical faculty, not a spiritual one, and he was carried on Al-Buraq, a shining white animal. This too indicates a physical journey, because the soul does not need a means of transportation of this nature. And Allah knows best.

An Interesting Story

In his book Dala'il An-Nubuwwah, Al-Hafiz Abu Nu`aym Al-Isbahani recorded via Muhammad bin `Umar Al-Waqidi who said: Malik bin Abi Ar-Rijjal told me from `Amr bin `Abdullah that Muhammad bin Ka`b Al-Qurazi said: "The Messenger of Allah sent Dihyah bin Khalifah to Caesar." He mentioned how he came to him, and described an incident that showed how wise Caesar was. He sent for the Arab merchants who were in Syria and Abu Sufyan Sakhr bin Harb and his companions were brought to him. He asked them the well-known questions that were recorded by Al-Bukhari and Muslim, as we shall discuss below, and Abu Sufyan tried hard to give the impression that this was an insignificant issue. (The narrator) said that Abu Sufyan (later) said: "By Allah, nothing stopped me from saying something to Heraclius to make him despise (Muhammad) but the fact that I did not want to tell a lie that would later be found out, and he would never believe me again after that. Then I told him about the night on which he was taken on the Night Journey. I said: `O King, shall I not tell you of something from which you will know that he is lying' He said, `What is it' I said: `He claims that he went out of our land, the land of Al-Haram, in one night, and came to your sanctuary in Jerusalem, then came back to us the same night, before morning came.' The Patriarch of Jerusalem was there, standing next to Caesar. The Patriarch of Jerusalem said: `I know that night.' Caesar looked at him and said, `How do you know about this' He said, `I never used to sleep at night until I closed the doors of the sanctuary. On that night I closed all the doors except for one, which I could not manage to close. I asked my workers and others who were with me to help me deal with it, but we could not move it. It was like trying to move a mountain. So I called the carpenters, and they looked at it and said: The lintel and some part of the structure has fallen onto it. We cannot move it until morning, when we will be able to see what the problem is. So I went back and left those two doors open. The next morning I went back, and saw that the stone at the corner of the sanctuary had a hole in it, and there were traces of an animal having been tethered there. I said to my companions: This door has not been closed last night except for a Prophet, who prayed last night in our sanctuary.''' And he mentioned the rest of the Hadith. In his book At-Tanwir fi Mawlid As-Siraj Al-Munir, Al-Hafiz Abu Al-Khattab `Umar bin Dihyah mentioned the Hadith of the Isra' narrated from Anas, and spoke well about it, then he said: "The reports of the Hadith of the Isra' reach the level of Mutawatir. They were narrated from `Umar bin Al-Khattab, `Ali, Ibn Mas`ud, Abu Dharr, Malik bin Sa`sa`ah, Abu Hurayrah, Abu Sa`id, Ibn `Abbas, Shaddad bin Aws, Ubayy bin Ka`b, `Abdur-Rahman bin Qarat, Abu Habbah Al-Ansari, Abu Layla Al-Ansari, `Abdullah bin `Amr, Jabir, Hudhayfah, Buraydah, Abu Ayyub, Abu Umamah, Samurah bin Jundub, Abu Al-Hamra', Suhayb Ar-Rumi, Umm Hani', and `A'ishah and `Asma', the daughters of Abu Bakr As-Siddiq, may Allah be pleased with them all. Some of them narrated the incident at length, and others narrated it more briefly, as was reported in the Musnad collections. Even though some reports do not fulfill the conditions of Sahih, nevertheless the Muslims agreed unanimously on the fact that the Isra' happened, and it was rejected only by the heretics and apostates.

(They intend to put out the Light of Allah with their mouths. But Allah will bring His Light to perfection even though the disbelievers hate (it).) (61:8).

Surah: 17 Ayah: 2 & Ayah: 3

وَءَاتَيْنَا مُوسَى ٱلْكِتَٰبَ وَجَعَلْنَٰهُ هُدًى لِّبَنِىٓ إِسْرَٰٓءِيلَ أَلَّا تَتَّخِذُوا۟ مِن دُونِى وَكِيلًا ۝

2. And We gave Mûsa (Moses) the Scripture and made it a guidance for the Children of Israel (saying): "Take not other than Me as (your) Wakîl (Protector, Lord, or Disposer of your affairs, etc.).

ذُرِّيَّةَ مَنْ حَمَلْنَا مَعَ نُوحٍ إِنَّهُۥ كَانَ عَبْدًا شَكُورًا ۝

3. "O offspring of those whom We carried (in the ship) with Nûh (Noah)! Verily, he was a grateful slave."

Transliteration

2. Waatayna moosa alkitaba wajaAAalnahu hudan libanee isra-eela alla tattakhithoo min doonee wakeelan   3. Thurriyyata man hamalna maAAa noohin innahu kana AAabdan shakooran

Tafsir Ibn Kathir

Musa and how He was given the Tawrah

When Allah mentions how He took His servant Muhammad, on the Journey by Night, He follows it by mentioning Musa, His servant and Messenger who also spoke with Him. Allah often mentions Muhammad and Musa together, may the peace and blessings of Allah be upon them both, and he mentions the Tawrah and the Qur'an together. So after mentioning the Isra', He says:

(And We gave Musa the Scripture), meaning the Tawrah.

(and made it), meaning the Scripture,

(a guidance), meaning a guide,

(for the Children of Israel (saying): "Take none...") means, lest they should take,

("... other than Me as (your) Wakil") means, `you have no protector, supporter or god besides Me,' because Allah revealed to every Prophet that he should worship Him alone with no partner or associate. Then Allah says:

(O offspring of those whom We carried (in the ship) with Nuh) by addressing the descendants of those who were carried in the ship with Nuh there is a reminder of the blessings, as if Allah is saying: `O descendants of those whom We saved and carried in the ship with Nuh, follow in the footsteps of your father,

(Verily, he was a grateful servant). `Remember the blessing I have granted you by sending Muhammad.' Imam Ahmad reported that Anas bin Malik said: "The Messenger of Allah said:

«إِنَّ اللَّهَ لَيَرْضَى عَنِ الْعَبْدِ أَنْ يَأْكُلَ الْأَكْلَةَ أَوْ يَشْرَبَ الشَّرْبَةَ فَيَحْمَدَ اللَّهَ عَلَيْهَا»

(Allah will be pleased with His servant if, when he eats something or drinks something, he praises Allah for it.)" This was also recorded by Muslim, At-Tirmidhi and An-Nasa'i. Malik said about Zayd bin Aslam: "He used to praise Allah in all circumstances." In this context, Al-Bukhari mentioned the Hadith of Abu Zar`ah narrating from Abu Hurayrah, who said that the Prophet said:

«أَنَا سَيِّدُ وَلَدِ آدَمَ يَوْمَ الْقِيَامَةِ»

(I will be the leader of the sons of Adam on the Day of Resurrection...) He quoted the Hadith at length, and in the Hadith, the Prophet said:

«فَيَأْتُونَ نُوحًا فَيَقُولُونَ: يَا نُوحُ إِنَّكَ أَنْتَ أَوَّلُ الرُّسُلِ إِلَى أَهْلِ الْأَرْضِ، وَقَدْ سَمَّاكَ اللَّهُ عَبْدًا شَكُورًا، فَاشْفَعْ لَنَا إِلَى رَبِّكَ»

(They will come to Nuh and will say, `O Nuh, you were the first of the Messengers sent to the people of earth, and Allah called you grateful servant, so intercede for us with your Lord.') And he quoted the Hadith in full.

Surah: 17 Ayah: 4, Ayah: 5, Ayah: 6, Ayah: 7 & Ayah: 8

وَقَضَيْنَآ إِلَىٰ بَنِىٓ إِسْرَٰٓءِيلَ فِى ٱلْكِتَٰبِ لَتُفْسِدُنَّ فِى ٱلْأَرْضِ مَرَّتَيْنِ وَلَتَعْلُنَّ عُلُوًّا كَبِيرًا ۝

4. And We decreed for the Children of Israel in the Scripture: indeed you would do mischief in the land twice and you will become tyrants and extremely arrogant!

فَإِذَا جَآءَ وَعْدُ أُولَىٰهُمَا بَعَثْنَا عَلَيْكُمْ عِبَادًا لَّنَآ أُوْلِى بَأْسٍ شَدِيدٍ فَجَاسُواْ خِلَٰلَ ٱلدِّيَارِ ۚ وَكَانَ وَعْدًا مَّفْعُولًا ۝

5. So, when the promise came for the first of the two, We sent against you slaves of Ours given to terrible warfare. They entered the very innermost parts of your homes. And it was a promise (completely) fulfilled.

ثُمَّ رَدَدْنَا لَكُمُ ٱلْكَرَّةَ عَلَيْهِمْ وَأَمْدَدْنَٰكُم بِأَمْوَٰلٍ وَبَنِينَ وَجَعَلْنَٰكُمْ أَكْثَرَ نَفِيرًا ۝

6. Then We gave you a return of victory over them. And We helped you with wealth and children and made you more numerous in man-power.

إِنْ أَحْسَنتُمْ أَحْسَنتُمْ لِأَنفُسِكُمْ ۖ وَإِنْ أَسَأْتُمْ فَلَهَا ۚ فَإِذَا جَآءَ وَعْدُ ٱلْأَخِرَةِ لِيَسُۥٓـُٔواْ وُجُوهَكُمْ وَلِيَدْخُلُواْ ٱلْمَسْجِدَ كَمَا دَخَلُوهُ أَوَّلَ مَرَّةٍ وَلِيُتَبِّرُواْ مَا عَلَوْاْ تَتْبِيرًا ۝

7. (And We said): "If you do good, you do good for your own selves, and if you do evil (you do it) against yourselves." Then, when the second promise came to pass, (We permitted your enemies) to disgrace your faces and to enter the mosque (of Jerusalem) as they had entered it before, and to destroy with utter destruction all that fell in their hands.

$$\text{عَسَىٰ رَبُّكُمْ أَن يَرْحَمَكُمْ ۚ وَإِنْ عُدتُّمْ عُدْنَا ۘ وَجَعَلْنَا جَهَنَّمَ لِلْكَافِرِينَ حَصِيرًا ﴿٨﴾}$$

8. (and We said in the Taurât (Torah)) "It may be that your Lord may show mercy unto you, but if you return (to sins), We shall return (to Our Punishment). And We have made Hell a prison for the disbelievers.

Transliteration

4. Waqadayna ila banee isra-eela fee alkitabi latufsidunna fee al-ardi marratayni walataAAlunna AAuluwwan kabeeran 5. Fa-itha jaa waAAdu oolahuma baAAathna AAalaykum AAibadan lana olee ba/sin shadeedin fajasoo khilala alddiyari wakana waAAdan mafAAoolan 6. Thumma radadna lakumu alkarrata AAalayhim waamdadnakum bi-amwalin wabaneena wajaAAalnakum akthara nafeeran 7. In ahsantum ahsantum li-anfusikum wa-in asa/tum falaha fa-itha jaa waAAdu al-akhirati liyasoo-oo wujoohakum waliyadkhuloo almasjida kama dakhaloohu awwala marratin waliyutabbiroo ma AAalaw tatbeeran 8. AAasa rabbukum an yarhamakum wa-in AAudtum AAudna wajaAAalna jahannama lilkafireena haseeran

Tafsir Ibn Kathir

It was mentioned in the Tawrah that the Jews would spread Mischief twice

Allah tells us that He made a declaration to the Children of Israel in the Scripture, meaning that He had already told them in the Book which He revealed to them, that they would cause mischief on the earth twice, and would become tyrants and extremely arrogant, meaning they would become shameless oppressors of people, Allah says:

(And We made known this decree to him, that the root of those (sinners) was to be cut off in the early morning.)(15:66), meaning, We already told him about that and informed him of it.

The First Episode of Mischief caused by the Jews, and their Punishment for it

(So, when the promise came for the first of the two) meaning the first of the two episodes of mischief.

(We sent against you servants of Ours given to terrible warfare.) means, `We unleashed soldiers against you from among Our creatures who were given to terrible warfare,' i.e., they had great strength and weapons and power. They entered the very innermost parts of your homes, meaning they took possession of your land and invaded the very innermost parts of your homes, going between and through your houses, coming and going freely with no fear of anyone. This was the promise (completely) fulfilled. The earlier and later commentators differed over the identity of these invaders. Many Isra'iliyyat (reports from Jewish sources) were narrated about this, but I did not want to make this book too long by mentioning them, because some of them are fabricated, concocted by their heretics, and others may be true, but we have no need of them, praise be to Allah. What Allah has told us in His Book (the Qur'an) is sufficient and we have no need of what is in the other books that came before. Neither Allah nor His Messenger required us to refer to them. Allah told His Messenger that when (the Jews) committed transgression and aggression, Allah gave their enemies power over them to destroy their country and enter the innermost parts of their homes. Their humiliation and subjugation was a befitting punishment, and your Lord is never unfair or unjust to His servants. They had rebelled and killed many of the Prophets and scholars. Ibn Jarir recorded that Yahya bin Sa`id said: "I heard Sa`id bin Al-Musayyib saying: `Nebuchadnezzar conquered Ash-Sham (Greater Syria, including Palestine), destroying Jerusalem and killing them, then he came to Damascus and found blood boiling in a censer. He asked them: What is this blood They said: We found our forefathers doing this. Because of that blood, he killed seventy thousand of the believers and others, then the blood stopped boiling. This report is Sahih from Sa`id bin Al-Musayyib, and this event is well-known, as he (Nebuchadnezzar) killed their nobles and scholars, and did not leave alive anyone who knew the Tawrah by heart. He took many prisoners from the sons of the Prophets and others, and did many other things that would take too long to mention here. If we had found anything that was correct or close enough, we could have written it and reported it here. And Allah knows best. Then Allah says:

((And We said): "If you do good, you do good for your own selves, and if you do evil (you do it) against yourselves.") As Allah says elsewhere:

(Whosoever does a righteous good deed, it is for (the benefit of) himself; and whosoever does evil, it is against himself.) (45:15)

The Second Episode of Mischief

Then Allah says:

(Then, when the second promise came to pass,) meaning, the second episode of mischief, when your enemies came again,

((We permitted your enemies) to disgrace your faces) meaning, to humiliate you and subdue you,

(and to enter the Masjid) meaning, Bayt Al-Maqdis (Jerusalem).

(as they had entered it before,) when they entered the very innermost parts of your homes.

(and to destroy) wrecking and inflicting ruin upon it.

(all that fell in their hands.) everything they could get their hands on.

(with utter destruction. It may be that your Lord may show mercy unto you) meaning that He may rid you of them.

(but if you return (to sins), We shall return (to Our punishment).) meaning, if you return to causing mischief,

(We shall return) means, We `will once again punish you in this world, along with the punishment and torment We save for you in the Hereafter.'

(And We have made Hell a prison (Hasir) for the disbelievers.) meaning, a place of permanent detention, a prison which cannot be avoided or escaped. Ibn `Abbas said, "Hasir here means a jail." Mujahid said, "They will be detained in it." Others said likewise. Al-Hasan said, "Hasir means a bed of Fire." Qatadah said: "The Children of Israel returned to aggres- sion, so Allah sent this group against them, Muhammad and his companions, who made them pay the Jizyah, with willing submission, and feeling themselves subdued."

Surah: 17 Ayah: 9 & Ayah: 10

إِنَّ هَـٰذَا ٱلْقُرْءَانَ يَهْدِى لِلَّتِى هِىَ أَقْوَمُ وَيُبَشِّرُ ٱلْمُؤْمِنِينَ ٱلَّذِينَ يَعْمَلُونَ ٱلصَّـٰلِحَـٰتِ أَنَّ لَهُمْ أَجْرًا كَبِيرًا ۝

9. Verily, this Qur'ân guides to that which is most just and right and gives glad tidings to the believers (in the Oneness of Allâh and His Messenger, Muhammad (peace be upon him)) who work deeds of righteousness, that they shall have a great reward (Paradise).

وَأَنَّ ٱلَّذِينَ لَا يُؤْمِنُونَ بِٱلْءَاخِرَةِ أَعْتَدْنَا لَهُمْ عَذَابًا أَلِيمًا ۝

10. And that those who believe not in the Hereafter for them We have prepared a painful torment (Hell).

Transliteration

9. Inna hatha alqur-ana yahdee lillatee hiya aqwamu wayubashshiru almu/mineena allatheena yaAAmaloona alssalihati anna lahum ajran kabeeran   10. Waanna allatheena la yu/minoona bial-akhirati aAAtadna lahum AAathaban aleeman

Tafsir Ibn Kathir

Praising the Qur'an

Allah praises His noble Book, the Qur'an, which He revealed to His Messenger Muhammad . It directs people to the best and clearest of ways.

(gives good news to those who believe,) in it a

(those who do righteous deeds,) in accordance with it, telling them

(that they will have a great reward,) i.e., on the Day of Resurrection. And He tells

(those who do not believe in the Hereafter,) that

(for them is a painful torment,) i.e. on the Day of Resurrection. As Allah says:

(... then announce to them a painful torment.) (84:24)

Surah: 17 Ayah: 11

$$وَيَدْعُ ٱلْإِنسَٰنُ بِٱلشَّرِّ دُعَآءَهُۥ بِٱلْخَيْرِ ۖ وَكَانَ ٱلْإِنسَٰنُ عَجُولًا ۝$$

11. And man invokes (Allâh) for evil as he invokes (Allâh) for good and man is ever hasty (i.e., if he is angry with somebody, he invokes (saying): "O Allâh! Curse him" and that one should not do, but one should be patient).

Transliteration

11. WayadAAu al-insanu bialshsharri duAAaahu bialkhayri wakana al-insanu AAajoolan

Tafsir Ibn Kathir

Man's Haste and Prayers against Himself

Allah tells us about man's haste and how he sometimes prays against himself or his children or his wealth, praying for something bad to happen for them, or for them to die or be destroyed, invoking curses, etc. If Allah were to answer his prayer, he would be destroyed because of it, as Allah says:

(And were Allah to hasten for mankind the evil...) (10:11) This is how it was interpreted by Ibn `Abbas, Mujahid and Qatadah. We have already discussed the Hadith:

$$«لَا تَدْعُوا عَلَى أَنْفُسِكُمْ، وَلَا عَلَى أَمْوَالِكُمْ أَنْ تُوَافِقُوا مِنَ اللهِ سَاعَةَ إِجَابَةٍ يَسْتَجِيبُ فِيهَا»$$

(Do not pray against yourselves or your wealth, for that might coincide with a time when Allah answers prayers.) What makes the son of Adam do that is his anxiety and haste. Allah says:

(And man is ever hasty.) Salman Al-Farisi and Ibn `Abbas mentioned the story of Adam, when he wanted to get up before his soul reached his feet. When his soul was breathed into him, it entered his body from his head downwards. When it reached his brain he sneezed, and said, "Al-Hamdu Lillah" (praise be to Allah), and Allah said, "May your Lord have mercy on you, O Adam." When it reached his eyes, he opened them, and when it reached his body and limbs he started to stare at them in wonder. He wanted to get up before it reached his feet, but he could not. He said, "O Lord, make it happen before night comes."

Surah: 17 Ayah: 12

وَجَعَلْنَا ٱلَّيْلَ وَٱلنَّهَارَ ءَايَتَيْنِ ۖ فَمَحَوْنَآ ءَايَةَ ٱلَّيْلِ وَجَعَلْنَآ ءَايَةَ ٱلنَّهَارِ مُبْصِرَةً لِّتَبْتَغُوا۟ فَضْلًا مِّن رَّبِّكُمْ وَلِتَعْلَمُوا۟ عَدَدَ ٱلسِّنِينَ وَٱلْحِسَابَ ۚ وَكُلَّ شَىْءٍ فَصَّلْنَٰهُ تَفْصِيلًا ۝

12. And We have appointed the night and the day as two Ayât (signs etc.). Then, We have obliterated the sign of the night (with darkness) while We have made the sign of day illuminating, that you may seek bounty from your Lord, and that you may know the number of the years and the reckoning. And We have explained everything (in detail) with full explanation.

Transliteration

12. WajaAAalna allayla waalnnahara ayatayni famahawna ayata allayli wajaAAalna ayata alnnahari mubsiratan litabtaghoo fadlan min rabbikum walitaAAlamoo AAadada alssineena waalhisaba wakulla shay-in fassalnahu tafseelan

Tafsir Ibn Kathir

The Night and Day are Signs of the Great Power of Allah

Allah reminds us of the great signs that He created, including the alternation of the night and day, so that people may rest at night, and go out and earn a living, do their work, and travel during the day, and so that they may know the number of days, weeks, months and years, so they will know the appointed times for paying debts, doing acts of worship, dealing with transactions, paying rents and so on. Allah says:

(that you may seek bounty from your Lord,) meaning, in your living and travels etc.

(and that you may know the number of the years and to count.) If time stood still and never changed, we would not know any of these things, as Allah says:

(Say: "Tell me! If Allah made the night continuous for you till the Day of Resurrection, which god besides Allah could bring you light Will you not then hear" Say: "Tell me! If Allah made the day continuous for you till the Day of Resurrection, which god besides Allah could bring you night wherein you rest Will you not then see" It is out of His mercy that He has made for you the night and the day that you may rest therein and that you may seek of His bounty - and in order that you may be grateful.) (28:71-73)

(Blessed be He Who has placed the big stars in the heaven, and has placed therein a great lamp (sun), and a moon giving light. And He it is Who has put the night and the day in succession, for such who desires to remember or desires to show his gratitude.) (25:61-62)

(and His is the alternation of night and day.) (23:80)

(He makes the night to go in the day and makes the day to go in the night. And He has subjected the sun and the moon. Each running (on a fixed course) for an appointed term. Verily, He is the All-Mighty, the Oft-Forgiving.) (39:5)

((He is the) Cleaver of the daybreak. He has appointed the night for resting, and the sun and the moon for reckoning. Such is the measuring of the All-Mighty, the All-Knowing.) (6:96),

(And a sign for them is the night. We withdraw therefrom the day, and behold, they are in darkness. And the sun runs on its fixed course for a term (appointed). That is the decree of the All-Mighty, the All-Knowing.) (36:37-38) Allah has made the night a sign having distinguishing features by which it is known. These features include the darkness and the appearance of the moon. The day also has distinguishing features by which it is known; the light and the appearance of the shining sun. He made a distinction between the light of the moon and the light of the sun, so that they may be distinguished from one another, as Allah says:

(It is He Who made the sun a shining thing and the moon a light and measured out for it stages that you might know the number of years and to count (periods of time). Allah did not create this but in truth.) (10:5) until,

(Ayat for those people who keep their duty to Allah, and fear Him much.) (10:6)

(They ask you about the crescent moons. Say: "These are signs to mark fixed periods of time for mankind and for the pilgrimage.") (2:189)

(Then, We have obliterated the sign of the night (with darkness) while We have made the sign of the day illuminating,) Ibn Jurayj reported that `Abdullah bin Kathir commented on this Ayah: "(It means) the darkness of the night and the twilight of the day." Ibn Jurayj reported that Mujahid said: "The sun is the sign of the day and the moon is the sign of the night.

(We have obliterated the sign of the night) this refers to the moon's blackness, which is how Allah has created it."

(And We have appointed the night and the day as two Ayat.) Ibn Abi Najih reported that Ibn `Abbas said: "By night and day, this is how Allah created them, may He be glorified."

Surah: 17 Ayah: 13 & Ayah: 14

وَكُلَّ إِنسَٰنٍ أَلْزَمْنَٰهُ طَٰٓئِرَهُۥ فِى عُنُقِهِۦ ۖ وَنُخْرِجُ لَهُۥ يَوْمَ ٱلْقِيَٰمَةِ كِتَٰبًا يَلْقَىٰهُ مَنشُورًا ﴿١٣﴾

13. And We have fastened every man's deeds to his neck, and on the Day of Resurrection, We shall bring out for him a book which he will find wide open.

$$\text{ٱقۡرَأۡ كِتَٰبَكَ كَفَىٰ بِنَفۡسِكَ ٱلۡيَوۡمَ عَلَيۡكَ حَسِيبࣰا ۝}$$

14. (It will be said to him): "Read your book. You yourself are sufficient as a reckoner against you this Day."

Transliteration

13. Wakulla insanin alzamnahu ta-irahu fee AAunuqihi wanukhriju lahu yawma alqiyamati kitaban yalqahu manshooran 14. Iqra/ kitabaka kafa binafsika alyawma AAalayka haseeban

Tafsir Ibn Kathir

Every Person will have the Book of his Deeds with Him

After mentioning time, and the deeds of the son of Adam that take place therein, Allah says:

(And We have fastened every man's Ta'irah (deeds) to his neck,) The word Ta'irah (lit. something that flies) refers to man's deeds which fly from him, as Ibn `Abbas, Mujahid and others said. It includes both good deeds and bad deeds, he will be forced to acknowledge them and will be rewarded or punished accordingly.

(So whosoever does good equal to the weight of a speck of dust shall see it. And whosoever does evil equal to the weight of a speck of dust shall see it.) (99:7-8). Allah says:

((Remember) that the two receivers (recording angels) receive (each human being), one sitting on the right and one on the left (to note his or her actions). Not a word does he (or she) utter but there is a watcher by him ready (to record it).) (50:17-18)

(But verily, over you (are appointed angels in charge of mankind) to watch you, Kiraman (Honorable) Katibin - writing down (your deeds), they know all that you do.) (82:10-12)

(You are only being requited for what you used to do.) (52:16)

(whosoever works evil, will have the recompense thereof.) (4:123) The meaning is that the deeds of the sons of Adam are preserved, whether they are great or small, and they are recorded night and day, morning and evening.

(and on the Day of Resurrection, We shall bring out for him a Book which he will find wide open.) meaning, `We will collect all of his deeds for him in a Book which will be given to him on the Day of Resurrection, either in his right hand, if he is one of the blessed, or in his left hand if he is one of the wretched.'

(wide open) means, it will be open for him and others to read all of his deeds, from the beginning of his life until the end.

(On that Day man will be informed of what (deeds) he sent forward, and what (deeds) he left behind. Nay! Man will be a witness against himself, though he may put forth his excuses.) (75:13-15) Allah says:

((It will be said to him): "Read your Book. You yourself are sufficient as a reckoner against you this Day.") meaning, you have not been treated unjustly and nothing has been recorded against you except what you have done, because you remember everything that you have done, and no one will forget anything that he did. Everyone will be able to read his Book, whether he is literate or illiterate.

(And We have fastened every man's Ta'irah (deeds) to his neck,) The neck is mentioned because it is a part of the body that has no counterpart, and when one is restrained by it, he has no escape. Ma`mar narrated from Qatadah, "His deeds,

(and on the Day of Resurrection, We shall bring out for him) We shall bring forth those deeds."

(a Book which he will find wide open.) Ma`mar said: Al-Hasan recited,

(one sitting on the right and one on the left.) (50:17) (And he said;) "O son of Adam, your Book has been opened for you, and two noble angels have been entrusted to accompany you, one on your right and one on your left. The one who is on your right records your good deeds, and the one who is on your left records your bad deeds. `So do whatever you want, a lot or a little, until you die, then I will fold up your Book and tie it to your neck with you in your grave. Then when you come out on the Day of Resurrection, you will find the Book wide open, so read your Book.' By Allah, the One Who makes you accountable for your own deeds is being perfectly just." These are some of the best words Al-Hasan ever spoke, may Allah have mercy on him.

Surah: 17 Ayah: 15

مَّنِ ٱهْتَدَىٰ فَإِنَّمَا يَهْتَدِى لِنَفْسِهِۦ ۖ وَمَن ضَلَّ فَإِنَّمَا يَضِلُّ عَلَيْهَا ۚ وَلَا تَزِرُ وَازِرَةٌ وِزْرَ أُخْرَىٰ ۗ وَمَا كُنَّا مُعَذِّبِينَ حَتَّىٰ نَبْعَثَ رَسُولًا ﴿١٥﴾

15. Whoever goes right, then he goes right only for the benefit of his own self. And whoever goes astray, then he goes astray to his own loss. No one laden with burdens can bear another's burden. And We never punish until We have sent a Messenger (to give warning).

Transliteration

15. Mani ihtada fa-innama yahtadee linafsihi waman dalla fa-innama yadillu AAalayha wala taziru waziratun wizra okhra wama kunna muAAaththibeena hatta nabAAatha rasoolan

Tafsir Ibn Kathir

No One will have to bear the Sins of Another

Allah tells us that whoever is guided and follows the truth, walking in the footsteps of the Prophet , he will gain the good consequences of that for himself.

(And whoever goes astray,) meaning from the truth, deviating from the way of guidance, he is wronging himself and will have to bear the consequences. Then Allah says:

(No one laden with burdens can bear another's burden.) no one will have to bear the sins of another, and he does not wrong anyone besides himself, as Allah says:

(and if one heavily laden calls another to (bear) his load, nothing of it will be lifted) (35:15) There is no contradiction between this and other Ayat:

(And verily, they shall bear their own loads, and other loads besides their own.) (29:13) and:

(and also of the burdens of those whom they misled without knowledge.) (16:25) For those who called others to do evil will bear the sin of their own deviation as well as the sin of those whom they led astray, without detracting the least amount from the burden of those people, and none of this burden shall be removed from them. This is the justice and mercy of Allah towards His servants. As Allah says:

(And We never punish until We have sent a Messenger (to give warning).)

No Punishment until a Messenger has been sent

Allah tells us that out of His justice, He does not punish anyone until He has established proof against him by sending a Messenger to him, as He says:

(Every time a group is cast therein, its keeper will ask: "Did no warner come to you" They will say: "Yes, indeed a warner did come to us, but we belied him and said: `Allah never sent down anything (of revelation); you are only in great error.'") (67:8-9) And,

(And those who disbelieved will be driven to Hell in groups, till, when they reach it, the gates thereof will be opened. And its keepers will say, "Did not the Messengers come to you from yourselves - reciting to you the verses of your Lord, and warning you of the meeting of this Day of yours" They will say: "Yes," but the Word of torment has been justified against the disbelievers!) (39:71) And,

(Therein they will cry: "Our Lord! Bring us out, we shall do righteous good deeds, not (the evil deeds) that we used to do." (Allah will reply:) "Did We not give you lives long enough, so that whosoever would receive admonition could receive it And the warner came to you. So taste you (the evil of your deeds). For the wrongdoers there is no helper.") (35:37) There are other Ayat which indicate that Allah will not make anyone enter Hell except after sending a Messenger to them.

The Issue of Small Children who die

Here there arises an issue over which the scholars in earlier and modern times have disagreed, may Allah have mercy on them. This is the issue of children who die when they are little, and their parents are disbelievers: what happens to them By the same token, what happens to the insane, the deaf, the senile and those who die during the circumstances of Fatrah, when no Message reached them Several Hadiths have been narrated on this topic, which I will quote here by the help and support of Allah. The First Hadith from Al-Aswad bin Sar ®299: Imam Ahmad reported from Al-Aswad bin Sari' that the Messenger of Allah said,

«أَرْبَعَةٌ يَحْتَجُّونَ يَوْمَ الْقِيَامَةِ: رَجُلٌ أَصَمُّ لَا يَسْمَعُ شَيْئًا، وَرَجُلٌ أَحْمَقُ، وَرَجُلٌ هَرِمٌ، وَرَجُلٌ مَاتَ فِي فَتْرَةٍ، فَأَمَّا الْأَصَمُّ فَيَقُولُ: رَبِّ قَدْ جَاءَ الْإِسْلَامُ وَمَا أَسْمَعُ شَيْئًا، وَأَمَّا الْأَحْمَقُ فَيَقُولُ: رَبِّ قَدْ جَاءَ الْإِسْلَامُ وَالصِّبْيَانُ يَحْذِفُونِي بِالْبَعْرِ، وَأَمَّا الْهَرِمُ فَيَقُولُ: رَبِّ لَقَدْ جَاءَ الْإِسْلَامُ وَمَا أَعْقِلُ شَيْئًا، وَأَمَّا الَّذِي مَاتَ فِي الْفَتْرَةِ فَيَقُولُ: رَبِّ مَا أَتَانِي لَكَ رَسُولٌ. فَيَأْخُذُ مَوَاثِيقَهُمْ لَيُطِيعُنَّهُ، فَيُرْسِلُ إِلَيْهِمْ أَنِ ادْخُلُوا النَّارَ، فَوَالَّذِي نَفْسُ مُحَمَّدٍ بِيَدِهِ، لَوْ دَخَلُوهَا لَكَانَتْ عَلَيْهِمْ بَرْدًا وَسَلَامًا»

(There are four who will present their case on the Day of Resurrection: a deaf man who never heard anything, an insane man, a very old and senile man, and a man who died during the Fatrah. As for the deaf man, he will say, "O Lord, Islam came but I never heard anything." As for the insane man, he will say, "O Lord, Islam came and the young boys were throwing camel dung at me." As for the senile man, he will say, "O Lord, Islam came and I did not understand anything." As for the one who died during the Fatrah, he will say, "O Lord, no Messenger from You came to me." Allah will accept their pledge of obedience to Him, then He will send word to them that they should enter the Fire. By the One in Whose Hand is the soul of Muhammad, if they enter it, it will be cool and safe for them.) There is a similar report with a chain from Qatadah from Al-Hasan from Abu Rafi` from Abu Hurayrah, but at the end it says:

«فَمَنْ دَخَلَهَا كَانَتْ عَلَيْهِ بَرْدًا وَسَلَامًا، وَمَنْ لَمْ يَدْخُلْهَا يُسْحَبُ إِلَيْهَا»

(Whoever enters it will find it cool and safe, and whoever does not enter it will be dragged into it.) This was also recorded by Ishaq bin Rahwayh from Mu`adh bin Hisham, and by Al-Bayhaqi in Al-I`tiqad. He said: "This is a Sahih chain." It was reported by Ibn Jarir from the Hadith of Ma`mar from Hammam from Abu Hurayrah, who attributed it to the Prophet . Then Abu Hurayrah said: "Recite, if you wish:

(And We never punish until We have sent a Messenger (to give warning))." This was also narrated by Ma`mar from `Abdullah bin Tawus from his father, from Abu Hurayrah, but it is Mauquf (it was not attributed directly to the Prophet).

The Second Hadith from Abu Hurayrah

He said that the Messenger of Allah said:

«كُلُّ مَوْلُودٍ يُولَدُ عَلَى الْفِطْرَةِ، فَأَبَوَاهُ يُهَوِّدَانِهِ أَوْ يُنَصِّرَانِهِ أَوْ يُمَجِّسَانِهِ، كَمَا تُنْتِجُ الْبَهِيمَةُ بَهِيمَةً جَمْعَاءَ، هَلْ تُحِسُّونَ فِيهَا مِنْ جَدْعَاءَ؟»

(Every newborn is born in a state of Fitrah (the natural state of man), then his parents make him into a Jew or Christian or Zoroastrian, as animals produce whole animals - do you see any that is born mutilated (with something missing)) According to one report they said: "O Messenger of Allah, what about those who die when they are little" He said,

«اللهُ أَعْلَمُ بِمَا كَانُوا عَامِلِين»

(Allah knows best what they would have done.) Imam Ahmad reported from Abu Hurayrah that the Prophet () as far as I know - the narrator was not sure if it was attributed to Musa - said:

«ذَرَارِيُّ الْمُسْلِمِينَ فِي الْجَنَّةِ يَكْفُلُهُمْ إِبْرَاهِيمُ عَلَيْهِ السَّلَام»

(The children of the Muslims are in Paradise, being taken care of by Ibrahim.) In Sahih Muslim it is reported from `Iyyad bin Hammad that the Messenger of Allah said that Allah said:

«إِنِّي خَلَقْتُ عِبَادِي حُنَفَاء»

(I have created My servants as Hunafa.) According to another version, the wording is "as Muslims."

The Third Hadith from Samurah

In his book Al-Mustakhraj `Ala Al-Bukhari, Al-Hafiz Abu Bakr Al-Barqani recorded the Hadith of `Awf Al-A`rabi, from Abu Raja' Al-`Utardi from Samurah that the Prophet said:

»كُلُّ مَوْلُودٍ يُولَدُ عَلَى الْفِطْرَةِ«

(Every newborn is born in a state of Fitrah.) The people called out to him: "O Messenger of Allah! What about the children of the idolators" He said,

»وَأَوْلَادُ الْمُشْرِكِينَ«

(And the children of the idolators too.) At-Tabarani reported that Samurah said: "We asked the Messenger of Allah about the children of the idolators, and he said,

»هُمْ خَدَمُ أَهْلِ الْجَنَّةِ«

(They are the servants of the people of Paradise.)

The Fourth Hadith from the Paternal Uncle of Hasna

Ahmad reported that Hasna' bint Mu`awiyah, from Bani Suraym, said that his paternal uncle said to him: "I said, `O Messenger of Allah, who is in Paradise' He said,

»النَّبِيُّ فِي الْجَنَّةِ، وَالشَّهِيدُ فِي الْجَنَّةِ، وَالْمَوْلُودُ فِي الْجَنَّةِ، وَالْوَئِيدُ فِي الْجَنَّةِ«

(Prophets are in Paradise, martyrs are in Paradise, infants are in Paradise and baby girls who were buried alive are in Paradise.)

It is Makruh to discuss this Matter

In order to discuss this issue we need good, sound proof, but people who have no knowledge of Shari`ah may try to speak about it. For this reason some of the scholars did not like to discuss it. This view has been narrated from Ibn `Abbas, Al-Qasim bin Muhammad bin Abi Bakr As-Siddiq, Muhammad bin Al-Hanafiyyah and others. Ibn Hibban recorded in his Sahih that Jarir bin Hazim said: I heard Abu Raja' Al-`Utardi saying that he heard Ibn `Abbas (may Allah be pleased with them both) saying, "While he was on the Minbar, the Messenger of Allah said:

»لَا يَزَالُ أَمْرُ هَذِهِ الْأُمَّةِ مُوَاتِيًا أَوْ مُقَارِبًا مَا لَمْ يَتَكَلَّمُوا فِي الْوِلْدَانِ وَالْقَدَرِ«

(This Ummah will be fine so long as they do not talk about children and the divine decree.)" Ibn Hibban said: "This means talking about the children of the idolators." Abu Bakr Al-Bazzar also recorded it via Jarir bin Hazim, then he said, "A group narrated it from Abu Raja' from Ibn `Abbas, but it is Mauquf".

Surah: 17 Ayah: 16

وَإِذَآ أَرَدْنَآ أَن نُّهْلِكَ قَرْيَةً أَمَرْنَا مُتْرَفِيهَا فَفَسَقُواْ فِيهَا فَحَقَّ عَلَيْهَا ٱلْقَوْلُ فَدَمَّرْنَٰهَا تَدْمِيرًا ۝

16. And when We decide to destroy a town (population), We (first) send a definite order (to obey Allâh and be righteous) to those among them (or We (first) increase in number those of its population) who lead a life of luxury. Then, they transgress therein, and thus the word (of torment) is justified against it (them). Then We destroy it with complete destruction.

Transliteration

16. Wa-itha aradna an nuhlika qaryatan amarna mutrafeeha fafasaqoo feeha fahaqqa AAalayha alqawlu fadammarnaha tadmeeran

Tafsir Ibn Kathir

Meanings of Amarna

The commentators differed over the meaning of this word. It was said that the phrase translated here as "Amarna those who live luxuriously. Then, they transgress therein" means, "We send Our decree upon them" as Allah says elsewhere:

(Our decree reaches it by night or by day) For (Amarna cannot mean "Our command") because Allah does not command or enjoin immorality. Or, they said it means that Allah subjugated them to commit immoral deeds, so they deserved the punishment. Or it was said that it means: "We commanded them to obey Us, but they committed immoral sins, so they deserved punishment." This was reported from Ibn Jurayj from Ibn `Abbas, and it is also the view of Sa`id bin Jubayr.

(Amarna those who live luxuriously. Then, they transgress therein,) `Ali bin Abi Talhah reported that Ibn `Abbas said: (this means) "We gave power to the evil people, so they committed sin therein (in the town), and because they did that, Allah destroyed them with the punishment." This is similar to the Ayah:

(And thus We have set up in every town great ones of its wicked people) (6:133) This was also the view of Abu Al-`Aliyah, Mujahid and Ar-Rabi' bin Anas.

(And when We decide to distroy a town (populaton), Amarna those who live luxuriously. Then, they transgress therein,) Al-`Awfi reported that Ibn `Abbas said, (it means) "We increase their numbers. This was also the view of `Ikrimah, Al-Hasan, Ad-Dahhak and Qatadah, and it was reported from Malik and Az-Zuhri.

Surah: 17 Ayah: 17

وَكَمْ أَهْلَكْنَا مِنَ ٱلْقُرُونِ مِنْ بَعْدِ نُوحٍ ۗ وَكَفَىٰ بِرَبِّكَ بِذُنُوبِ عِبَادِهِۦ خَبِيرًۢا بَصِيرًا

17. And how many generations have We destroyed after Nûh (Noah)! And Sufficient is your Lord as an All-Knower and All-Beholder of the sins of His slaves.

Transliteration

17. Wakam ahlakna mina alqurooni min baAAdi noohin wakafa birabbika bithunoobi AAibadihi khabeeran baseeran

Tafsir Ibn Kathir

A Threat to Quraysh

Warning the disbelievers of the Quraysh for rejecting His Messenger Muhammad , Allah says that He destroyed other nations who rejected the Messengers after Nuh. This indicates that during the centuries between Adam and Nuh, humans were following Islam, as Ibn `Abbas said: "Between Adam and Nuh there were ten generations, during all of which humans were following Islam." The meaning (of the Ayah) is: "You disbelievers are not more dear to Allah than they were, and you have rejected the most noble of the Messengers and the best of creation, so you are more deserving of punishment."

(And sufficient is your Lord as All-Knower and Seer of the sins of His servants.) means, He knows everything they do, good and evil, and nothing at all is hidden from Him, may He be glorified and exalted.

Surah: 17 Ayah: 18 & Ayah: 19

مَّن كَانَ يُرِيدُ ٱلْعَاجِلَةَ عَجَّلْنَا لَهُۥ فِيهَا مَا نَشَآءُ لِمَن نُّرِيدُ ثُمَّ جَعَلْنَا لَهُۥ جَهَنَّمَ يَصْلَىٰهَا مَذْمُومًا مَّدْحُورًا

18. Whoever wishes for the quick-passing (transitory enjoyment of this world), We readily grant him what We will for whom We like. Then, afterwards, We have appointed for him Hell; he will burn therein disgraced and rejected, (- far away from Allâh's Mercy).

وَمَنْ أَرَادَ ٱلْءَاخِرَةَ وَسَعَىٰ لَهَا سَعْيَهَا وَهُوَ مُؤْمِنٌ فَأُو۟لَٰٓئِكَ كَانَ سَعْيُهُم مَّشْكُورًا

19. And whoever desires the Hereafter and strives for it, with the necessary effort due for it (i.e. do righteous deeds of Allâh's Obedience) while he is a believer (in the Oneness of Allâh - Islâmic Monotheism) - then such are the ones whose striving shall be appreciated, (thanked and rewarded by Allâh).

Transliteration

18. Man kana yureedu alAAajilata AAajjalna lahu feeha ma nashao liman nureedu thumma jaAAalna lahu jahannama yaslaha mathmooman madhooran 19. Waman arada al-akhirata wasaAAa laha saAAyaha wahuwa mu/minun faola-ika kana saAAyuhum mashkooran

Tafsir Ibn Kathir

The Reward of Those who desire this World and Those who desire the Hereafter

Allah tells us that not everyone who desires this world and its luxuries gets what he wants. That is attained by those whom Allah wants to have it, and they get what He wills that they should get. This Ayah narrows down the general statements made in other Ayat. Allah says:

(We readily grant him what We will for whom We like. Then, afterwards, We have appointed for him Hell) meaning, in the Hereafter,

(he will burn therein) means, he will enter it until it covers him on all sides,

(disgraced) means, blamed for his bad behaviour and evil deeds, because he chose the transient over the eternal,

(rejected.) means, far away (from Allah's mercy), humiliated and put to shame.

(And whoever desires the Hereafter) wanting the Hereafter and its blessings and delights,

(and strives for it, with the necessary effort due for it) seeking it in the right way, which is following the Messenger .

(while he is a believer,) means, his heart has faith, i.e., he believes in the reward and punishment,

(then such are the ones whose striving shall be appreciated, (rewarded by Allah).)

Surah: 17 Ayah: 20 & Ayah: 21

كُلاًّ نُّمِدُّ هَـٰٓؤُلَآءِ وَهَـٰٓؤُلَآءِ مِنْ عَطَآءِ رَبِّكَ ۚ وَمَا كَانَ عَطَآءُ رَبِّكَ مَحْظُورًا ۝

20. To each - these as well as those - We bestow from the Bounties of your Lord. And the Bounties of your Lord can never be forbidden.

ٱنظُرْ كَيْفَ فَضَّلْنَا بَعْضَهُمْ عَلَىٰ بَعْضٍ ۚ وَلَلْآخِرَةُ أَكْبَرُ دَرَجَـٰتٍ وَأَكْبَرُ تَفْضِيلًا ۝

21. See how We prefer one above another (in this world), and verily, the Hereafter will be greater in degrees and greater in preferment.

Chapter 17: Al-Israa (The Night Journey or Bani Isra'il), Verses 001-111

Transliteration

20. Kullan numiddu haola-i wahaola-i min AAata-i rabbika wama kana AAatao rabbika mahthooran 21. Onthur kayfa faddalna baAAdahum AAala baAAdin walal-akhiratu akbaru darajatin waakbaru tafdeelan

Tafsir Ibn Kathir

On each meaning, on each of the two groups, those who desire this world and those who desire the Hereafter, We bestow what they want

(from the bounties of your Lord.) means, He is the One Who is in control of all things, and He is never unjust. He gives to each what he deserves, whether it is eternal happiness or doom. His decree is unstoppable, no one can withhold what He gives or change what He wants. Allah says:

(And the bounties of your Lord can never be forbidden.) meaning, no one can withhold or prevent them. Qatadah said,

(And the bounties of your Lord can never be forbidden.) "(It means) they can never decrease".

(And the Bounties of your Lord can never be forbidden) Al-Hasan and others said, "(It means) they can never be prevented." Then Allah says:

(See how We prefer one above another,) meaning in this world, so that some are rich and some are poor, and others are in between; some are beautiful, some are ugly and others are in between; some die young while others live to a great age, and some die in between.

(and verily, the Hereafter will be greater in degrees and greater in preferment.) means, the differences between them in the Hereafter will be greater than the differences between them in this world. Some of them will be in varying levels of Hell, in chains and fetters, while others will be in the lofty degrees of Paradise, with its blessings and delights. The people of Hell will vary in their positions and levels, just as the people of Paradise will. In Paradise there are one hundred levels, and the distance between one level and another is like the distance between heaven and earth. It is recorded in the Two Sahihs that the Prophet said:

«إِنَّ أَهْلَ الدَّرَجَاتِ الْعُلَى لَيَرَوْنَ أَهْلَ عِلِّيِّينَ كَمَا تَرَوْنَ الْكَوْكَبَ الْغَابِرَ فِي أُفُقِ السَّمَاءِ»

(The people of the highest levels (of Paradise) will see the people of `Illiyin as if they are looking at distant stars on the horizon.) Allah says:

(and verily, the Hereafter will be greater in degrees and greater in preferment.)

Surah: 17 Ayah: 22

لَّا تَجْعَلْ مَعَ ٱللَّهِ إِلَٰهًا ءَاخَرَ فَتَقْعُدَ مَذْمُومًا مَّخْذُولًا ﴿٢٢﴾

22. Set not up with Allâh any other ilâh (god), (O man)! (This verse is addressed to Prophet Muhammad (peace be upon him) but its implication is general to all mankind), or you will sit down reproved, forsaken (in the Hell-fire).

Transliteration

22. La tajAAal maAAa Allahi ilahan akhara fataqAAuda mathmooman makhthoolan

Tafsir Ibn Kathir

Do not associate Anything in Worship with Allah

Addressing those who are responsible among this Ummah, Allah says, "Do not admit any partner into your worship of your Lord."

(or you will sit down reproved,) meaning, because of associating others with Him.

(forsaken.) means, because the Lord, may He be exalted, will not help you; He will leave you to the one whom you worshipped, and he has no power either to benefit or to harm, because the Only One Who has the power to benefit or to harm is Allah alone, with no partner or associate. Imam Ahmad reported that `Abdullah bin Mas`ud said: "The Messenger of Allah said:

«مَنْ أَصَابَتْهُ فَاقَةٌ فَأَنْزَلَهَا بِالنَّاسِ لَمْ تُسَدَّ فَاقَتُهُ، وَمَنْ أَنْزَلَهَا بِاللهِ أَرْسَلَ اللهُ لَهُ بِالْغِنَى إِمَّا آجِلًا وَإِمَّا غِنًى عَاجِلًا»

(Whoever is afflicted with poverty and goes and asks people for help, will never get rid of his poverty, but if he asks Allah for help, then Allah will grant him the means of independence sooner or later.) This was also recorded by Abu Dawud and At-Tirmidhi, who said, "Hasan Sahih Gharib".

Surah: 17 Ayah: 23 & Ayah: 24

۞ وَقَضَىٰ رَبُّكَ أَلَّا تَعْبُدُوٓا۟ إِلَّآ إِيَّاهُ وَبِٱلْوَٰلِدَيْنِ إِحْسَٰنًا ۚ إِمَّا يَبْلُغَنَّ عِندَكَ ٱلْكِبَرَ أَحَدُهُمَآ أَوْ كِلَاهُمَا فَلَا تَقُل لَّهُمَآ أُفٍّ وَلَا تَنْهَرْهُمَا وَقُل لَّهُمَا قَوْلًا كَرِيمًا

23. And your Lord has decreed that you worship none but Him. And that you be dutiful to your parents. If one of them or both of them attain old age in your life, say not to them a word of disrespect, nor shout at them but address them in terms of honor.

وَٱخْفِضْ لَهُمَا جَنَاحَ ٱلذُّلِّ مِنَ ٱلرَّحْمَةِ وَقُل رَّبِّ ٱرْحَمْهُمَا كَمَا رَبَّيَانِى صَغِيرًا

24. And lower unto them the wing of submission and humility through mercy, and say: "My Lord! Bestow on them Your Mercy as they did bring me up when I was young."

Transliteration

23. Waqada rabbuka alla taAAbudoo illa iyyahu wabialwalidayni ihsanan imma yablughanna AAindaka alkibara ahaduhuma aw kilahuma fala taqul lahuma offin wala tanharhuma waqul lahuma qawlan kareeman 24. Waikhfid lahuma janaha alththulli mina alrrahmati waqul rabbi irhamhuma kama rabbayanee sagheeran

Tafsir Ibn Kathir

The Command to Worship Allah Alone and to be Dutiful to One's Parents

Allah commands us to worship Him alone, with no partner or associate. The word Qada (normally having the meaning of decree) here means "commanded". Mujahid said that

(And He has Qada) means enjoined. This is also how Ubayy bin Ka`b, Ibn Mas`ud and Ad-Dahhak bin Muzahim recited the Ayah as:

«وَوَصَّى رَبُّكَ أَلَّا تَعْبُدُوا إِلَّا إِيَّاه»

"And your Lord has Wassa (enjoined) that you worship none but Him." The idea of worshipping Allah is connected to the idea of honoring one's parents. Allah says:

(And that you be dutiful to your parents.) Here He commands good treatment of parents, as He says elsewhere:

(give thanks to Me and to your parents. Unto Me is the final destination) (31:14)

(If one of them or both of them attain old age in your life, say not to them a word of disrespect,) means, do not let them hear anything offensive from you, not even say "Uff!" which is the mildest word of disrespect,

(and do not reprimand them) means, do not do anything horrible to them.

(and do not reprimand them) `Ata' bin Rabah said that it meant, "Do not raise your hand against them." When Allah forbids speaking and behaving in an obnoxious manner, He commands speaking and behaving in a good manner, so He says:

(but address them in terms of honor.) meaning gently, kindly, politely, and with respect and appreciation.

(And lower unto them the wing of submission and humility through mercy,) means, be humble towards them in your actions.

(and say: "My Lord! Bestow on them Your Mercy as they did bring me up when I was young.") means, say this when they grow old and when they die. Ibn `Abbas said: "But then Allah revealed:

(It is not (proper) for the Prophet and those who believe to ask Allah's forgiveness for the idolators...)" (9:13) There are many Hadiths which speak about honoring one's parents, such as the Hadith narrated through a number of chains of narration from Anas and others, which states that the Prophet climbed up on the Minbar, and then said, ((Amin, Amin, Amin.)) It was said, "O Messenger of Allah, why did you say Amin" He said:

«أَتَانِي جِبْرِيلُ فَقَالَ: يَا مُحَمَّدُ رَغِمَ أَنْفُ رَجُلٍ ذُكِرْتَ عِنْدَهُ فَلَمْ يُصَلِّ عَلَيْكَ، قُلْ: آمِينَ، فَقُلْتُ: آمِينَ، ثُمَّ قَالَ: رَغِمَ أَنْفُ رَجُلٍ دَخَلَ عَلَيْهِ شَهْرُ رَمَضَانَ ثُمَّ خَرَجَ فَلَمْ يُغْفَرْ لَهُ، قُلْ: آمِينَ، فَقُلْتُ: آمِينَ، ثُمَّ قَالَ: رَغِمَ أَنْفُ رَجُلٍ أَدْرَكَ وَالِدَيْهِ أَوْ أَحَدَهُمَا فَلَمْ يُدْخِلَاهُ الْجَنَّةَ، قُلْ: آمِينَ، فَقُلْتُ: آمِين»

(Jibril came to me and said, "O Muhammad, he is doomed who hears you mentioned and does not say Salla upon you." He said, "Say Amin," so I said Amin. Then he said, "He is doomed who sees the month of Ramadan come and go, and he has not been forgiven." He said, "Say Amin," so I said Amin. Then he said, "He is doomed who grows up and both his parents or one of them are still alive, and they do not cause him to enter Paradise." He said, "Say Amin," so I said Amin.)

Another Hadith Imam Ahmad reported from Abu Hurayrah that the Prophet said:

«رَغِمَ أَنْفُ، ثُمَّ رَغِمَ أَنْفُ ثُمَّ رَغِمَ أَنْفُ رَجُلٍ أَدْرَكَ أَحَدَ أَبَوَيْهِ أَوْ (كِلَيْهِمَا) عِنْدَ الْكِبَرِ وَلَمْ يَدْخُلِ الْجَنَّةَ»

He is doomed, he is doomed, he is doomed, the man whose parents, one or both of them, reach old age while he is alive and he does not enter Paradise.) This version is Sahih although no one recorded it other than Muslim.

Another Hadith

Imam Ahmad recorded Mu`awiyah bin Jahimah As-Salami saying that Jahimah came to the Prophet and said: "O Messenger of Allah, I want to go out to fight and I have come to seek your advice." He said,

Chapter 17: Al-Israa (The Night Journey or Bani Isra'il), Verses 001-111

«فَهَلْ لَكَ مِنْ أُمٍّ»

(Do you have a mother) He said, "Yes." The Prophet said,

«فَالْزَمْهَا فَإِنَّ الْجَنَّةَ عِنْدَ رِجْلَيْهَا»

(Then stay with her, for Paradise is at her feet.) Similar incidents were also recorded by others. This was recorded by An-Nasa'i and Ibn Majah.

Another Hadith

Imam Ahmad recorded that Al-Miqdam bin Ma`dikarib said that the Prophet said:

«إِنَّ اللهَ يُوصِيكُمْ بِآبَائِكُمْ إِنَّ اللهَ يُوصِيكُمْ بِأُمَّهَاتِكُمْ إِنَّ اللهَ يُوصِيكُمْ بِأُمَّهَاتِكُمْ إِنَّ اللهَ يُوصِيكُمْ بِأُمَّهَاتِكُمْ إِنَّ اللهَ يُوصِيكُمْ بِالْأَقْرَبِ فَالْأَقْرَبِ»

(Allah enjoins you concerning your fathers, Allah enjoins you concerning your mothers, Allah enjoins you concerning your mothers, Allah enjoins you concerning your mothers, Allah enjoins you concerning your close relatives then the next in closeness.) This was recorded by Ibn Majah from the Hadith of `Abdullah bin `Ayyash.

Another Hadith

Ahmad recorded that a man from Banu Yarbu` said: "I came to the Prophet while he was talking to the people, and I heard him saying,

«يَدُ الْمُعْطِي الْعُلْيَا، أُمَّكَ وَأَبَاكَ، وَأُخْتَكَ وَأَخَاكَ، ثُمَّ أَدْنَاكَ أَدْنَاكَ»

(The hand of the one who gives is superior. (Give to) your mother and your father, your sister and your brother, then the closest and next closest.)"

Surah: 17 Ayah: 25

رَّبُّكُمْ أَعْلَمُ بِمَا فِي نُفُوسِكُمْ ۚ إِن تَكُونُوا۟ صَٰلِحِينَ فَإِنَّهُۥ كَانَ لِلْأَوَّٰبِينَ غَفُورًا

25. Your Lord knows best what is in your inner-selves. If you are righteous, then, verily, He is Ever Most Forgiving to those who turn unto Him again and again in obedience, and in repentance.

Transliteration

25. Rabbukum aAAlamu bima fee nufoosikum in takoonoo saliheena fa-innahu kana lil-awwabeena ghafooran

Tafsir Ibn Kathir

Omissions comitted against Parents are pardoned with Good Relations and Repentance

Sa`id bin Jubayr said: "This refers to a man who said something that he did not think would be offensive to his parents." According to another report: "He did not mean anything bad by that." So Allah said:

(Your Lord knows best what is in your souls. If you are righteous,)

(He is Ever Most Forgiving to those who turn to Him in repentance.) Qatadah said: "To the obedient who pray."

(He is Ever Most Forgiving to those who turn to Him in repentance.) Shu`bah narrated from Yahya bin Sa`id from Sa`id bin Al-Musayyib; "This refers to those who commit sin then repent, and commit sin then repent." `Ata' bin Yasar, Sa`id bin Jubayr and Mujahid said: "They are the ones who return to goodness." Mujahid narrated from `Ubayd bin `Umayr, concerning this Ayah: "This is the one who, when he remembers his sin when he is alone, he seeks the forgiveness of Allah." Mujahid agreed with him on that. Ibn Jarir said: "The best view on this matter is of those who said that it refers to the one who repents after committing sin, who comes back from disobedience to obedience and who leaves that which Allah hates for that which He loves and is pleased with. " What he said is correct, for Allah says,

(Verily, to Us will be their return) (88:25). And according to a Sahih Hadith, the Messenger of Allah would say when he returned from a journey,

»آيِبُونَ تَائِبُونَ، عَابِدُونَ لِرَبِّنَا حَامِدُونَ«

(We have returned repenting, worshipping and praising our Lord.)

Surah: 17 Ayah: 26, Ayah: 27 & Ayah: 28

وَءَاتِ ذَا ٱلْقُرْبَىٰ حَقَّهُۥ وَٱلْمِسْكِينَ وَٱبْنَ ٱلسَّبِيلِ وَلَا تُبَذِّرْ تَبْذِيرًا ۝

26. And give to the kindred his due and to the Miskîn (poor) and to the wayfarer. But spend not wastefully (your wealth) in the manner of a spendthrift . (Tafsir At-Tabarî).

إِنَّ ٱلْمُبَذِّرِينَ كَانُوٓا۟ إِخْوَٰنَ ٱلشَّيَـٰطِينِ وَكَانَ ٱلشَّيْطَـٰنُ لِرَبِّهِۦ كَفُورًا ۝

27. Verily, spendthrifts are brothers of the Shayâtîn (devils), and the Shaitân (Devil - Satan) is ever ungrateful to his Lord.

Chapter 17: Al-Israa (The Night Journey or Bani Isra'il), Verses 001-111

وَإِمَّا تُعْرِضَنَّ عَنْهُمُ ٱبْتِغَآءَ رَحْمَةٍ مِّن رَّبِّكَ تَرْجُوهَا فَقُل لَّهُمْ قَوْلاً مَّيْسُوراً ﴿٢٨﴾

28. And if you (O Muhammad (peace be upon him)) turn away from them (kindred, poor, wayfarer whom We have ordered you to give their rights, but if you have no money at the time they ask you for it) and you are awaiting a mercy from your Lord for which you hope, then, speak unto them a soft kind word (i.e. Allâh will give me and I shall give you).

Transliteration

26. Waati tha alqurba haqqahu waalmiskeena waibna alssabeeli wala tubaththir tabtheeran 27. Inna almubaththireena kanoo ikhwana alshshayateeni wakana alshshaytanu lirabbihi kafooran 28. Wa-imma tuAAridanna AAanhumu ibtighaa rahmatin min rabbika tarjooha faqul lahum qawlan maysooran

Tafsir Ibn Kathir

The Command to maintain the Ties of Kinship and the Prohibition of Extravagance

When Allah mentions honoring one's parents, He follows this with the command to treat one's relatives well and to maintain the ties of kinship. According to the Hadith:

«أُمَّكَ وَأَبَاكَ، ثُمَّ أَدْنَاكَ أَدْنَاكَ»

«ثُمَّ الْأَقْرَبَ فَالْأَقْرَبَ»

(Your mother and your father, then your closest relatives and the next closest.) According to another Hadith:

«مَنْ أَحَبَّ أَنْ يُبْسَطَ لَهُ فِي رِزْقِهِ وَيُنْسَأَ لَهُ فِي أَجَلِهِ، فَلْيَصِلْ رَحِمَه»

(Whoever would like to see his provision expanded and his life extended, let him maintain his ties of kinship.)

(But spend not wastefully (your wealth) in the manner of a spendthrift.) When Allah commands spending, He forbids extravagance. Spending should be moderate, as stated in another Ayah:

(And those who, when they spend, are neither extravagant nor stingy). (25:67) Then He says, to discourage extravagance:

(Verily, the spendthrifts are brothers of the Shayatin,) They have this trait in common. Ibn Mas`ud said: "This refers spending extravagantly when it is not appropriate." Ibn `Abbas said likewise. Mujahid said: "If a man spends all his wealth on appropriate things, then he is not a spendthrift, but if he spends a little inappropriately, then he is a spendthrift." Qatadah said: "Extravagance means spending money on sin in disobeying Allah, and on wrongful and corrupt things." Imam Ahmad recorded that Anas bin Malik said: "A man came from Banu Tamim to the Messenger of Allah and said: `O Messenger of Allah, I have a lot of wealth, I have a family, children, and the refinements of city life, so tell me how I should spend and what I should do.' The Messenger of Allah said:

《تُخْرِجُ الزَّكَاةَ مِنْ مَالِكَ إِنْ كَانَ، فَإِنَّهَا طُهْرَةٌ تُطَهِّرُكَ، وَتَصِلُ أَقْرِبَاءَكَ، وَتَعْرِفُ حَقَّ السَّائِلِ وَالْجَارِ وَالْمِسْكِينِ》

(Pay the Zakah on your wealth if any is due, for it is purification that will make you pure, maintain your ties of kinship, pay attention to the rights of beggars, neighbors and the poor.) He said: `O Messenger of Allah, make it less for me.' He (recited):

(وَءَاتِ ذَا الْقُرْبَى حَقَّهُ وَالْمِسْكِينَ وَابْنَ السَّبِيلِ وَلاَ تُبَذِّرْ تَبْذِيرًا)

(And give to the kinsman his due, and to the Miskin (poor) and to the wayfarer. But spend not wastefully in the manner of a spendthrift.) The man said, `That is enough for me, O Messenger of Allah. If I pay Zakah to your messenger, will I be absolved of that duty before Allah and His Messenger' The Messenger of Allah said:

《نَعَمْ، إِذَا أَدَّيْتَهَا إِلَى رَسُولِي فَقَدْ بَرِئْتَ مِنْهَا وَلَكَ أَجْرُهَا، وَإِثْمُهَا عَلَى مَنْ بَدَّلَهَا》

(Yes, if you give it to my messenger, you will have fulfilled it, and you will have the reward for it, and the sin is on the one who changes it.)"

(Verily, the spendthrifts are brothers of the Shayatin,) meaning, they are their brothers in extravagance, foolishness, failing to obey Allah and committing sin. Allah said:

(and the Shaytan is ever ungrateful to his Lord.) meaning, he is an ingrate, because he denied the blessings of Allah and did not obey Him, turning instead to disobedience and rebellion.

(And if you turn away from them and you are awaiting a mercy from your Lord) `If your relatives and those to whom We have commanded you to give, ask you for something, and you do not have anything, and you turn away from them because you have nothing to give,

(then, speak unto them a soft, kind word.) meaning, with a promise. This was the opinion of Mujahid, `Ikrimah, Sa`id bin Jubayr, Al-Hasan, Qatadah and others.

Surah: 17 Ayah: 29 & Ayah: 30

وَلَا تَجْعَلْ يَدَكَ مَغْلُولَةً إِلَىٰ عُنُقِكَ وَلَا تَبْسُطْهَا كُلَّ ٱلْبَسْطِ فَتَقْعُدَ مَلُومًا مَّحْسُورًا

29. And let not your hand be tied (like a miser) to your neck, nor stretch it forth to its utmost reach (like a spendthrift), so that you become blameworthy and in severe poverty.

إِنَّ رَبَّكَ يَبْسُطُ ٱلرِّزْقَ لِمَن يَشَآءُ وَيَقْدِرُ ۚ إِنَّهُۥ كَانَ بِعِبَادِهِۦ خَبِيرًۢا بَصِيرًا

30. Truly, your Lord enlarges the provision for whom He wills and straitens (for whom He wills). Verily, He is Ever All-Knower, All-Seer of His slaves.

Transliteration

29. Wala tajAAal yadaka maghloolatan ila AAunuqika wala tabsutha kulla albasti fataqAAuda malooman mahsooran 30. Inna rabbaka yabsutu alrrizqa liman yashao wayaqdiru innahu kana biAAibadihi khabeeran baseeran

Tafsir Ibn Kathir

Moderation in Spending

Allah enjoins moderation in living. He condemns miserliness and forbids extravagance.

(And let not your hand be tied (like a miser) to your neck,) this means, do not be miserly and stingy, never giving anything to anyone, as the Jews - may the curses of Allah be upon them - said, "Allah's Hand is tied up (i.e., He does not give and spend of His bounty)". They attributed miserliness to Him, Exalted and Sanctified be the Most Generous Bestower!

(nor overextend it (like a spendthrift)) means, nor be extravagant in spending and giving more than you can afford, or paying more than you earn, lest you become blameworthy and find yourself in severe poverty. If you are a miser, people will blame you and condemn you, and no longer rely on you. When you spend more than you can afford, you will find yourself without anything to spend, so you will be worn out, like an animal that cannot walk, so it becomes weak and incapable. It is described as worn out, which is similar in meaning to exhausted. As Allah says:

(Then look again: "Can you see any rifts" Then look again and yet again, your sight will return to you in a state of humiliation and worn out.) (67:3-4) meaning, unable to see any faults. Similarly, Ibn `Abbas, Al-Hasan, Qatadah, Ibn Jurayj, Ibn Zayd and others understood this Ayah as miserliness and extravagance. It was reported in the Two Sahihs from the Hadith of Abu Az-Zinad from Al-A`raj that Abu Hurayrah heard the Messenger of Allah say:

«مَثَلُ الْبَخِيلِ وَالْمُنْفِقِ كَمَثَلِ رَجُلَيْنِ عَلَيْهِمَا جُبَّتَانِ مِنْ حَدِيدٍ مِنْ ثُدِيِّهِمَا إِلَى تَرَاقِيهِمَا، فَأَمَّا الْمُنْفِقُ فَلَا يُنْفِقُ إِلَّا سَبَغَتْ أَوْ وَفَرَتْ عَلَى جِلْدِهِ حَتَّى تُخْفِيَ بَنَانَهُ وَتَعْفُوَ أَثَرَهُ، وَأَمَّا الْبَخِيلُ فَلَا يُرِيدُ أَنْ يُنْفِقَ شَيْئًا إِلَّا لَزِقَتْ كُلُّ حَلْقَةٍ مِنْهَا مَكَانَهَا، فَهُوَ يُوَسِّعُهَا فَلَا تَتَّسِع»

(The parable of the miser and the almsgiver is that of two persons wearing iron cloaks from their chests to their collar-bones. When the almsgiver gives in charity, the cloak becomes spacious until it covers his whole body to such an extent that it hides his fingertips and covers his tracks (obliterates his tracks - or, his sins will be forgiven). And when the miser wants to spend, it (the iron cloak) sticks and (its) every ring gets stuck to its place, and he tries to widen it, but it does not become wide.) This version was recorded by Al-Bukhari in the Book of Zakah. In the Two Sahihs it is recorded that Mu`awiyah bin Abi Muzarrid narrated from Sa`id bin Yasar that Abu Hurayrah said: "The Messenger of Allah said:

«مَا مِنْ يَوْمٍ يُصْبِحُ الْعِبَادُ فِيهِ إِلَّا وَمَلَكَانِ يَنْزِلَانِ مِنَ السَّمَاءِ يَقُولُ أَحَدُهُمَا: اللَّهُمَّ أَعْطِ مُنْفِقًا خَلَفًا، وَيَقُولُ الْآخَرُ: اللَّهُمَّ أَعْطِ مُمْسِكًا تَلَفًا»

(There is no day when a person wakes up but two angels come down from heaven. One of them says, `O Allah, compensate the one who gives (in charity),' and the other one says, `O Allah, destroy the one who withholds.')" Muslim recorded from Abu Hurayrah that the Prophet said:

«مَا نَقَصَ مَالٌ مِنْ صَدَقَةٍ، وَمَا زَادَ اللهُ عَبْدًا أَنْفَقَ إِلَّا عِزًّا، وَمَنْ تَوَاضَعَ لِلَّهِ رَفَعَهُ اللهُ»

(Wealth never decreases because of Sadaqah (charity). Allah never increases a servant who gives in charity except in honor, and whoever is humble for the sake of Allah, Allah will raise him in status.) According to a Hadith narrated by Abu Kathir from `Abdullah bin `Amr, who attributed it to the Prophet:

«إِيَّاكُمْ وَالشُّحَّ فَإِنَّهُ أَهْلَكَ مَنْ كَانَ قَبْلَكُمْ، أَمَرَهُمْ بِالْبُخْلِ فَبَخِلُوا، وَأَمَرَهُمْ بِالْقَطِيعَةِ فَقَطَعُوا، وَأَمَرَهُمْ بِالْفُجُورِ فَفَجَرُوا»

Chapter 17: Al-Israa (The Night Journey or Bani Isra'il), Verses 001-111

(Beware of stinginess for it destroyed the people who came before you. It commanded them to be miserly, so they were miserly; and it commanded them to cut the ties of kinship, so they cut them; and it commanded them to commit immoral actions, so they did so.)

(Truly, your Lord expands the provision for whom He wills and straitens (for whom He wills).) This Ayah is telling us that Allah is the One Who provides or withholds, the Bestower Who is running the affairs of His creation as He wills. He makes rich whomever He wills, and He makes poor whomever He wills, by the wisdom that is His. He said: /

(Verily, He is Ever All-Knower, All-Seer of His servants.) meaning, He knows and sees who deserves to be rich and who deserves to be poor. In some cases, richness may be decreed so that a person gets carried away, leading to his own doom. In other cases, poverty may be a punishment. We seek refuge with Allah from both.

Surah: 17 Ayah: 31

وَلَا تَقْتُلُوٓاْ أَوْلَٰدَكُمْ خَشْيَةَ إِمْلَٰقٍ ۖ نَّحْنُ نَرْزُقُهُمْ وَإِيَّاكُمْ ۚ إِنَّ قَتْلَهُمْ كَانَ خِطْـًٔا كَبِيرًا ۝

31. And kill not your children for fear of poverty. We provide for them and for you. Surely, the killing of them is a great sin.

Transliteration

31. Wala taqtuloo awladakum khashyata imlaqin nahnu narzuquhum wa-iyyakum inna qatlahum kana khit-an kabeeran

Tafsir Ibn Kathir

Prohibition of killing Children

This Ayah indicates that Allah is more compassionate towards His servants than a father to his child, because He forbids killing children just as He enjoins parents to take care of their children in matters of inheritance. The people of Jahiliyyah would not allow their daughters to inherit from them, and some would even kill their daughters lest they make them more poor. Allah forbade that and said:

(And kill not your children for fear of poverty.) meaning, lest they may make you poor in the future. This is why Allah mentions the children's provision first:

(We shall provide for them as well as for you.) In Surat Al-An`am, Allah says:

(kill not your children because of poverty.) (6:151)

(We provide sustenance for you and for them) (6:151) and,

(Surely, the killing of them is a great sin.) means, a major sin. In Two Sahihs it is recorded that `Abdullah bin Mas`ud said: "I said, `O Messenger of Allah, which sin is the worst' He said,

«أَنْ تَجْعَلَ لِلَّهِ نِدًّا وَهُوَ خَلَقَكَ . قُلْتُ: ثُمَّ أَيٌّ؟ قَالَ: أَنْ تَقْتُلَ وَلَدَكَ خَشْيَةَ أَنْ يَطْعَمَ مَعَكَ . قُلْتُ: ثُمَّ أَيٌّ؟ قَالَ: أَنْ تُزَانِيَ بِحَلِيلَةِ جَارِكَ»

(To appoint rivals of Allah when He has created you.) I asked, `Then what' He said, (To kill your child lest he should eat with you.) I asked, `Then what' He said, (To commit adultery with your neighbor's wife.)"

Surah: 17 Ayah: 32

وَلَا تَقْرَبُوا۟ ٱلزِّنَىٰٓ ۖ إِنَّهُۥ كَانَ فَـٰحِشَةً وَسَآءَ سَبِيلًا ﴿٣٢﴾

32. And come not near to the unlawful sexual intercourse. Verily, it is a Fâhishah (i.e. anything that transgresses its limits: a great sin), and an evil way (that leads one to Hell unless Allâh forgives him).

Transliteration

32. Wala taqraboo alzzina innahu kana fahishatan wasaa sabeelan

Tafsir Ibn Kathir

The Command to avoid Zina (Unlawful Sex) and Everything that leads to it

Allah says, forbidding His servants to commit Zina or to approach it or to do anything that may lead to it:

(And come not near to unlawful sex. Verily, it is a Fahishah (immoral sin)) meaning a major sin,

(and an evil way.) meaning, a terrible way to behave. Imam Ahmad recorded Abu Umamah saying that a young man came to the Prophet and said, "O Messenger of Allah! Give me permission to commit Zina (unlawful sex)." The people surrounded him and rebuked him, saying, "Stop! Stop!" But the Prophet said,

«ائْذَنُهُ»

(Come close) The young man came to him, and he said,

«اجْلِسْ»

(Sit down) so he sat down. The Prophet said,

«أَتُحِبُّهُ لِأُمِّكَ»

(Would you like it (unlawful sex) for your mother) He said, "No, by Allah, may I be ransomed for you." The Prophet said,

«وَلَا النَّاسُ يُحِبُّونَهُ لِأُمَّهَاتِهِم»

(Neither do the people like it for their mothers.) The Prophet said,

«أَفَتُحِبُّهُ لِابْنَتِكَ؟»

(Would you like it for your daughter) He said, "No, by Allah, may I be ransomed for you." The Prophet said,

«وَلَا النَّاسُ يُحِبُّونَهُ لِبَنَاتِهِم»

(Neither do the people like it for their daughters.) The Prophet said,

«أَفَتُحِبُّهُ لِأُخْتِكَ؟»

(Would you like it for your sister) He said, "No, by Allah, may I be ransomed for you." The Prophet said,

«وَلَا النَّاسُ يُحِبُّونَهُ لِأَخَوَاتِهِم»

(Neither do the people like it for their sisters.) The Prophet said,

«أَفَتُحِبُّهُ لِعَمَّتِكَ؟»

(Would you like it for your paternal aunt) He said, "No, by Allah, O Allah's Messenger! may I be ransomed for you." The Prophet said,

«وَلَا النَّاسُ يُحِبُّونَهُ لِعَمَّاتِهِم»

(Neither do the people like it for their paternal aunts.) The Prophet said,

«أَفَتُحِبُّهُ لِخَالَتِكَ؟»

(Would you like it for your maternal aunt) He said, "No, by Allah, O Allah's Messenger! may I be ransomed for you." The Prophet said,

«وَلَا النَّاسُ يُحِبُّونَهُ لِخَالَاتِهِم»

(Neither do the people like it for their maternal aunts.) Then the Prophet put his hand on him and said,

«اللَّهُمَّ اغْفِرْ ذَنْبَهُ، وَطَهِّرْ قَلْبَهُ، وَأَحْصِنْ فَرْجَهُ»

(O Allah, forgive his sin, purify his heart and guard his chastity.) After that the young man never paid attention to anything of that nature.

Surah: 17 Ayah: 33

وَلَا تَقْتُلُوا۟ ٱلنَّفْسَ ٱلَّتِى حَرَّمَ ٱللَّهُ إِلَّا بِٱلْحَقِّ ۗ وَمَن قُتِلَ مَظْلُومًا فَقَدْ جَعَلْنَا لِوَلِيِّهِۦ سُلْطَـٰنًا فَلَا يُسْرِف فِّى ٱلْقَتْلِ ۖ إِنَّهُۥ كَانَ مَنصُورًا ۝

33. And do not kill anyone whose killing Allâh has forbidden, except for a just cause. And whoever is killed wrongfully (Mazlûman intentionally with hostility and oppression and not by mistake), We have given his heir the authority ((to demand Qisâs - Law of Equality in punishment - or to forgive, or to take Diyah (blood money)) But let him not exceed limits in the matter of taking life (i.e. he should not kill except the killer only). Verily, he is helped (by the Islâmic law).

Transliteration

33. Wala taqtuloo alnnafsa allatee harrama Allahu illa bialhaqqi waman qutila mathlooman faqad jaAAalna liwaliyyihi sultanan fala yusrif fee alqatli innahu kana mansooran

Tafsir Ibn Kathir

Prohibition of Unlawful Killing. Allah forbids killing with no legitimate reason.

It was reported in the Two Sahihs that the Messenger of Allah said:

«لَا يَحِلُّ دَمُ امْرِئٍ مُسْلِمٍ يَشْهَدُ أَنْ لَا إِلَهَ إِلَّا اللهُ وَأَنَّ مُحَمَّدًا رَسُولُ اللهِ، إِلَّا بِإِحْدَى ثَلَاثٍ: النَّفْسُ بِالنَّفْسِ، وَالزَّانِي الْمُحْصَنُ، وَالتَّارِكُ لِدِينِهِ الْمُفَارِقُ لِلْجَمَاعَةِ»

(The blood of a Muslim who bears witness to La ilaha illallah and that Muhammad is the Messenger of Allah, is not permissible (to be shed) except in three cases: a soul for a soul (i.e., in the case of murder), an adulterer who is married, and a person who leaves his religion and deserts the Jama'ah.) The following is recorded in the books of the Sunan:

«لَزَوَالُ الدُّنْيَا عِنْدَ اللهِ أَهْوَنُ مِنْ قَتْلِ مُسْلِمٍ»

(If the world were to be destroyed, it would be of less importance to Allah than the killing of a Muslim.)

(And whoever is killed wrongfully, We have given his heir the authority.) The authority is over the killer. The heir has the choice; if he wishes, he may have him killed in retaliation, or he may forgive him in return for the payment of the Diyah (blood money), or he may forgive him with no payment, as is reported in the Sunnah. The great scholar and Imam Ibn `Abbas understood from the general meaning of this Ayah that Mu`awiyah should take power, because he was the heir of `Uthman, who had been killed wrongfully, may Allah be pleased with him, and Mu`awiyah did eventually take power, as Ibn `Abbas said on the basis of this Ayah. This is one of the stranger of matters.

(But let him not exceed limits in the matter of taking life.) They said: this means the heir should not go to extremes in killing the killer, such as mutilating the body or taking revenge on persons other than the killer.

(Verily, he is helped.) means, the heir is helped against the killer by the Shari`ah and by divine decree.

Surah: 17 Ayah: 34 & Ayah: 35

وَلَا تَقْرَبُواْ مَالَ ٱلْيَتِيمِ إِلَّا بِٱلَّتِي هِيَ أَحْسَنُ حَتَّىٰ يَبْلُغَ أَشُدَّهُۥ وَأَوْفُواْ بِٱلْعَهْدِ إِنَّ ٱلْعَهْدَ كَانَ مَسْـُٔولًا ۝

34. And come not near to the orphan's property except to improve it, until he attains the age of full strength. And fulfil (every) covenant. Verily! the covenant, will be questioned about.

وَأَوْفُواْ ٱلْكَيْلَ إِذَا كِلْتُمْ وَزِنُواْ بِٱلْقِسْطَاسِ ٱلْمُسْتَقِيمِ ذَٰلِكَ خَيْرٌ وَأَحْسَنُ تَأْوِيلًا ۝

35. And give full measure when you measure, and weigh with a balance that is straight. That is good (advantageous) and better in the end.

Transliteration

34. Wala taqraboo mala alyateemi illa biallatee hiya ahsanu hatta yablugha ashuddahu waawfoo bialAAahdi inna alAAahda kana mas-oolan 35. Waawfoo alkayla itha kiltum wazinoo bialqistasi almustaqeemi thalika khayrun waahsanu ta/weelan

Tafsir Ibn Kathir

The Command to handle the Orphan's Wealth properly and to be Honest in Weights and Measures

(And come not near to the orphan's property except to improve it, until he attains the age of full strength.) meaning, do not dispose of the orphan's wealth except in a proper manner.

(but consume it (the orphan's property) not wastefully and hastily fearing that they should grow up, and whoever (among guardians) is rich, he should take no wages, but if he is poor, let him have for himself what is just and reasonable (according to his labor).) (4:6) In Sahih Muslim it is recorded that the Messenger of Allah said to Abu Dharr:

«يَا أَبَا ذَرَ إِنِّي أَرَاكَ ضَعِيفًا، وَإِنِّي أُحِبُّ لَكَ مَا أُحِبُّ لِنَفْسِي: لَا تَأَمَّرَنَّ عَلَى اثْنَيْنِ، وَلَا تَوَلَّيَنَّ مَالَ الْيَتِيمِ»

(O Abu Dharr, I see that you are weak (in adiministering), and I like for you that which I like for myself. Do not let yourself be appointed as Amir over two people, and do not let yourself be appointed as guardian of an orphan's property.)

(And fulfill (every) covenant.) meaning, everything that you promise people, and the covenants that you agree to, because the person who makes a covenant or a promise will be asked about it:

(Verily, the covenant will be questioned about.)

(And give full measure when you measure.) meaning, do not try to make it weigh less nor wrong people with their belongings.

(and weigh with a balance) meaning scales,

(that is straight.) meaning that which is not distorted nor that which will cause confusion.

(that is good) for you, in your daily life and in your Hereafter. So Allah says:

(and better in the end.) meaning, with regard to your ultimate end in the Hereafter.

(That is good (advantageous) and better in the end.) Sa`id narrated that Qatadah said that this means "Better in reward and a better end. " Ibn `Abbas used to say: "O

Chapter 17: Al-Israa (The Night Journey or Bani Isra'il), Verses 001-111

people, you are entrusted with two things for which the people who came before you were destroyed - these weights and measures."

Surah: 17 Ayah: 36

وَلَا تَقْفُ مَا لَيْسَ لَكَ بِهِ عِلْمٌ إِنَّ ٱلسَّمْعَ وَٱلْبَصَرَ وَٱلْفُؤَادَ كُلُّ أُوْلَٰٓئِكَ كَانَ عَنْهُ مَسْئُولاً ۝

36. And follow not (O man i.e., say not, or do not or witness not) that of which you have no knowledge. Verily! The hearing, and the sight, and the heart, of each of those one will be questioned (by Allâh).

Transliteration

36. Wala taqfu ma laysa laka bihi AAilmun inna alssamAAa waalbasara waalfu-ada kullu ola-ika kana AAanhu mas-oolan

Tafsir Ibn Kathir

Do not speak without Knowledge

`Ali bin Abi Talhah reported that Ibn `Abbas said: "This means) do not say (anything of which you have no knowledge)." Al-`Awfi said: "Do not accuse anyone of that of which you have no knowledge." Muhammad bin Al-Hanafiyyah said: "It means bearing false witness." Qatadah said: "Do not say, `I have seen', when you did not see anything, or `I have heard', when you did not hear anything, or `I know', when you do not know, for Allah will ask you about all of that." In conclusion, what they said means that Allah forbids speaking without knowledge and only on the basis of suspicion, which is mere imagination and illusions. As Allah says:

(Avoid much suspicion; indeed some suspicions are sins.) (49:12) According to a Hadith:

«إِيَّاكُمْ وَالظَّنَّ فَإِنَّ الظَّنَّ أَكْذَبُ الْحَدِيثِ»

(Beware of suspicion, for suspicion is the falsest of speech.) The following Hadith is found in Sunan Abu Dawud:

«بِئْسَ مَطِيَّةُ الرَّجُلِ: زَعَمُوا»

(What an evil habit it is for a man to say, `They claimed...') According to another Hadith:

«إِنَّ أَفْرَى الْفِرَى أَنْ يُرِيَ الرَّجُلُ عَيْنَيْهِ مَا لَمْ تَرَيَا»

(The worst of lies is for a man to claim to have seen something that he has not seen.) In the Sahih it says:

«مَنْ تَحَلَّمَ حُلْمًا كُلِّفَ يَوْمَ الْقِيَامَةِ أَنْ يَعْقِدَ بَيْنَ شَعِيرَتَيْنِ وَلَيْسَ بِفَاعِلٍ»

(Whoever claims to have seen a dream (when he has not seen) will be told on the Day of Resurrection to make a knot between two barley grains, and he will not be able to do it.)

(each of those ones) means these faculties, hearing, sight and the heart,

(will be questioned.) means, the person will be asked about them on the Day of Resurrection, and they will be asked about him and what he did with them.

Surah: 17 Ayah: 37 & Ayah: 38

وَلَا تَمْشِ فِى ٱلْأَرْضِ مَرَحًا ۖ إِنَّكَ لَن تَخْرِقَ ٱلْأَرْضَ وَلَن تَبْلُغَ ٱلْجِبَالَ طُولًا ۝

37. And walk not on the earth with conceit and arrogance. Verily, you can neither rend nor penetrate the earth, nor can you attain a stature like the mountains in height.

كُلُّ ذَٰلِكَ كَانَ سَيِّئُهُۥ عِندَ رَبِّكَ مَكْرُوهًا ۝

38. All the bad aspects of these (the above mentioned things) are hateful to your Lord.

Transliteration

37. Wala tamshi fee al-ardi marahan innaka lan takhriqa al-arda walan tablugha aljibala toolan 38. Kullu thalika kana sayyi-ohu AAinda rabbika makroohan

Tafsir Ibn Kathir

Condemnation of strutting

Allah forbids His servants to strut and walk in a boastful manner:

(And walk not on the earth with conceit and arrogance.) meaning, walking in boastful manner and acting proud, like those who are arrogant oppressors.

(Verily, you can neither rend nor penetrate the earth) means, you cannot penetrate the earth with your walking. This was the opinion of Ibn Jarir.

Surah: 17 Ayah: 39

ذَٰلِكَ مِمَّآ أَوْحَىٰٓ إِلَيْكَ رَبُّكَ مِنَ ٱلْحِكْمَةِ ۗ وَلَا تَجْعَلْ مَعَ ٱللَّهِ إِلَٰهًا ءَاخَرَ فَتُلْقَىٰ فِى جَهَنَّمَ مَلُومًا مَّدْحُورًا ۝

39. This is (part) of Al-Hikmah (wisdom, good manners and high character) which your Lord has revealed to you (O Muhammad (peace be upon him)) And set not up with Allâh any other ilâh (god) lest you should be thrown into Hell, blameworthy and rejected, (from Allâh's Mercy).

Transliteration

39. Thalika mimma awha ilayka rabbuka mina alhikmati wala tajAAal maAAa Allahi ilahan akhara fatulqa fee jahannama malooman madhooran

Tafsir Ibn Kathir

Everything previously mentioned is Revelation and Wisdom

Allah says: `What We have commanded you to do is part of good manners, and what We have forbidden you are evil qualities. We have revealed this to you, O Muhammad, so that you may command the people likewise.'

(And set not up with Allah any other god lest you should be thrown into Hell, blameworthy) meaning, your own self will blame you, as will Allah and His creation.

(rejected) means far removed from everything good. Ibn `Abbas and Qatadah said: "(It means) cast out." This is an address to the Ummah via the Messenger, for he is infallible.

Surah: 17 Ayah: 40

أَفَأَصْفَىٰكُمْ رَبُّكُم بِٱلْبَنِينَ وَٱتَّخَذَ مِنَ ٱلْمَلَٰٓئِكَةِ إِنَٰثًا ۚ إِنَّكُمْ لَتَقُولُونَ قَوْلًا عَظِيمًا ۝

40. Has then your Lord (O pagans of Makkah) preferred for you sons, and taken for Himself from among the angels daughters. Verily you indeed utter an awful saying.

Transliteration

40. Afaasfakum rabbukum bialbaneena waittakhatha mina almala-ikati inathan innakum lataqooloona qawlan AAatheeman

Tafsir Ibn Kathir

Refutation of Those Who claim that the Angels are Daughters of Allah

Allah refutes the lying idolators who claim, may the curse of Allah be upon them, that the angels are the daughters of Allah. They made the angels, who are the servants of Ar-Rahman (the Most Beneficent), females, and called them daughters of Allah, then they worshipped them. They were gravely wrong on all three counts. Allah says, denouncing them:

(Has then your Lord preferred for you sons,) meaning, has He given only you sons

(and taken for Himself from among the angels daughters) meaning, has He chosen for Himself, as you claim, daughters Then Allah denounces them even more severely, and says:

(Verily, you indeed utter an awful saying.) meaning, in your claim that Allah has children, then you say that His children are female, which you do not like for yourselves and may even kill them by burying them alive. That is indeed a division most unfair! Allah says:

(And they say: "The Most Beneficent (Allah) has begotten a child." Indeed you have brought forth (said) a terrible evil thing. Whereby the heavens are almost torn, and the earth split asunder, and the mountains fall in ruins. That they ascribe a son child to the Most Beneficent. But it is not suitable for (the majesty of) the Most Beneficent that he should beget a child. There is none in the heavens and the earth but comes unto the Most Beneficent as a servant. Verily, He knows each one of them, and has counted them a full counting. And every one of them will come to Him alone on the Day of Resurrection.) (19:88-95)

Surah: 17 Ayah: 41

وَلَقَدْ صَرَّفْنَا فِى هَـٰذَا ٱلْقُرْءَانِ لِيَذَّكَّرُواْ وَمَا يَزِيدُهُمْ إِلَّا نُفُورًا ۝

41. And surely, We have explained (Our Promises, Warnings and (set forth many) examples) in this Qur'ân that they (the disbelievers) may take heed, but it increases them in naught save aversion.

Transliteration

41. Walaqad sarrafna fee hatha alqur-ani liyaththakkaroo wama yazeeduhum illa nufooran

Tafsir Ibn Kathir

(And surely, We have explained in this Qur'an) meaning, `We have explained Our warni- ngs so that they may remember the proof, evidence and exhorta- tions contained there- in, and be prevented from Shirk, wrong- doing and scandal.'

(but it increases them in naught) the wrong- doers among them (save aversion.) aversion towards the truth; they go further away from it.

Surah: 17 Ayah: 42 & Ayah: 43

قُل لَّوْ كَانَ مَعَهُۥٓ ءَالِهَةٌ كَمَا يَقُولُونَ إِذًا لَّٱبْتَغَوْاْ إِلَىٰ ذِى ٱلْعَرْشِ سَبِيلًا ﴿٤٢﴾

42. Say (O Muhammad (peace be upon him) to these polytheists, pagans): "If there had been other âlihah (gods) along with Him as they assert, then they would certainly have sought out a way to the Lord of the Throne (seeking His Pleasures and to be near to Him).

سُبْحَٰنَهُۥ وَتَعَٰلَىٰ عَمَّا يَقُولُونَ عُلُوًّا كَبِيرًا ﴿٤٣﴾

43. Glorified and High be He! High above (the great falsehood) that they say! (i.e. forged statements that there are other gods along with Allâh, but He is Allâh, the One, the Self-Sufficient Master, whom all creatures need. He begets not, nor was He begotten, and there is none comparable or coequal unto Him).

Transliteration

42. Qul law kana maAAahu alihatun kama yaqooloona ithan laibtaghaw ila thee alAAarshi sabeelan 43. Subhanahu wataAAala AAamma yaqooloona AAuluwwan kabeeran

Tafsir Ibn Kathir

Allah says: `Say, O Muhammad, to these idolators who claim that Allah has a partner among His creation, and who worship others besides Him that they may bring them nearer to Him: if the matter is as you say, and there is another god besides Him whom you worship in order to draw closer to Him and so that he will intercede for you with Him, then those whom you worship would themselves worship Him and seek means to draw closer to Him. So worship Him alone, just as those on whom you call besides Him worship Him. You have no need of a deity to be an intermediary between you and Him, for He does not like or accept that, rather He hates it and rejects it, and has forbidden that through all of His Messengers and Prophets.' Then He glorifies and sanctifies Himself far above all that, and says:

(Glorified and Exalted is He high above what they say!) meaning these idolators who transgress and do wrong when they claim that there are other gods besides Him.

(high above) means, far above. He is Allah, the One, the Self-Sufficient Master, Whom all creatures need. He begets not, nor was He begotten, and there is none comparable or coequal unto Him.

Surah: 17 Ayah: 44

تُسَبِّحُ لَهُ ٱلسَّمَٰوَٰتُ ٱلسَّبْعُ وَٱلْأَرْضُ وَمَن فِيهِنَّ ۚ وَإِن مِّن شَىْءٍ إِلَّا يُسَبِّحُ بِحَمْدِهِۦ وَلَٰكِن لَّا تَفْقَهُونَ تَسْبِيحَهُمْ ۗ إِنَّهُۥ كَانَ حَلِيمًا غَفُورًا ﴿٤٤﴾

44. The seven heavens and the earth and all that is therein, glorify Him and there is not a thing but glorifies His Praise. But you understand not their glorification. Truly, He is Ever Forbearing, Oft-Forgiving.

Transliteration

44. Tusabbihu lahu alssamawatu alssabAAu waal-ardu waman feehinna wa-in min shay-in illa yusabbihu bihamdihi walakin la tafqahoona tasbeehahum innahu kana haleeman ghafooran

Tafsir Ibn Kathir

Everything glorifies Allah

Allah says: the seven heavens and the earth and all that is therein, meaning the creatures that dwell therein, sanctify Him, exalt Him, venerate Him, glorify Him and magnify Him far above what these idolators say, and they bear witness that He is One in His Lordship and Divinity. In everything there is a sign of Allah indicating that He is One. As Allah says:

(Whereby the heavens are almost torn, and the earth is split asunder, and the mountains fall in ruins, That they ascribe child to the Most Beneficent) (19:90-91).

(and there is not a thing but glorifies His praise.) there is no created being that does not celebrate the praises of Allah.

(But you understand not their glorification.) means, `You do not understand them, O mankind, because it is not like your languages.' This applies to all creatures generally, animal, inanimate and botanical. This is the better known of the two opinions according to the most reliable of two opinions. It was reported in Sahih Al-Bukhari that Ibn Mas`ud said: "We used to hear the Tasbih of the food as it was being eaten." Imam Ahmad recorded that (Mu`adh bin Anas said that) the Messenger of Allah came upon some people who were sitting on their mounts and talking to one another. He said to them:

«ارْكَبُوهَا سَالِمَةً وَدَعُوهَا سَالِمَةً، وَلَا تَتَّخِذُوهَا كَرَاسِيَّ لِأَحَادِيثِكُمْ فِي الطُّرُقِ وَالْأَسْوَاقِ، فَرُبَّ مَرْكُوبَةٍ خَيْرٌ مِنْ رَاكِبِهَا، وَأَكْثَرُ ذِكْرًا اللهِ مِنْهُ»

(Ride them safely then leave them safely. Do not use them as chairs for you to have conversations in the streets and marketplaces, because the one that is ridden may be better than the one who rides it, and may remember Allah more than he does.) An-Nasa'i recorded in his Sunan that `Abdullah bin `Amr said: "The Messenger of Allah forbade us from killing frogs."

(Truly, He is Ever Forbearing, Oft-Forgiving.) means, He does not hasten to punish those who disobey Him, rather He gives them time and waits, then if they persist in their stubborn Kufr, He seizes them with a punishment of the All-Mighty, All-Capable. It was recorded in the Two Sahihs that:

«إِنَّ اللَّهَ لَيُمْلِي لِلظَّالِمِ حَتَّى إِذَا أَخَذَهُ لَمْ يُفْلِتْهُ»

(Allah will let the wrongdoer carry on until, when He does seize him, He will never let him go.) Then the Messenger of Allah recited:

(وَكَذَلِكَ أَخْذُ رَبِّكَ إِذَا أَخَذَ الْقُرَى وَهِيَ ظَالِمَةٌ)

(Such is the punishment of your Lord when He seizes the (population of) towns while they are doing wrong.) (11:02) Allah says:

(And many a township did I give respite while it was given to wrongdoing.) (22:45) until the end of two Ayat.

(And many a township did We destroy while they were given to wrongdoing.) (22:48) Whoever gives up his disbelief and disobedience, and turns back to Allah in repentance, Allah will accept his repentance, as He says:

(And whoever does evil or wrongs himself but afterwards seeks Allah's forgiveness) (4:110) Here, Allah says:

(Truly, He is Ever Forbearing, Oft-Forgiving.) At the end of Surah Fatir, He says:

(Verily, Allah grasps the heavens and the earth lest they should move away from their places, and if they were to move away from their places, there is not one that could grasp them after Him. Truly, He is Ever Most Forbearing, Oft-Forgiving...) until His saying;

(And if Allah were to punish men)(35:41-45)

Surah: 17 Ayah: 45 & Ayah: 46

وَإِذَا قَرَأْتَ الْقُرْآنَ جَعَلْنَا بَيْنَكَ وَبَيْنَ الَّذِينَ لَا يُؤْمِنُونَ بِالْآخِرَةِ حِجَابًا مَّسْتُورًا ﴿٤٥﴾

45. And when you (Muhammad (peace be upon him)) recite the Qur'ân, We put between you and those who believe not in the Hereafter, an invisible veil (or screen their hearts, so they hear or understand it not).

وَجَعَلْنَا عَلَىٰ قُلُوبِهِمْ أَكِنَّةً أَن يَفْقَهُوهُ وَفِي آذَانِهِمْ وَقْرًا ۚ وَإِذَا ذَكَرْتَ رَبَّكَ فِي الْقُرْآنِ وَحْدَهُ وَلَّوْا عَلَىٰ أَدْبَارِهِمْ نُفُورًا ﴿٤٦﴾

46. And We have put coverings over their hearts lest they should understand it (the Qur'ân), and in their ears deafness. And when you make mention of your Lord

Alone (Lâ ilâha illallâh (none has the right to be worshipped but Allâh) Islâmic Monotheism in the Qur'ân, they turn on their backs, fleeing in extreme dislike.

Transliteration

45. Wa-itha qara/ta alqur-ana jaAAalna baynaka wabayna allatheena la yu/minoona bial-akhirati hijaban mastooran 46. WajaAAalna AAala quloobihim akinnatan an yafqahoohu wafee athanihim waqran wa-itha thakarta rabbaka fee alqur-ani wahdahu wallaw AAala adbarihim nufooran

Tafsir Ibn Kathir

The Veil over the Hearts of the Idolators

Allah says to His Messenger Muhammad : `When you recite Qur'an to these idolators, We put an invisible veil between you and them.' Qatadah and Ibn Zayd said, "It is coverings over their hearts," as Allah says:

(And they say: "Our hearts are under coverings (screened) from that to which you invite us; and in our ears is deafness, and between us and you is a screen) meaning, there is something that is stopping and preventing your words from reaching us.

(an invisible veil.) meaning something which covers, or that cannot be seen, so there is a barrier between them and guidance. This is the interpretation that Ibn Jarir (may Allah have mercy on him) thought was correct. Al-Hafiz Abu Ya`la Al-Mawusili recorded that Asma' bint Abi Bakr (may Allah be pleased with her) said, "When the Ayah,

(Perish the two hands of Abu Lahab and perish he!) (111:1) was revealed, the one-eyed woman Umm Jamil (the wife of Abu Lahab) came with a stone pestle in her hand, screaming, `What was sent to us is somebody blameworthy, or, we reject somebody blameworthy (Abu Musa - one of the narrators - said, it is I who am not sure what was said); we shun his religion and disobey whatever he commands!' The Messenger of Allah was sitting with Abu Bakr by his side. Abu Bakr, may Allah be pleased with him, said, `This woman has come and I am afraid she will see you.' The Prophet said,

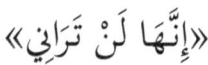

(Certainly she will not see me.) and he recited Qur'an through which he was protected from her:

(And when you recite the Qur'an, We put between you and those who believe not in the Hereafter, an invisible veil). She came and found Abu Bakr, but she did not see the Prophet . She said, `O Abu Bakr, I have heard that your companion is lampooning me.' Abu Bakr said, `No, by the Lord of this House (the Ka`bah), he is not lampooning you.' Then she went away, saying, `The Quraysh know that I am the daughter of their master.'"

(And We have put coverings over their hearts,) Akinnah (coverings) is the plural of Kinan, which covers the heart.

(lest they should understand it,) means, lest they should understand the Qur'an.

(and in their ears deafness) something that will stop them from hearing the Qur'an in such a way that they will understand it and be guided by it.

(And when you make mention of your Lord Alone in the Qur'an,) means, when you declare Allah to be One in your recitation, and say La Ilaha Illallah,

(they turn) means they turn away

(on their backs, fleeing in extreme dislike.) As Allah says:

(And when Allah Alone is mentioned, the hearts of those who believe not in the Hereafter are filled with disgust (from the Oneness of Allah).) (39:45) z

(And when you make mention of your Lord Alone in the Qur'an,) Commenting on this Ayah, Qatadah said that when the Muslims said La Ilaha Illallah, the idolators disliked this and found it intolerable. Iblis and his troops hated it, but Allah insisted on supporting it so that it would prevail over those who opposed it. Whoever uses it against his opponent will prevail, and whoever fights for it will be victorious. Only the Muslims of the Arabian Peninsula, which can be traversed by a rider in a few nights, knew it and accepted it, out of all mankind.

Surah: 17 Ayah: 47 & Ayah: 48

نَّحْنُ أَعْلَمُ بِمَا يَسْتَمِعُونَ بِهِۦٓ إِذْ يَسْتَمِعُونَ إِلَيْكَ وَإِذْ هُمْ نَجْوَىٰٓ إِذْ يَقُولُ ٱلظَّٰلِمُونَ إِن تَتَّبِعُونَ إِلَّا رَجُلًا مَّسْحُورًا ۝

47. We know best of what they listen to, when they listen to you. And when they take secret counsel, then, the Zâlimûn (polytheists and wrong-doers) say: "You follow none but a bewitched man."

ٱنظُرْ كَيْفَ ضَرَبُوا۟ لَكَ ٱلْأَمْثَالَ فَضَلُّوا۟ فَلَا يَسْتَطِيعُونَ سَبِيلًا ۝

48. See what examples they have put forward for you. So they have gone astray, and never can they find a way.

Transliteration

47. Nahnu aAAlamu bima yastamiAAoona bihi ith yastamiAAoona ilayka wa-ith hum najwa ith yaqoolu aththalimoona in tattabiAAoona illa rajulan mashooran 48. Onthur kayfa daraboo laka al-amthala fadalloo fala yastateeAAoona sabeelan

Tafsir Ibn Kathir

The Secret Counsel of Quraysh after hearing the Qur'an

Allah tells His Prophet about what the leaders of Quraysh discussed when they came and listened to him reciting Qur'an in secret, without their people knowing about it. They said that he was Mashur which according to the better-known view means someone affected by magic (Sihr); it may also mean a man who has a lung, i.e., a mere human being, as if they were saying that if you follow Muhammad, you will only be following a human being. This second suggestion does not sound correct, because what they meant here was that he was under the influence of Sihr (magic) which made him see dreams in which he learned these words that he recited. Some of them said he was a poet, or a soothsayer, or crazy, or a sorcerer. Allah says:

(See what examples they have put forward for you. So they have gone astray, and never can they find a way.) meaning, they will never be guided to the truth and will never find a way to reach it. Muhammad bin Ishaq said in As-Sirah: "Muhammad bin Muslim bin Shihab Az-Zuhri told me that it happened that Abu Sufyan bin Harb, Abu Jahl bin Hisham and Al-Akhnas bin Shurayq bin `Amr bin Wahb Ath-Thaqafi, the ally of Bani Zahrah, went out one night to listen to the Messenger of Allah when he was praying at night in his house. Each one of them took up a position for listening, and none of them knew that the others were also there. They stayed listening to him all night until dawn came. When they left, they met up on the road, each of them blaming the others, saying to one another; `Do not come back again, lest you give the wrong impression (i.e., that you like what you hear).' Then they went away until the second night came, when each of them came back to his place and spent the night listening. When dawn came they left, then when they met up on the road, each of them blamed the others, saying the same as they had said the previous night. Then they went away until the third night came, when each of them came back to his place and spent the night listening. When dawn came they left, then when they met up on the road, they said to one another, `Let us not leave until we promise not to come back,' so they made a promise to that effect, and went their separate ways. In the morning, Al-Akhnas bin Shurayq took his stick and went to the house of Abu Sufyan bin Harb, where he said, `Tell me, O Abu Hanzalah (i.e., Abu Sufyan), what do you think of what you have heard from Muhammad' Abu Sufyan said, `O Abu Tha`labah (i.e., Al-Akhnas), by Allah, I have heard something I understand and I know what is meant by it, and I have heard things I do not understand and do not know what is meant by it.' Al-Akhnas said: `Me too, by the One by Whom you swore.' Then he left and went to Abu Jahl, and entered his house. He said, `O Abu Al-Hakam (i.e., Abu Jahl), what do you think of what you have heard from Muhammad' He said, `What did you hear' He said, `We and Banu `Abd Manaf competed for honor and position: they fed people so we fed people, they engaged in battle so we engaged in battle, they gave so we gave, until we were neck and neck, like race horses. Then they said, we have a Prophet among us who receives revelation from heaven. How could we compete with that By Allah we will never believe in him.' Then Al-Akhnas got up and left him."

Surah: 17 Ayah: 49, Ayah: 50, Ayah: 51 & Ayah: 52

وَقَالُوٓا۟ أَءِذَا كُنَّا عِظَٰمًا وَرُفَٰتًا أَءِنَّا لَمَبْعُوثُونَ خَلْقًا جَدِيدًا ۝

49. And they say: "When we are bones and fragments (destroyed), should we really be resurrected (to be) a new creation?"

قُلْ كُونُوا۟ حِجَارَةً أَوْ حَدِيدًا ۝

50. Say (O Muhammad (peace be upon him)) "Be you stones or iron,"

أَوْ خَلْقًا مِّمَّا يَكْبُرُ فِى صُدُورِكُمْ ۚ فَسَيَقُولُونَ مَن يُعِيدُنَا ۖ قُلِ ٱلَّذِى فَطَرَكُمْ أَوَّلَ مَرَّةٍ ۚ فَسَيُنْغِضُونَ إِلَيْكَ رُءُوسَهُمْ وَيَقُولُونَ مَتَىٰ هُوَ ۖ قُلْ عَسَىٰٓ أَن يَكُونَ قَرِيبًا ۝

51. "Or some created thing that is yet greater (or harder) in your breasts (thoughts to be resurrected, even then you shall be resurrected)" Then, they will say: "Who shall bring us back (to life)?" Say: "He Who created you first!" Then, they will shake their heads at you and say: "When will that be?" Say: "Perhaps it is near!"

يَوْمَ يَدْعُوكُمْ فَتَسْتَجِيبُونَ بِحَمْدِهِۦ وَتَظُنُّونَ إِن لَّبِثْتُمْ إِلَّا قَلِيلًا ۝

52. On the Day when He will call you, and you will answer (His Call) with (words of) His Praise and Obedience, and you will think that you have stayed (in this world) but a little while!

Transliteration

49. Waqaloo a-itha kunna AAithaman warufatan a-inna lamabAAoothoona khalqan jadeedan 50. Qul koonoo hijaratan aw hadeedan 51. Aw khalqan mimma yakburu fee sudoorikum fasayaqooloona man yuAAeeduna quli allathee fatarakum awwala marratin fasayunghidoona ilayka ruoosahum wayaqooloona mata huwa qul AAasa an yakoona qareeban 52. Yawma yadAAookum fatastajeeboona bihamdihi watathunnoona in labithtum illa qaleelan

Tafsir Ibn Kathir

Refutation of Those Who do not believe in Life after Death

Allah tells us about the disbelievers who think it very unlikely that the Resurrection will happen and who say, in a tone of denial,

(When we are bones and fragments.) meaning earth. This was the view of Mujahid. `Ali bin Abi Talhah reported from Ibn `Abbas that it means dust.

(should we really be resurrected (to be) a new creation) meaning, on the Day of Resurrection after we have disintegrated and become nothing, and have been forgotten. Allah tells us about them elsewhere:

(They say: "Shall we indeed be returned to (our) former state of life Even after we are crumbled bones" They say: "It would in that case, be a return with loss!") (79:10-12). And,

(And he puts forth for Us a parable, and forgets his own creation.) until the end of two Ayat. (36:78-79) Allah commands His Messenger to respond to them, so He says:

(Say (O Muhammad): "Be you stones or iron,") - which are more difficult to restore than bones and fragments,

(Or some created thing that is yet greater (or harder) in your breasts.) Ibn Ishaq narrated from Ibn Abi Najih from Mujahid: "I asked Ibn `Abbas about that, and he said: `This is death.'" `Atiyah reported that Ibn `Umar explained of this Ayah: "If you were dead I would still resurrect you." This was also the view of Sa`id bin Jubayr, Abu Salih, Al-Hasan, Qatadah, Ad-Dahhak and others. This means that if you were to assume that you would become dead, which is the opposite of living, Allah will resurrect you when He wills, for nothing can stop Him when He wills a thing.

(Or some created thing that is yet greater (or harder) in your breasts.) Mujahid said: "This means the heavens, earth and mountains." According to another report, "Whatever you want to be, go ahead, Allah will still resurrect you after you die."

(Then, they will say: "Who shall bring us back (to life)") meaning, who will resurrect us if we are stones or iron or some other strong created thing

(Say: "He Who created you first!") meaning, He Who created you when you were nothing, then you became human beings, walking about. He is able to create you anew, no matter what you have become.

(And He it is Who originates the creation, then He will repeat it; and this is easier for Him.) (30:27)

(Then, they will shake their heads at you) Ibn `Abbas and Qatadah said, "They will move their heads in a gesture of mockery." This view expressed by Ibn `Abbas and Qatadah is what the Arabs understand from the language, because the word used Fasayunghidun indicates an up-and-down movement Nughad. A word derived from the same root, Naghd, is used to refer to the young of the ostrich, because when it walks, it walks quickly and moves its head. The same word is used to describe a tooth when it becomes loose and is detached from its place.

(and say: "When will that be") This shows that they thought it very unlikely that it would happen, as Allah says:

(And they say: "When will this promise (i.e. Resurrection) be fulfilled, if you are truthful") (36:48)

(Those who believe not therein seek to hasten it (the Hour)) (42:18)

(Say: "Perhaps it is near!") meaning, beware of it, for it is at hand and will no doubt come to you, and what will be will be.

(On the Day when He will call you,) meaning the Lord, may He be blessed and exalted:

(When He will call you by a single call, behold, you will come out from the earth) (30:25) meaning, when He commands you to come out from the earth, for nothing can oppose Him or prevent His command from being fulfilled. Rather, it is as He says:

(And Our commandment is but one as the twinkling of an eye) (54:50)

(Verily, Our Word unto a thing when We intend it, is only that We say unto it: "Be!" - and it is) (16:40)

(But it will be only a single Zajrah. When behold, they find themselves (on the surface of the earth) alive (after their death).) (79:13-14), meaning, it will be just one definitive command, then the people will have come out from the inside of the earth to its surface, as Allah says:

(On the Day when He will call you, and you will answer with (words of) His praise) meaning, you will all rise up in response to His command and in obedience to His will.

(and you will think) means, on the Day when you rise up from your graves,

(that you have stayed) in this earthly abode,

(but a little while.) This is like the Ayah:

(The Day they see it, (it will be) as if they had not tarried (in this world) except an afternoon or a morning.) (79:46). Allah says:

(The Day when the Trumpet will be blown: that Day, We shall gather the blue or blind-eyed with thirst. They will speak in a very low voice to each other (saying): "You stayed not longer than ten (days)." We know very well what they will say, when the best among them in knowledge and wisdom will say: "You stayed no longer than a day!") (20:102-104).

(And on the Day that the Hour will be established, they will swear that they stayed not but an hour - thus were they ever deluded.) (30:55)

(He will say: "What number of years did you stay on earth" They will say: "We stayed a day or part of a day. Ask of those who keep account." He will say: "You stayed not but a little, if you had only known!") (23:112-114).

Surah: 17 Ayah: 53

وَقُل لِّعِبَادِى يَقُولُوا۟ ٱلَّتِى هِىَ أَحْسَنُ ۚ إِنَّ ٱلشَّيْطَـٰنَ يَنزَغُ بَيْنَهُمْ ۚ إِنَّ ٱلشَّيْطَـٰنَ كَانَ لِلْإِنسَـٰنِ عَدُوًّا مُّبِينًا ﴿٥٣﴾

53. And say to My slaves (i.e. the true believers of Islâmic Monotheism) that they should (only) say those words that are the best. (Because) Shaitân (Satan) verily, sows disagreements among them. Surely, Shaitân (Satan) is to man a plain enemy.

Transliteration

53. Waqul liAAibadee yaqooloo allatee hiya ahsanu inna alshshaytana yanzaghu baynahum inna alshshaytana kana lil-insani AAaduwwan mubeenan

Tafsir Ibn Kathir

People should speak Good Words with Politeness

Allah commands His servant Muhammad () to tell the believing servants of Allah that they should address one another in their conversations and discussions with the best and politest of words, for if they do not do that, Shaytan will sow discord among them, and words will lead to actions, so that evil and conflicts and fights will arise among them. For Shaytan is the enemy of Adam and his descendants, and has been since he refused to prostrate to Adam. His enmity is obvious and manifest. For this reason it is forbidden for a man to point at his Muslim brother with an iron instrument, for Shaytan may cause him to strike him with it. (Imam Ahmad recorded that Abu Hurayrah said: "The Messenger of Allah said:

«لَا يُشِيرَنَّ أَحَدُكُمْ إِلَى أَخِيهِ بِالسِّلَاحِ، فَإِنَّهُ لَا يَدْرِي أَحَدُكُمْ لَعَلَّ الشَّيْطَانَ أَنْ يَنْزِعَ فِي يَدِهِ فَيَقَعَ فِي حُفْرَةٍ مِنَ النَّارِ»

(No one of you should point at his brother with a weapon, for he does not know whether Shaytan will cause him to strike him with it and thus be thrown into a pit of Fire.) Al-Bukhari and Muslim recorded this Hadith with the chain of narration from `Abdur-Razzaq.

Surah: 17 Ayah: 54 & Ayah: 55

رَّبُّكُمْ أَعْلَمُ بِكُمْ ۖ إِن يَشَأْ يَرْحَمْكُمْ أَوْ إِن يَشَأْ يُعَذِّبْكُمْ ۚ وَمَآ أَرْسَلْنَـٰكَ عَلَيْهِمْ وَكِيلًا ﴿٥٤﴾

54. Your Lord knows you best, if He wills, He will have mercy on you, or if He wills, He will punish you. And We have not sent you (O Muhammad (peace be upon him)) as a guardian over them.

وَرَبُّكَ أَعْلَمُ بِمَن فِى ٱلسَّمَٰوَٰتِ وَٱلْأَرْضِ ۗ وَلَقَدْ فَضَّلْنَا بَعْضَ ٱلنَّبِيِّۦنَ عَلَىٰ بَعْضٍ ۖ وَءَاتَيْنَا دَاوُۥدَ زَبُورًا ۝

55. And your Lord knows best all who are in the heavens and the earth. And indeed, We have preferred some of the Prophets above others, and to Dâwûd (David) We gave the Zabûr (Psalms).

Transliteration

54. Rabbukum aAAlamu bikum in yasha/ yarhamkum aw in yasha/ yuAAaththibkum wama arsalnaka AAalayhim wakeelan   55. Warabbuka aAAlamu biman fee alssamawati waal-ardi walaqad faddalna baAAda alnnabiyyeena AAala baAAdin waatayna dawooda zabooran

Translation

54. Your Lord knows you best, if He will, He will have mercy on you, or if He will, He will punish you. And We have not sent you (O Muhammad SAW) as a guardian over them.

55. And your Lord knows best all who are in the heavens and the earth. And indeed, We have preferred some of the Prophets above others, and to Dawûd (David) We gave the Zabûr (Psalms).

Tafsir Ibn Kathir

Allah says:

(Your Lord knows you best;) O mankind, meaning, He knows best who among you deserves to be guided and who does not deserve to be guided.

(if He wills, He will have mercy on you,) by helping you to obey Him and turn to Him.

(or if He wills, He will punish you. And We have not sent you) - O Muhammad -

(as a guardian over them.) meaning, `We have sent you as a warner, so whoever obeys you, will enter Paradise and whoever disobeys you, will enter Hell.'

(And your Lord knows best all who are in the heavens and the earth.) meaning, their status or level of obedience or disobedience.

The Preference of some Prophets above Others

(And indeed, We have preferred some of the Prophets above others.) As Allah says:

(Those Messengers! We preferred some of them to others; to some of them Allah spoke (directly); others He raised to degrees (of honor.)) (2:253) This does not contradict the report in the Two Sahihs which says that the Messenger of Allah said:

«لَا تُفَضِّلُوا بَيْنَ الْأَنْبِيَاءِ»

(Don't give superiority to any Prophet among (Allah's) Prophets.) What is meant in this Hadith is giving a superiority based on whims and fanaticism or sectarian feelings, not on the basis of evidence. If there is solid evidence, we have to follow it. There is no dispute that the Messengers are better than the rest of the Prophets, and that the mighty Messengers of Great Resolve are the best of all. They are the five mentioned in two Ayat of the Qur'an, in Surat Al-Ahzab:

(And (remember) when We took from the Prophets their covenant, and from you and from Nuh, Ibrahim, Musa and `Isa son of Maryam.) (33:7) and in Surat Ash-Shura:

(He has ordained for you the same religion which He ordained for Nuh, and that which We have revealed to you, and that which We ordained for Ibrahim, Musa and `Isa saying you should establish religion and make no divisions in it.) (42:13) There is no dispute that Muhammad is the best of them, then Ibrahim, then Musa, then `Isa (peace be upon them all), according to the best-known view. We have discussed the evidence for this in detail elsewhere, and Allah is the source of help. Allah's saying,

(and to Dawud We gave the Zabur.) is an indication of his virtue and honor. Al-Bukhari recorded from Abu Hurayrah that the Prophet said:

«خُفِّفَ عَلَى دَاوُدَ الْقُرْآنُ، فَكَانَ يَأْمُرُ بِدَوَابِّهِ فَتُسْرَجُ، فَكَانَ يَقْرَؤُهُ قَبْلَ أَنْ يَفْرُغَ»

(The Qur'an (i.e. revealed Scripture of Zabur) was made easy for Dawud, so he would call for his mounts to be saddled, and he would finish reciting it (i.e., the Zabur) before the job was done.)

Surah: 17 Ayah: 56 & Ayah: 57

قُلِ ٱدْعُوا۟ ٱلَّذِينَ زَعَمْتُم مِّن دُونِهِۦ فَلَا يَمْلِكُونَ كَشْفَ ٱلضُّرِّ عَنكُمْ وَلَا تَحْوِيلًا ۝

56. Say (O Muhammad (peace be upon him)) "Call unto those - besides Him - whom you pretend (to be gods like angels, 'Isâ (Jesus), 'Uzair (Ezra), and others.). They have neither the power to remove the adversity from you nor even to shift it from you to another person."

أُو۟لَـٰٓئِكَ ٱلَّذِينَ يَدْعُونَ يَبْتَغُونَ إِلَىٰ رَبِّهِمُ ٱلْوَسِيلَةَ أَيُّهُمْ أَقْرَبُ وَيَرْجُونَ رَحْمَتَهُۥ وَيَخَافُونَ عَذَابَهُۥٓ إِنَّ عَذَابَ رَبِّكَ كَانَ مَحْذُورًا ۝

57. Those whom they call upon (like 'Isâ (Jesus) - son of Maryam (Mary), 'Uzair (Ezra), angel) desire (for themselves) means of access to their Lord (Allâh), as to which of them should be the nearest; and they ('Iesa (Jesus), 'Uzair (Ezra), angels and others) hope for His Mercy and fear His Torment. Verily, the Torment of your Lord is (something) to be afraid of!

Transliteration

56. Quli odAAu allatheena zaAAamtum min doonihi fala yamlikoona kashfa alddurri AAankum wala tahweelan 57. Ola-ika allatheena yadAAoona yabtaghoona ila rabbihimu alwaseelata ayyuhum aqrabu wayarjoona rahmatahu wayakhafoona AAathabahu inna AAathaba rabbika kana mahthooran

Tafsir Ibn Kathir

The gods of the Idolators can neither benefit nor harm; rather they themselves seek to draw close to Allah

Allah says:

(Say) O Muhammad to these idolators who worship things other than Allah,

(Call upon those - besides Him whom you pretend.) such as idols and rivals of Allah. Even if you turn to them,

(They have neither the power to remove the adversity from you) they have no such power at all,

(nor even to shift (it from you to another person.)) to lift the distress from you and give it to someone else. The meaning is that the only one Who is able to do that is Allah Alone, with no partner or associate, Who is the One Who creates and issues commands.

(Say: "Call upon those whom you pretend) Al-`Awfi reported from Ibn `Abbas, "The people of Shirk used to say, `we worship the angels and the Messiah and `Uzayr,' while these (the angels and the Messiah and `Uzayr) themselves call upon Allah."

(Those whom they call upon, desire) Al-Bukhari recorded from Sulayman bin Mahran Al-A`mash, from Ibrahim, from Abu Ma`mar, from `Abdullah:

(Those whom they call upon, desire a means of access to their Lord,) "Some of the Jinn used to be worshipped, then they became Muslims." According to another report: "Some humans used to worship some of the Jinn, then those Jinn became Muslim, but those humans adhered to their religion (of worshipping the Jinn)."

(they hope for His mercy and fear His torment.) Worship cannot be complete or perfect unless it is accompanied by both fear and hope. Fear stops one from doing things that are forbidden, and hope makes one do more good deeds.

(Verily, the torment of your Lord is (something) to be afraid of!) meaning, one should beware of it and be afraid lest it happen. We seek refuge with Allah from that.

Surah: 17 Ayah: 58

$$\text{وَإِن مِّن قَرْيَةٍ إِلَّا نَحْنُ مُهْلِكُوهَا قَبْلَ يَوْمِ ٱلْقِيَـٰمَةِ أَوْ مُعَذِّبُوهَا عَذَابًا شَدِيدًا ۚ كَانَ ذَٰلِكَ فِى ٱلْكِتَـٰبِ مَسْطُورًا ۝}$$

58. And there is not a town (population) but We shall destroy it before the Day of Resurrection, or punish it with a severe torment. That is written in the Book (of our Decrees)

Transliteration

58. Wa-in min qaryatin illa nahnu muhlikooha qabla yawmi alqiyamati aw muAAaththibooha AAathaban shadeedan kana thalika fee alkitabi mastooran

Tafsir Ibn Kathir

The Destruction or Torment of all Disbelieving Towns before the Hour begins

Here Allah tells us that He has decreed and it is written in Al-Lawh Al-Mahfuz (The Preserved Tablet) which is with Him, that there is no town that He will not destroy by wiping out all its people or by punishing them,

(with a severe torment.) either by killing them or sending calamities upon them as He wills. This will be because of their sins, as Allah says of the past nations:

(We wronged them not, but they wronged themselves.) (11:101)

(So it tasted the evil result of its affair (disbelief), and the consequence of its affair (disbelief) was loss.) (65:9)

(And many a town (population) revolted against the command of its Lord and His Messengers;) (65:8) and many Ayat.

Surah: 17 Ayah: 59

$$\text{وَمَا مَنَعَنَا أَن نُّرْسِلَ بِٱلْـَٔايَـٰتِ إِلَّا أَن كَذَّبَ بِهَا ٱلْأَوَّلُونَ ۚ وَءَاتَيْنَا ثَمُودَ ٱلنَّاقَةَ مُبْصِرَةً فَظَلَمُوا۟ بِهَا ۚ وَمَا نُرْسِلُ بِٱلْـَٔايَـٰتِ إِلَّا تَخْوِيفًا ۝}$$

59. And nothing stops Us from sending the Ayât (proofs, evidences, signs) but that the people of old denied them. And We sent the she-camel to Thamûd as a clear sign, but they did her wrong. And We sent not the signs except to warn, and to make them afraid (of destruction).

Chapter 17: Al-Israa (The Night Journey or Bani Isra'il), Verses 001-111

Transliteration

59. Wama manaAAana an nursila bial-ayati illa an kaththaba biha al-awwaloona waatayna thamooda alnnaqata mubsiratan fathalamoo biha wama nursilu bial-ayati illa takhweefan

Tafsir Ibn Kathir

The Reason why Allah did not send Signs or Miracles

Sa`id bin Jubayr said, "The idolators said: `O Muhammad, you claim that before you there were Prophets, among whom was one to whom the wind was subjugated, and another who could bring the dead back to life. If you want us to believe in you, ask your Lord to turn As-Safa' into gold for us.' Allah conveyed to him by inspiration (Wahy): `I have heard what they have said. If you wish, I will do what they say, but if they do not believe after that, the punishment will come down upon them, because after the sign has been sent, there is no room for speculation. Or if you wish, I will be patient with your people and give them more time.' He said:

«يَارَبِّ اسْتَأْنِ بِهِم»

(O Lord, give them more time.)" This was also narrated by Qatadah, Ibn Jurayj and others. Imam Ahmad recorded that Ibn `Abbas said, "The people of Makkah asked the Prophet to turn As-Safa' into gold for them, and to remove the mountains (from around Makkah) so that they could cultivate the land. It was said to him (by Allah): `If you wish, I will be patient and give them more time, or if you wish, I will do what they are asking, but if they then disbelieve, they will be destroyed as the nations before them were destroyed.' He said,

«لَا، بَلِ اسْتَأْنِ بِهِم»

(No, be patient and give them more time.) Then Allah revealed:

(And nothing stops Us from sending the Ayat but that the people of old denied them.) An-Nasa'i also reported this from the Hadith of Jarir. Imam Ahmad recorded that Ibn `Abbas said: The Quraysh said to the Prophet, "Ask your Lord to turn As-Safa' into gold and we will believe in you." He said,

«وَتَفْعَلُونَ؟»

(Will you really do that) They said, "Yes." So he asked his Lord, and Jibril came to him and said: "Your Lord conveys His Salam to you and says, `If you wish, I will turn As-Safa' into gold for them, then whoever of them disbelieves after that, will be punished with a torment the like of which has never be seen in creation; or if you wish, I will open the gates of repentance and mercy for them.'" He said,

«بَلْ بَابُ التَّوْبَةِ وَالرَّحْمَةِ»

(Rather the gates of repentance and mercy.)

(And We sent not the signs except to make them afraid (of destruction).) Qatadah said, "Allah makes people afraid with whatever signs He wills, so that they may learn a lesson and remember and return to Him. We were told that Al-Kufah was shaken at the time of Ibn Mas`ud, who said: `O people, your Lord is rebuking you, so pay heed!'" Similarly, it was reported that Al-Madinah was struck by several earthquakes at the time of `Umar bin Al-Khattab. `Umar said: "You have changed, by Allah, and if such a quake were to strike again, I will subject you to such and such." The Prophet said, in a Hadith whose authenticity is agreed upon:

«إِنَّ الشَّمْسَ وَالْقَمَرَ آيَتَانِ مِنْ آيَاتِ اللهِ وَإِنَّهُمَا لَا يَنْكَسِفَانِ لِمَوْتِ أَحَدٍ وَلَا لِحَيَاتِهِ، وَلَكِنَّ اللهَ عَزَّ وَجَلَّ يُخَوِّفُ بِهِمَا عِبَادَهُ، فَإِذَا رَأَيْتُمْ ذَلِكَ فَافْزَعُوا إِلَى ذِكْرِهِ وَدُعَائِهِ وَاسْتِغْفَارِهِ ثُمَّ قَالَ: يَا أُمَّةَ مُحَمَّدٍ وَاللهِ مَا أَحَدٌ أَغْيَرُ مِنَ اللهِ أَنْ يَزْنِيَ عَبْدُهُ أَوْ تَزْنِيَ أَمَتُهُ، يَا أُمَّةَ مُحَمَّدٍ وَاللهِ لَوْ تَعْلَمُونَ مَا أَعْلَمُ لَضَحِكْتُمْ قَلِيلًا وَلَبَكَيْتُمْ كَثِيرًا»

(The sun and the moon are two of the signs of Allah, and they are not eclipsed for the death or life of anyone. Allah uses them to make His servants afraid, so if you see them, hasten to remember Him, call on Him and seek His forgiveness.) Then he said: (O Ummah of Muhammad, by Allah, no one has a greater sense of jealousy than Allah if He sees His servant, or female servant, committing Zina (illegal sexual intercourse). O Ummah of Muhammad, if you knew what I know, you would laugh little and weep much.)

Surah: 17 Ayah: 60

وَإِذْ قُلْنَا لَكَ إِنَّ رَبَّكَ أَحَاطَ بِٱلنَّاسِ وَمَا جَعَلْنَا ٱلرُّءْيَا ٱلَّتِىٓ أَرَيْنَٰكَ إِلَّا فِتْنَةً لِّلنَّاسِ وَٱلشَّجَرَةَ ٱلْمَلْعُونَةَ فِى ٱلْقُرْءَانِ ۚ وَنُخَوِّفُهُمْ فَمَا يَزِيدُهُمْ إِلَّا طُغْيَٰنًا كَبِيرًا

60. And (remember) when We told you: "Verily! Your Lord has encompassed mankind (i.e. they are in His Grip)." And We made not the vision which we showed you (O Muhammad as an actual eye-witness and not as a dream on the night of Al-Isrâ') but a trial for mankind, and (likewise) the accursed tree (Zaqqûm, mentioned) in the Qur'ân. We warn and make them afraid but it only

increases them in naught save great disbelief, oppression and disobedience to Allâh.

Transliteration

60. Wa-ith qulna laka inna rabbaka ahata bialnnasi wama jaAAalna alrru/ya allatee araynaka illa fitnatan lilnnasi waalshshajarata almalAAoonata fee alqur-ani wanukhawwifuhum fama yazeeduhum illa tughyanan kabeeran

Tafsir Ibn Kathir

Allah has encompassed Mankind and made the Vision of His Prophet a Trial for Them

Allah says to His Messenger, encouraging him to convey the Message and informing him that He is protecting him from the people, that He is able to deal with them and that they are in His grasp and under His domination and control.

(And (remember) when We told you: "Verily, your Lord has encompassed mankind..") Mujahid, `Urwah bin Az-Az-Zubayr, Al-Hasan, Qatadah and others said, "This means, He protected you from them."

(And We made not the vision which We showed you but a trial for mankind,) Al-Bukhari recorded that Ibn `Abbas said:

(And We made not the vision which We showed you but a trial for mankind,) "This is the vision which the Messenger of Allah saw with his own eyes on the night when he was taken on the Night Journey (Al-Isra')·

and (likewise) the accursed tree in the Qur a0n. refers to the Tree of Zaqqum." This was also recorded by Ahmad, `Abdur-Razzaq and others. It was also reported by Al-`Awfi from Ibn `Abbas. It was also interpreted as referring to the Night of the Isra' by Mujahid, Sa`id bin Jubayr, Al-Hasan, Masruq, Ibrahim, Qatadah, `Abdur-Rahman bin Zayd and several others. We have already quoted at length a comprehensive collection of Hadith about the Isra' at the beginning of this Surah, praise be to Allah. We have also already stated that some people gave up their Islam after they had been following the truth, because their hearts and minds could not comprehend that, and they denied what their knowledge could not grasp, but Allah caused it to increase and strengthen the faith of others, and so He says:

(but a trial), meaning a test. As for the cursed tree, this is the Tree of Zaqqum. When the Messenger of Allah told them that he had seen Paradise and Hell, and seen the Tree of Zaqqum, they did not believe that, and Abu Jahl, upon whom be the curses of Allah, even said, "Bring us some dates and butter," and he started eating them and saying, "Let us have some Zaqqum, we don't know any other Zaqqum but this." This was narrated by Ibn `Abbas, Masruq, Abu Malik, Al-Hasan Al-Basri and others. Everyone who interpreted the Ayah to refer to the Night of the Isra', also interpreted it to refer to the Tree of Zaqqum.

((We) make them afraid) meaning, 'We make the disbelievers afraid with Our warnings and punishments and torment.'

(but it only increases them in naught save great disbelief, oppression and disobedience to Allah.) means, it only pushes them further into their disbelief and misguidance, and this is because Allah has forsaken them.

Surah: 17 Ayah: 61 & Ayah: 62

وَإِذْ قُلْنَا لِلْمَلَـٰٓئِكَةِ ٱسْجُدُواْ لِـَٔادَمَ فَسَجَدُوٓاْ إِلَّآ إِبْلِيسَ قَالَ ءَأَسْجُدُ لِمَنْ خَلَقْتَ طِينًا ۝

61. And (remember) when We said to the angels: "Prostrate unto Adam." They prostrated except Iblîs (Satan). He said: "Shall I prostrate to one whom You created from clay?"

قَالَ أَرَءَيْتَكَ هَـٰذَا ٱلَّذِى كَرَّمْتَ عَلَىَّ لَئِنْ أَخَّرْتَنِ إِلَىٰ يَوْمِ ٱلْقِيَـٰمَةِ لَأَحْتَنِكَنَّ ذُرِّيَّتَهُۥٓ إِلَّا قَلِيلًا ۝

62. (Iblîs (Satan)) said: "See this one whom You have honored above me, if You give me respite (keep me alive) to the Day of Resurrection, I will surely seize and mislead his offspring (by sending them astray) all but a few!"

Transliteration

61. Wa-ith qulna lilmala-ikati osjudoo li-adama fasajadoo illa ibleesa qala aasjudu liman khalaqta teenan 62. Qala araaytaka hatha allathee karramta AAalayya la-in akhkhartani ila yawmi alqiyamati laahtanikanna thurriyyatahu illa qaleelan

Tafsir Ibn Kathir

The Story of Adam and Iblis

Allah mentions here the enmity of Iblis, may the curse of Allah be upon him and his progeny. This is an ancient hatred, dating from the time that Allah created Adam, when He commanded the angels to prostrate to Adam, and all of them prostrated except Iblis, who was too arrogant and he haughtily refused to prostrate to him. He said in a tone indicating contempt:

(He said: "Shall I prostrate myself to one whom You created from clay") According to another Ayah, he said:

(I am better than he. You created me from fire, and You created him from clay.) (7:12) He also said, speaking to the Lord with disbelief and insolence, but the Lord bore it patiently:

(He said: "See this one whom You have honored above me...") `Ali bin Abi Talhah reported that Ibn `Abbas said, "He is saying, `I am going to dominate his offspring, all but a few.'" Mujahid said (it means), "I am going to surround them." Ibn Zayd said (it means), "I am going to lead them astray." All of them are close in meaning, and the meaning of the Ayah is, "Do You see this one whom You have honored and made greater than me If You give me time, I will lead his descendants astray, all but a few of them."

Surah: 17 Ayah: 63, Ayah: 64 & Ayah: 65

قَالَ اذْهَبْ فَمَن تَبِعَكَ مِنْهُمْ فَإِنَّ جَهَنَّمَ جَزَآؤُكُمْ جَزَآءً مَّوْفُورًا ۝

63. (Allâh) said: "Go, and whosoever of them follows you, surely Hell will be the recompense of you (all) an ample recompense.

وَٱسْتَفْزِزْ مَنِ ٱسْتَطَعْتَ مِنْهُم بِصَوْتِكَ وَأَجْلِبْ عَلَيْهِم بِخَيْلِكَ وَرَجِلِكَ وَشَارِكْهُمْ فِى ٱلْأَمْوَٰلِ وَٱلْأَوْلَٰدِ وَعِدْهُمْ وَمَا يَعِدُهُمُ ٱلشَّيْطَٰنُ إِلَّا غُرُورًا ۝

64. "And befool them gradually those whom you can among them with your voice (i.e. songs, music, and any other call for Allâh's disobedience), make assaults on them with your cavalry and your infantry, share with them wealth and children (by tempting them to earn money by illegal ways -usury, or by committing illegal sexual intercourse), and make promises to them." But Satan promises them nothing but deceit.

إِنَّ عِبَادِى لَيْسَ لَكَ عَلَيْهِمْ سُلْطَٰنٌ وَكَفَىٰ بِرَبِّكَ وَكِيلًا ۝

65. "Verily! My slaves (i.e. the true believers of Islâmic Monotheism) - you have no authority over them. And All-Sufficient is your Lord as a Guardian."

Transliteration

63. Qala ithhab faman tabiAAaka minhum fa-inna jahannama jazaokum jazaan mawfooran   64. Waistafziz mani istataAAta minhum bisawtika waajlib AAalayhim bikhaylika warajlika washarikhum fee al-amwali waal-awladi waAAidhum wama yaAAiduhumu alshshaytanu illa ghurooran   65. Inna AAibadee laysa laka AAalayhim sultanun wakafa birabbika wakeelan

Tafsir Ibn Kathir

When Iblis asked for respite, Allah said to him:

`(Go,) I will give you respite.' According to another Ayah (Allah) said:

(Verily, you are of those allowed respite till the Day of the time appointed.) (38:80-81). Then Allah warned him and those who follow him among the progeny of Adam about Hell:

((Allah) said: "Go, and whosoever of them follows you, surely, Hell will be the recompense of you (all)) meaning, for your deeds.

(an ample recompense.) Mujahid said, "Sufficient recompense." Qatadah said, "It will be abundant for you and will not be decreased for you."

(And fool them gradually those whom you can among them with your voice,) It was said that this refers to singing. Mujahid said, "With idle entertainment and singing," meaning, influence them with that.

(And fool them gradually those whom you can among them with your voice,) Ibn `Abbas said, "Every caller who calls people to disobey Allah." This was the view of Qatadah, and was also the opinion favored by Ibn Jarir.

(Ajib upon them with your cavalry and your infantry.) Send your troops and cavalry and infantry against them. The meaning is, send whatever forces you have at your disposal against them. This is a command (related to the divine decree), as Allah says elsewhere:

(See you not that We have sent the Shayatin against the disbelievers to push them to do evil.) (19:83), meaning, to provoke them and drive them towards evil.

(Ajlib upon them with your cavalry and your infantry,) Ibn `Abbas and Mujahid said, "Everyone who rides or walks to go and commit sin and disobey Allah." Qatadah said, "He has infantry and cavalry among the Jinn and among humans. They are the ones who obey him." The Arabs use the verb Ajlaba when describing somebody shouting at another person. Hence it is forbidden in races to shout at one another and push one another. From this root is also derived the word Jalabah, which means raising voices.

(and share with them wealth and children,) Ibn `Abbas and Mujahid said, "This means what he commands them to do of spending money in disobedience to Allah, may He be exalted."

(and children,) Ibn' Abbas, as reported by Al-`Awfi, Mujahid and Ad-Dahhak said, "This means the children of Zina (i.e., illegitimate children)." `Ali bin Abi Talhah reported that Ibn `Abbas said, "This means the children whom they used to kill out of folly, without knowledge." Qatadah reported that Al-Hasan Al-Basri said: "Allah caused Shaytan to take a share of wealth and children by making them Magians, Jews and Christians, and making them follow any religion other than Islam, and by making them give a part of their wealth to the Shaytan." Qatadah said the same.

(and share with them wealth and children.) The fact that only wealth and children are mentioned in this Ayah, does not mean that it is limited only to those things. Everything in which a person disobeys Allah or obeys the Shaytan means that he is sharing with him. It was reported in Sahih Muslim from `Iyad bin Himar that the Messenger of Allah said:

«يَقُولُ اللهُ عَزَّ وَجَلَّ إِنِّي خَلَقْتُ عِبَادِي حُنَفَاءَ فَجَاءَتْهُمُ الشَّيَاطِينُ فَاجْتَالَتْهُمْ عَنْ دِينِهِمْ وَحَرَّمَتْ عَلَيْهِمْ مَا أَحْلَلْتُ لَهُمْ»

Chapter 17: Al-Israa (The Night Journey or Bani Isra'il), Verses 001-111

(Allah the Mighty and Exalted says, "I have created My servants as Hunafa' (monotheists), then the Shayatin come to them and lead them astray from their religion and (tell that) what I have permitted for them is forbidden to them.") According to the Two Sahihs, the Messenger of Allah said:

«لَوْ أَنَّ أَحَدَهُمْ إِذَا أَرَادَ أَنْ يَأْتِيَ أَهْلَهُ قَالَ: بِسْمِ اللهِ اللَّهُمَّ جَنِّبْنَا الشَّيْطَانَ وَجَنِّبِ الشَّيْطَانَ مَا رَزَقْتَنَا فَإِنَّهُ إِنْ يُقَدَّرْ بَيْنَهُمَا وَلَدٌ فِي ذَلِكَ لَمْ يَضُرَّهُ الشَّيْطَانُ أَبَدًا»

(When one of you wants to have intercourse with his wife, let him say, `In the Name of Allah. O Allah, keep us away from Shaytan and keep Shaytan away from what you bestow on us (children).' Then if a child is decreed for them from that, the Shaytan will never harm him.)

("...and make promises to them." But Shaytan promises them nothing but deceit.) As Allah tells us, Iblis will say, on the Day when the matter is decided:

(Verily, Allah promised you a promise of truth. And I too promised you, but I betrayed you.) (14:22)

(Verily, My servants, you have no authority over them.) Here Allah tells us that He supports His believing servants, and guards and protects them against the accursed Shaytan. Allah says:

(And All-Sufficient is your Lord as a Guardian.) meaning, as a Protector, Supporter and Helper.

Surah: 17 Ayah: 66

رَّبُّكُمُ ٱلَّذِى يُزْجِى لَكُمُ ٱلْفُلْكَ فِى ٱلْبَحْرِ لِتَبْتَغُوا۟ مِن فَضْلِهِۦٓ ۚ إِنَّهُۥ كَانَ بِكُمْ رَحِيمًا ۝

66. Your Lord is He Who drives the ship for you through the sea, in order that you may seek of His Bounty. Truly He is Ever Most Merciful towards you.

Transliteration

66. Rabbukumu allathee yuzjee lakumu alfulka fee albahri litabtaghoo min fadlihi innahu kana bikum raheeman

Tafsir Ibn Kathir

Ships are a Sign of the Mercy of Allah

Allah tells us of His kindness towards His servants by subjugating for them ships on the sea. He makes it easy for them to use ships to serve their interests, seeking His bounty through trade between one region and another. He says:

(Truly, He is ever Most Merciful towards you.) meaning, He does this for you out of His grace and mercy towards you.

Surah: 17 Ayah: 67

وَإِذَا مَسَّكُمُ ٱلضُّرُّ فِى ٱلْبَحْرِ ضَلَّ مَن تَدْعُونَ إِلَّآ إِيَّاهُ فَلَمَّا نَجَّىٰكُمْ إِلَى ٱلْبَرِّ أَعْرَضْتُمْ وَكَانَ ٱلْإِنسَـٰنُ كَفُورًا ۝

67. And when harm touches you upon the sea, those that you call upon vanish from you except Him (Allâh Alone). But when He brings you safe to land, you turn away (from Him). And man is ever ungrateful.

Transliteration

67. Wa-itha massakumu alddurru fee albahri dalla man tadAAoona illa iyyahu falamma najjakum ila albarri aAAradtum wakana al-insanu kafooran

Tafsir Ibn Kathir

When Harm befalls Them, the Disbelievers do not remember anyone except Allah

Allah tells us that when harm befalls people, they call on Him, turning to Him and sincerely beseeching Him. Hence Allah says:

(And when harm touches you upon the sea, those that you call upon vanish from you except Him.) meaning, everything they worship besides Allah disappears from their hearts and minds. Similar happened to `Ikrimah bin Abi Jahl when he fled from the Messenger of Allah after the conquest of Makkah, and headed for Ethiopia. He set out across the sea to go to Ethiopia, but a stormy wind arose. The people said to one another: "None can save you except Allah Alone." `Ikrimah said to himself, "By Allah if none can benefit on the sea except Allah then no doubt none can benefit on land except Allah. `O Allah! I promise You that if You bring me safely out of this, I will go and put my hand in the hand of Muhammad and surely, I will find him full of pity, kindness and mercy.'" They came out of it safely and were delivered from the sea. Then `Ikrimah went to the Messenger of Allah , and declared his Islam, and he became a good Muslim, may Allah be pleased with him.

(But when He brings you safe to land, you turn away.) means, you forget what you remembered of Divine Oneness (Tawhid) when you were on the sea, and you turn away from calling on Him Alone with no partner or associate.

(And man is ever ungrateful.) means, by nature he forgets and denies His blessings, except for those whom Allah protects.

Surah: 17 Ayah: 68

أَفَأَمِنتُمْ أَن يَخْسِفَ بِكُمْ جَانِبَ ٱلْبَرِّ أَوْ يُرْسِلَ عَلَيْكُمْ حَاصِبًا ثُمَّ لَا تَجِدُوا۟ لَكُمْ وَكِيلًا ۝

68. Do you then feel secure that He will not cause a side of the land to swallow you up, or that He will not send against you a violent sand-storm? Then, you shall find no Wakîl (guardian - one to guard you from the torment).

Transliteration

68. Afaamintum an yakhsifa bikum janiba albarri aw yursila AAalaykum hasiban thumma la tajidoo lakum wakeelan

Tafsir Ibn Kathir

Does not the Punishment of Allah come on Land too

Allah says, do you think that by emerging onto dry land you will be safe from His vengeance and punishment, that a side of the land will not swallow you up or He will not send against you a Hasib - which is a kind of rain that carries stones This was the view of Mujahid and others. As Allah says:

(Verily, We sent against them, except the family of Lut, them We saved in the last hour of the night, As a favor from Us.) (54:34-35) Elsewhere, Allah says:

(and We rained on them stones of Sijjil, in a well-arranged manner one after another)

(Do you feel secure that He, Who is over the heaven (Allah), will not cause the earth to sink with you, and then it should quake Or do you feel secure that He, Who is over the heaven (Allah), will not send against you a Hasib Then you shall know how (terrible) has been My warning) (67: 16-17)

(Then, you shall find no guardian.) no helper to turn the punishment away from you and save you.

Surah: 17 Ayah: 69

أَمْ أَمِنتُمْ أَن يُعِيدَكُمْ فِيهِ تَارَةً أُخْرَىٰ فَيُرْسِلَ عَلَيْكُمْ قَاصِفًا مِّنَ ٱلرِّيحِ فَيُغْرِقَكُم بِمَا كَفَرْتُمْ ثُمَّ لَا تَجِدُوا۟ لَكُمْ عَلَيْنَا بِهِۦ تَبِيعًا ۝

69. Or do you feel secure that He will not send you back a second time to sea and send against you a hurricane of wind and drown you because of your disbelief? Then you will not find any avenger therein against Us?

Transliteration

69. Am amintum an yuAAeedakum feehi taratan okhra fayursila AAalaykum qasifan mina alrreehi fayughriqakum bima kafartum thumma la tajidoo lakum AAalayna bihi tabeeAAan

Tafsir Ibn Kathir

Perhaps He will send You back to the Sea

Allah says,

(Or do you feel secure), `you who turn away from Us after acknowledging Our Oneness at sea once you are back upon dry land,'

(that He will not send you back) to sea a second time

(and send against you a Qasif) which will destroy your masts and sink your vessels. Ibn `Abbas and others said, "Al-Qasif is the wind of the sea which destroys vessels and sinks them."

(and drown you because of your disbelief) means because of your rejection and turning away from Allah.

(Then you will not find any avenger therein against Us.) Ibn `Abbas said that this means a helper. Mujahid said, "A helper who will avenge you," i.e., take revenge on your behalf. Qatadah said it means, "We are not afraid that anyone will pursue Us with anything of that nature (i.e., vengeance)."

Surah: 17 Ayah: 70

﴿ وَلَقَدْ كَرَّمْنَا بَنِىٓ ءَادَمَ وَحَمَلْنَٰهُمْ فِى ٱلْبَرِّ وَٱلْبَحْرِ وَرَزَقْنَٰهُم مِّنَ ٱلطَّيِّبَٰتِ وَفَضَّلْنَٰهُمْ عَلَىٰ كَثِيرٍ مِّمَّنْ خَلَقْنَا تَفْضِيلًا ۝ ﴾

70. And indeed We have honored the Children of Adam, and We have carried them on land and sea, and have provided them with At-Tayyibât (lawful good things), and have preferred them above many of those whom We have created with a marked preferment.

Transliteration

70. Walaqad karramna banee adama wahamalnahum fee albarri waalbahri warazaqnahum mina alttayyibati wafaddalnahum AAala katheerin mimman khalaqna tafdeelan

Tafsir Ibn Kathir

The Honor and noble Nature of Man

Allah tells us how He has honored the sons of Adam and made them noble by creating them in the best and most perfect of forms, as He says:

(Verily, We created man in the best stature (mould).) (95:4) He walks upright on his two feet and eats with his hand, whilet other living creatures walk on four feet and eat with their mouths, and He has given him hearing, sight and a heart with which to understand all of that, to benefit from it, and distinguish between things to know which are good for him and which are harmful, in both worldly and religious terms.

(and We have carried them on land) means, on animals such as cattle, horses and mules, and also on the sea in ships and boats, great and small.

(and have provided them with At-Tayyibat,) meaning agricultural produce, fruits, meat, and milk with all kinds of delicious and desirable flavors and colors and beautiful appearance, and fine clothes of all kinds of shapes colors and sizes, which they make for themselves or are brought to them by others from other regions and areas.

(and have preferred them above many of those whom We have created with a marked preferment.) means, over all living beings and other kinds of creation. This Ayah indicates that human are also preferred over the angels.

Surah: 17 Ayah: 71 & Ayah: 72

يَوْمَ نَدْعُواْ كُلَّ أُنَاسٍ بِإِمَامِهِمْ ۖ فَمَنْ أُوتِىَ كِتَبَهُۥ بِيَمِينِهِۦ فَأُوْلَٰٓئِكَ يَقْرَءُونَ كِتَبَهُمْ وَلَا يُظْلَمُونَ فَتِيلًا ۝

71. (And remember) the Day when We shall call together all human beings with their (respective) Imâm (their Prophets, or their records of good and bad deeds, or their Holy Books like the Qur'ân, the Taurât (Torah), the Injeel (Gospel)) So whosoever is given his record in his right hand, such will read their records, and they will not be dealt with unjustly in the least.

وَمَن كَانَ فِى هَٰذِهِۦٓ أَعْمَىٰ فَهُوَ فِى ٱلْءَاخِرَةِ أَعْمَىٰ وَأَضَلُّ سَبِيلًا ۝

72. And whoever is blind in this world (i.e., does not see Allâh's Signs and believes not in Him), will be blind in the Hereafter, and more astray from the Path.

Transliteration

71. Yawma nadAAoo kulla onasin bi-imamihim faman ootiya kitabahu biyameenihi faola-ika yaqraoona kitabahum wala yuthlamoona fateelan   72. Waman kana fee hathihi aAAma fahuwa fee al-akhirati aAAma waadallu sabeelan

Tafsir Ibn Kathir

Everyone will be called by his Imam on the Day of Resurrection

Allah tells us that on the Day of Resurrection, he will call each people to account by its Imam. The scholars differed as to the meaning of this (i.e. Imam. Mujahid and Qatadah said that it meant each nation would be called to account by its Prophet. Some of the Salaf said this is the greatest honor for the people of Hadith, because their leader is the Prophet. Ibn Zayd said it means they would be called to account by their Book which was revealed to their Prophet with its laws. This was also the view favored by Ibn Jarir. Ibn Abi Najih narrated that Mujahid said, "With their Books." It may be that what is meant here is what Al-`Awfi narrated from Ibn `Abbas concerning this Ayah,

((And remember) the Day when We shall call together all human beings with their (respective) Imam), which is that it refers to the Book (or record) of their deeds. This was also the view of Abu Al-`Aliyah, Al-Hasan and Ad-Dahhak. This view is the most correct, because Allah says:

(and all things We have recorded with numbers (as a record) in a Clear Book (Fi Imamin Mubin)) (36:12)

(And the Book (one's record) will be placed, and you will see the criminals, fearful of that which is (recorded) therein) (18:49)

(And you will see each nation humbled to their knees, each nation will be called to its record (of deeds). This Day you shall be recompensed for what you used to do. This Our record speaks about you with truth. Verily, We were recording what you used to do.) (45:28-29) This does not contradict the fact that the Prophet will be brought forward when Allah judges between his Ummah, for he will inevitably be a witness against his Ummah over their deeds. But what is meant here by Imam is the Book of deeds. Allah says:

((And remember) the Day when We shall call together all human beings with their (respective) Imam. So whosoever is given his record in his right hand, such will read their records,) means, because of their happiness and joy at what is recorded therein of good deeds - they will read it and want to read it. As Allah says:

(Then as for him who will be given his record in his right hand will say: "Here! read my record!) until His saying,

(But as for him who will be given his record in his left hand,) (69:19-29)

(and they will not be dealt with unjustly in the least (Fatilan).) We have already mentioned that the Fatil is the long thread in the groove of a date-pit. Al-Hafiz Abu Bakr Al-Bazzar recorded a Hadith from Abu Hurayrah according to which the Prophet said, concerning the Ayah,

((And remember) the Day when We shall call together all human beings with their (respective) Imam.)

«يُدْعَى أَحَدُهُمْ فَيُعْطَى كِتَابَهُ بِيَمِينِهِ، وَيُمَدُّ لَهُ فِي جِسْمِهِ، وَيَبْيَضُّ وَجْهُهُ، وَيُجْعَلُ عَلَى رَأْسِهِ تَاجٌ مِنْ لُؤْلُؤَةٍ يَتَلَأْلَأُ، فَيَنْطَلِقُ إِلَى أَصْحَابِهِ فَيَرَوْنَهُ مِنْ بَعِيدٍ،

فَيَقُولُونَ: اللَّهُمَّ آتِنَا بِهَذَا، وَبَارِكْ لَنَا فِي هَذَا، فَيَأْتِيهِمْ فَيَقُولُ لَهُمْ: أَبْشِرُوا فَإِنَّ لِكُلِّ رَجُلٍ مِنْكُمْ مِثْلَ هَذَا، وَأَمَّا الْكَافِرُ فَيَسْوَدُّ وَجْهُهُ، وَيُمَدُّ لَهُ فِي جِسْمِهِ، وَيَرَاهُ أَصْحَابُهُ فَيَقُولُونَ: نَعُوذُ بِاللهِ مِنْ هَذَا، أَوْ مِنْ شَرِّ هَذَا اللَّهُمَّ لَا تَأْتِنَا بِهِ فَيَأْتِيهِمْ فَيَقُولُونَ: اللَّهُمَّ أَخْزِهِ. فَيَقُولُ: أَبْعَدَكُمُ اللهُ فَإِنَّ لِكُلِّ رَجُلٍ مِنْكُمْ مِثْلَ هَذَا«

(One of you will be called and will be given his Book in his right hand. He will be in a good physical state, with a white face, and there will be placed on his head a crown of shining pearls. He will go to his companions and they will see him from afar, and will say, "O Allah, let him come to us and bless us with this." Then he will come to them and will say to them, "Rejoice, for every man among you will be like this." As for the disbeliever, his face will be black and his body will be enlarged. His companions will see him from afar and will say, "We seek refuge in Allah from this, or from the evil of this, O Allah, do not let him come to us." "Then he will come to them and they will say, O Allah, humiliate him!" He will say, "May Allah cast you away, every man among you will be like this.") Then Al-Bazzar said: "This was only reported through this chain."

(And whoever is blind in this) Ibn `Abbas, Mujahid, Qatadah and Ibn Zayd said: this means in this worldly life.

(blind) means, blind to the signs and proofs of Allah.

(then he will be blind in the Hereafter,) as he was blind in this world.

(and most astray from the path.) most astray as he was in this world. We seek refuge with Allah from that.

Surah: 17 Ayah: 73, Ayah: 74 & Ayah: 75

وَإِن كَادُوا۟ لَيَفْتِنُونَكَ عَنِ ٱلَّذِىٓ أَوْحَيْنَآ إِلَيْكَ لِتَفْتَرِىَ عَلَيْنَا غَيْرَهُۥ ۖ وَإِذًۭا لَّٱتَّخَذُوكَ خَلِيلًۭا ۝

73. Verily, they were about to tempt you away from that which We have revealed (the Qur'ân) unto you (O Muhammad (peace be upon him)) to fabricate something other than it against Us, and then they would certainly have taken you a Khalil (an intimate friend)!

وَلَوْلَآ أَن ثَبَّتْنَـٰكَ لَقَدْ كِدتَّ تَرْكَنُ إِلَيْهِمْ شَيْـًۭٔا قَلِيلًۭا ۝

74. And had We not made you stand firm, you would nearly have inclined to them a little.

إِذًا لَّأَذَقْنَـٰكَ ضِعْفَ ٱلْحَيَوٰةِ وَضِعْفَ ٱلْمَمَاتِ ثُمَّ لَا تَجِدُ لَكَ عَلَيْنَا نَصِيرًا ۝

75. In that case We would have made you taste a double portion (of punishment) in this life and a double portion (of punishment) after death. And then you would have found none to help you against Us.

Transliteration

73. Wa-in kadoo layaftinoonaka AAani allathee awhayna ilayka litaftariya AAalayna ghayrahu wa-ithan laittakhathooka khaleelan 74. Walawla an thabbatnaka laqad kidta tarkanu ilayhim shay-an qaleelan 75. Ithan laathaqnaka diAAfa alhayati wadiAAfa almamati thumma la tajidu laka AAalayna naseeran

Tafsir Ibn Kathir

How the Prophet would have been punished if He had given in at all to the Disbelievers' Demands that He change some of the Revelation

Allah tells us how He supported His Prophet and protected him and kept him safe from the evil plots of the wicked transgressors. Allah is the One Who took care of him and helped him, and would not leave him to any of His creation. He is the One Who is His Helper, Supporter and Protector, the One Who is to help him achieve victory and make His religion prevail over those who resist him and oppose him and fight him in the east and in the west. May Allah send peace and blessings upon him until the Day of Judgement.

Surah: 17 Ayah: 76 & Ayah: 77

وَإِن كَادُوا۟ لَيَسْتَفِزُّونَكَ مِنَ ٱلْأَرْضِ لِيُخْرِجُوكَ مِنْهَا ۖ وَإِذًا لَّا يَلْبَثُونَ خِلَـٰفَكَ إِلَّا قَلِيلًا ۝

76. And Verily, they were about to frighten you so much as to drive you out from the land. But in that case they would not have stayed (therein) after you, except for a little while.

سُنَّةَ مَن قَدْ أَرْسَلْنَا قَبْلَكَ مِن رُّسُلِنَا ۖ وَلَا تَجِدُ لِسُنَّتِنَا تَحْوِيلًا ۝

77. (This was Our) Sunnah (rule or way) with the Messengers We sent before you (O Muhammad (peace be upon him)) and you will not find any alteration in Our Sunnah (rule or way).

Transliteration

76. Wa-in kadoo layastafizzoonaka mina al-ardi liyukhrijooka minha wa-ithan la yalbathoona khilafaka illa qaleelan

Chapter 17: Al-Israa (The Night Journey or Bani Isra'il), Verses 001-111

77. Sunnata man qad arsalna qablaka min rusulina wala tajidu lisunnatina tahweelan

Tafsir Ibn Kathir

The Reason why these Ayat were revealed

This was revealed concerning the disbelievers among the Quraysh, when they wanted to expel the Messenger of Allah from among themselves. So Allah issued a warning to them in this Ayah, telling them that if they expelled him, they would not stay in Makkah for very long after that. And this is what happened after he migrated from them when their persecution became so intense. Only a year and a half after that, Allah brought him and them together on the battlefield of Badr, without any pre-arranged appointment, and He caused him to prevail over them and defeat them, so he killed their leaders and took their families as captives. Hence Allah said:

(A Sunnah with which We sent) meaning this is what We usually do to those who reject Our Messengers and persecute them by driving the Messenger out from among themselves - the punishment comes to them. If it were not for the fact that the Prophet was the Messenger of Mercy, vengeance would have come upon them such as had never been seen before in this world. So Allah says:

(And Allah would not punish them while you are among them.) (8:33)

Surah: 17 Ayah: 78 & Ayah: 79

أَقِمِ ٱلصَّلَوٰةَ لِدُلُوكِ ٱلشَّمْسِ إِلَىٰ غَسَقِ ٱلَّيْلِ وَقُرْءَانَ ٱلْفَجْرِ ۖ إِنَّ قُرْءَانَ ٱلْفَجْرِ كَانَ مَشْهُودًا ۝

78. Perform As-Salât (Iqamât-as-Salât) from mid-day till the darkness of the night (i.e. the Zuhr, 'Asr, Maghrib, and 'Ishâ' prayers), and recite the Qur'ân in the early dawn (i.e. the morning prayer). Verily, the recitation of the Qur'ân in the early dawn is ever witnessed (attended by the angels in charge of mankind of the day and the night).

وَمِنَ ٱلَّيْلِ فَتَهَجَّدْ بِهِۦ نَافِلَةً لَّكَ عَسَىٰٓ أَن يَبْعَثَكَ رَبُّكَ مَقَامًا مَّحْمُودًا ۝

79. And in some parts of the night (also) offer the Salât (prayer) with it (i.e. recite the Qur'an in the prayer), as an additional prayer (Tahajjud optional prayer - Nawâfil) for you (O Muhammad (peace be upon him)) It may be that your Lord will raise you to Maqâm Mahmûd (a station of praise and glory, i.e. the honor of intercession on the Day of Resurrection.).

Transliteration

78. Aqimi alssalata lidulooki alshshamsi ila ghasaqi allayli waqur-ana alfajri inna qur-ana alfajri kana mashhoodan 79. Wamina allayli fatahajjad bihi nafilatan laka AAasa an yabAAathaka rabbuka maqaman mahmoodan

Tafsir Ibn Kathir

The Command to offer the Prayers at their appointed Times

Allah says, commanding His Messenger to offer the prescribed prayers at the appointed times:

(Perform the Salat from midday.) Hushaym narrated from Mughirah from Ash-Sha`bi from Ibn `Abbas: "Midday means when the sun is at its zenith." This was also reported by Nafi` from Ibn `Umar, and by Malik in his Tafsir from Az-Zuhri from Ibn `Umar. This was the opinion of Abu Barzah Al-Aslami and Mujahid, and of Al-Hasan, Ad-Dahhak, Abu Ja`far Al-Baqir and Qatadah. It is also understood to (generally) refer to the times of the five prayers. Allah said;

(from midday till the darkness of the night,) meaning darkness, or it was said, sunset. This was understood to mean Zuhr `Asr, Maghrib and `Isha'.

(and recite the Qur'an in the early dawn.) meaning Salat Al-Fajr. The details of the timings of the prayers were reported in the Mutawatir Sunnah from the words and deeds of the Prophet , and this is what the people of Islam have followed until the present day, passing it down from generation to generation, century after century, as we have stated in the appropriate place, praise be to Allah.

The Meeting of the Angels at the Times of Fajr and `Asr Prayers

(Verily the recitation of the Qur'an in the early down is ever witnessed.) Ibn Mas`ud reported from Abu Hurayrah (may Allah be pleased with them both) that the Prophet said concerning this Ayah :

(and recite the Qur'an in the early dawn. Verily, the recitation of the Qur'an in the early dawn is ever witnessed.)

»تَشْهَدُهُ مَلَائِكَةُ اللَّيْلِ وَمَلَائِكَةُ النَّهَارِ«

(It is witnessed by the angels of the night and the angels of the day.) Al-Bukhari narrated from Abu Hurayrah that the Prophet said:

»فَضْلُ صَلَاةِ الْجَمِيعِ عَلَى صَلَاةِ الْوَاحِدِ خَمْسٌ وَعِشْرُونَ دَرَجَةً، وَتَجْتَمِعُ مَلَائِكَةُ اللَّيْلِ وَمَلَائِكَةُ النَّهَارِ فِي صَلَاةِ الْفَجْرِ«

(The prayer offered in congregation is twenty-five degrees better than the prayer offered individually, and the angels of the night and the angels of the day meet at Salat Al-Fajr.) Abu Hurayrah said: Recite, if you wish:

Chapter 17: Al-Israa (The Night Journey or Bani Isra'il), Verses 001-111

(and recite the Qur'an in the early dawn. Verily, the recitation of the Qur'an in the early dawn is ever witnessed.) Imam Ahmad recorded from Ibn Mas`ud and Abu Hurayrah that the Prophet said, concerning the Ayah:

(and recite the Qur'an in the early dawn. Verily, the recitation of the Qur'an in the early dawn is ever witnessed.)

«تَشْهَدُهُ مَلَائِكَةُ اللَّيْلِ وَمَلَائِكَةُ النَّهَارِ»

(It is witnessed by the angels of the night and the angels of the day.) This was recorded by At-Tirmidhi, An-Nasa'i, and Ibn Majah. At-Tirmidhi said, "It is Hasan Sahih." According to the version recorded in the Two Sahihs from Abu Hurayrah, the Prophet said:

«يَتَعَاقَبُونَ فِيكُمْ مَلَائِكَةٌ بِاللَّيْلِ وَمَلَائِكَةٌ بِالنَّهَارِ، وَيَجْتَمِعُونَ فِي صَلَاةِ الصُّبْحِ وَفِي صَلَاةِ الْعَصْرِ، فَيَعْرُجُ الَّذِينَ بَاتُوا فِيكُمْ فَيَسْأَلُهُمْ رَبُّهُمْ وَهُوَ أَعْلَمُ بِكُمْ كَيْفَ تَرَكْتُمْ عِبَادِي؟ فَيَقُولُونَ: أَتَيْنَاهُمْ وَهُمْ يُصَلُّونَ، وَتَرَكْنَاهُمْ وَهُمْ يُصَلُّونَ»

(The angels of the night and the angels of the day come amongst you in successive groups (in shifts). They meet at the Morning prayer (Fajr) and at the Mid-afternoon prayer ('Asr). Those who stayed among you at ascend, and their Lord asks them, although He knows best about you, "How did you leave My servants" They say, "We came to them when they were praying and we left them when they were praying.") `Abdullah bin Mas`ud said, "The two guards meet at Salat Al-Fajr, and one group ascends while the other stays where it is. " These were the comments of Ibrahim An-Nakha`i, Mujahid, Qatadah and others on the Tafsir of this Ayah.

The Command to pray Tahajjud

And in some parts of the night (also) offer the Salah with it as an additional prayer for you.) Here Allah commands him (the Prophet) to offer further prayers at night after the prescribed prayers. It was reported in Sahih Muslim from Abu Hurayrah that when the Messenger of Allah was asked which prayer is best after the prescribed prayers, he said,

«صَلَاةُ اللَّيْلِ»

(The Night prayer) Allah commanded His Messenger to pray the Night prayer after offering the prescribed prayers, and the term Tahajjud refers to prayer that is offered after sleeping. This was the view of `Alqamah, Al-Aswad, Ibrahim An-Nakha`i and others. It is also well-known from the Arabic language itself. A number of Hadiths report that the Messenger of Allah used to pray Tahajjud after he had slept. These include reports from Ibn `Abbas, `A'ishah and other Companions, may Allah be pleased with them. This has been discussed in detail in the appropriate place, praise be to Allah. Al-Hasan Al-Basri said, "This is what comes after `Isha', or it could mean what comes after sleeping."

(an additional prayer (Nawafil)) means the Night prayer has been made an extra prayer specifically for the Prophet , because all his previous and future sins had been forgiven. But for other members of his Ummah, offering optional prayers may expiate for whatever sins they may commit. This was the view of Mujahid, and it was reported in Al-Musnad from Abu Umamah Al-Bahili.

(It may be that your Lord will raise you to Maqam Mahmud.) meaning, `do that which you are commanded to do, and We will raise you to a station of praise and glory (Maqam Mahmud) on the Day of Resurrection, where all of creation will praise you,' as will their Creator, may He be glorified and exalted. Ibn Jarir said, "Most of the commentators said, `This is the position to which Muhammad will be raised on the Day of Resurrection, to intercede for the people so that their Lord will relieve them of some of the hardships they are facing on that Day.'" It was reported that Hudhayfah said, "Mankind will be gathered in one arena, where they will all hear the call and will all be seen. They will be standing barefoot and naked as they were created, and no person shall speak except by the leave of Allah. He will call out, `O Muhammad,' and he will respond,

»لَبَّيْكَ وَسَعْدَيْكَ، وَالْخَيْرُ فِي يَدَيْكَ وَالشَّرُّ لَيْسَ إِلَيْكَ، وَالْمَهْدِيُّ مَنْ هَدَيْتَ، وَعَبْدُكَ بَيْنَ يَدَيْكَ، وَمِنْكَ وَإِلَيْكَ لَا مَنْجَى وَلَا مَلْجَأَ مِنْكَ إِلَّا إِلَيْكَ، تَبَارَكْتَ وَتَعَالَيْتَ سُبْحَانَكَ رَبَّ الْبَيْتِ«

(At your service, all goodness is in Your Hands and evil is not to be attributed to You. The one who is guided is the one whom You guide. Your servant is before You, from You, and to You and there is no salvation or refuge from You except with You. May You be blessed and exalted, Glory be to You, Lord of the House (the Ka`bah).) This is the position of praise and honor (Maqam Mahmud) which was mentioned by Allah." Ibn `Abbas said, "The position of praise and honor is the position of intercession." Ibn Abi Najih reported something similar from Mujahid, and this was also the view of Al-Hasan Al-Basri. Qatadah said, "He is the first one for whom the earth will be opened on the Day of Resurrection, and he will be the first one to intercede." So the scholars consider this the position of praise and glory to which Allah referred in the Ayah:

(It may be that your Lord will raise you to Maqam Mahmud.) I, Ibn Kathir, say: the Messenger of Allah will have honors in the Day of Resurrection in which no one else will have a share, honors which will not be matched by anyone else. He is the first one for whom the earth will be opened and he will come forth riding to the gathering place. He will have a banner under which Adam and anyone else will gather, and he will have the Hawd (Lake) to which no one else will have more access than he. He will have the right of the Grand Intercession with Allah when He comes to judge between His creation. This will be after the people ask Adam, then Nuh, then Ibrahim, then Musa, then `Isa to intercede, and each of them will say, "I am not able for that." Then they will come to Muhammad , and he will say,

«أَنَا لَهَا أَنَا لَهَا»

(I can do that, I can do that.) We will mention this in more detail shortly, If Allah wills. Part of that will be that he will intercede for some people who had been commanded to be taken to Hell, and they will be brought back. He is the first Prophet whose Ummah will be judged, and the first to take them across the Bridge over the Fire, and the first to intercede in Paradise, as was reported in Sahih Muslim. In the Hadith about the Trumpet, it says that none of the believers will enter Paradise except through his intercession. He will be the first to enter Paradise, and his Ummah will be the first nation to enter. He will intercede for the status to be raised for people whose deeds could not get them there. He is the one who will reach Al-Wasilah, which is the highest position in Paradise, which befits no one but him. When Allah gives permission for intercession on behalf of sinners, the angels, Prophets and believers will intercede, and he will intercede for people whose number is known only to Allah. No one will intercede like him and no one will match him in intercession. This has been explained in comprehensive detail at the end of the Book of Sirah, in the chapter on the specific qualities. Praise be to Allah. Now with the help of Allah we will mention the Hadiths that were reported concerning Al-Maqam Al-Mahmud. Al-Bukhari recorded that Ibn `Umar said: "On the Day of Resurrection, the people will be humbled to their knees, each nation following its Prophet and saying, `O so-and-so, intercede,' `O so-and-so, intercede,' until the power of intercession is given to Muhammad , and that will be the day when Allah raises him to a position of praise and glory. Ibn Jarir recorded that `Abdullah bin `Umar said that the Messenger of Allah said:

«إِنَّ الشَّمْسَ لَتَدْنُو حَتَّى يَبْلُغَ الْعَرَقُ نِصْفَ الْأُذُنِ، فَبَيْنَمَا هُمْ كَذَلِكَ اسْتَغَاثُوا بِآدَمَ فَيَقُولُ: لَسْتُ بِصَاحِبِ ذَلِكَ، ثُمَّ بِمُوسَى فَيَقُولُ كَذَلِكَ، ثُمَّ بِمُحَمَّدٍ فَيَشْفَعُ بَيْنَ الْخَلْقِ فَيَمْشِي حَتَّى يَأْخُذَ بِحَلَقَةِ بَابِ الْجَنَّةِ، فَيَوْمَئِذٍ يَبْعَثُهُ اللهُ مَقَامًا مَحْمُودًا»

(The sun will come close until the sweat reaches halfway up one's ears. When the people are in that state, they will ask Adam for help, and he will say, "I am not the one to do that." Then they will ask Musa, and he will say likewise, then they will ask Muhammad, and he will intercede for the people and will go and take hold of the handle of the gate of Paradise, and that will be the Day when Allah resurrects him to a position of praise and glory.) Al-Bukhari also recorded it in the Book of Zakah, where he added:

«فَيَوْمَئِذٍ يَبْعَثُهُ اللهُ مَقَامًا مَحْمُودًا، يَحْمَدُهُ أَهْلُ الْجَمْعِ كُلُّهُم»

(That will be the Day when Allah resurrects him to a position of praise and glory, and all the people will praise him.) Abu Dawud At-Tayalisi recorded that `Abdullah said, "Then Allah will give permission for intercession, and Ar-Ruh Al-Quddus, Jibril, will stand up, then Ibrahim, the close Friend of Allah will stand up, then `Isa or Musa will stand up - Abu Az-Za`ra' said, `I do not know which of them, ' -- then your Prophet will stand up and will intercede, and no one after him will intercede as much as he does. This is the position of praise and glory to which Allah referred:

(It may be that your Lord will raise you to Maqam Mahmud.)"

The Hadith of Abu Hurayrah

Imam Ahmad (may Allah have mercy on him) recorded that Abu Hurayrah said, "Some meat was brought to the Messenger of Allah , and he lifted up the arm, which he used to like, and took one bite, then he said:

«أَنَا سَيِّدُ النَّاسِ يَوْمَ الْقِيَامَةِ، وَهَلْ تَدْرُونَ مِمَّ ذَاكَ؟ يَجْمَعُ اللهُ الْأَوَّلِينَ وَالْآخِرِينَ فِي صَعِيدٍ وَاحِدٍ، يُسْمِعُهُمُ الدَّاعِي، وَيَنْفُذُهُمُ الْبَصَرُ، وَتَدْنُو الشَّمْسُ فَيَبْلُغُ النَّاسَ مِنَ الْغَمِّ وَالْكَرْبِ مَا لَا يُطِيقُونَ، وَلَا يَحْتَمِلُونَ فَيَقُولُ بَعْضُ النَّاسِ لِبَعْضٍ: أَلَا تَرَوْنَ مَا أَنْتُمْ فِيهِ مِمَّا قَدْ بَلَغَكُمْ، أَلَا تَنْظُرُونَ مَنْ يَشْفَعُ لَكُمْ إِلَى رَبِّكُمْ؟ فَيَقُولُ بَعْضُ النَّاسِ لِبَعْضٍ:

عَلَيْكُمْ بِآدَمَ، فَيَأْتُونَ آدَمَ عَلَيْهِ السَّلَامُ فَيَقُولُونَ: يَا آدَمُ أَنْتَ أَبُو الْبَشَرِ خَلَقَكَ اللهُ بِيَدِهِ وَنَفَخَ فِيكَ مِنْ رُوحِهِ، وَأَمَرَ الْمَلَائِكَةَ فَسَجَدُوا لَكَ، فَاشْفَعْ لَنَا إِلَى رَبِّكَ أَلَا تَرَى مَا نَحْنُ فِيهِ، أَلَا تَرَى مَا قَدْ بَلَغَنَا؟ فَيَقُولُ آدَمُ: إِنَّ رَبِّي قَدْ غَضِبَ الْيَوْمَ غَضَبًا لَمْ يَغْضَبْ قَبْلَهُ مِثْلَهُ وَلَنْ يَغْضَبَ بَعْدَهُ مِثْلَهُ، وَإِنَّهُ قَدْ نَهَانِي عَنِ الشَّجَرَةِ فَعَصَيْتُ، نَفْسِي نَفْسِي نَفْسِي، اذْهَبُوا إِلَى غَيْرِي اذْهَبُوا إِلَى نُوحٍ، فَيَأْتُونَ نُوحًا فَيَقُولُونَ: يَا نُوحُ أَنْتَ أَوَّلُ الرُّسُلِ إِلَى أَهْلِ الْأَرْضِ،

Chapter 17: Al-Israa (The Night Journey or Bani Isra'il), Verses 001-111

وَقَدْ سَمَّاكَ اللهُ عَبْدًا شَكُورًا، اشْفَعْ لَنَا إِلَى رَبِّكَ أَلَا تَرَى مَا نَحْنُ فِيهِ، أَلَا تَرَى مَا قَدْ بَلَغَنَا؟ فَيَقُولُ نُوحٌ: إِنَّ رَبِّي قَدْ غَضِبَ الْيَوْمَ غَضَبًا لَمْ يَغْضَبْ قَبْلَهُ مِثْلَهُ وَلَنْ يَغْضَبَ بَعْدَهُ مِثْلَهُ قَطُّ، وَإِنَّهُ قَدْ كَانَتْ لِي دَعْوَةٌ دَعَوْتُهَا عَلَى قَوْمِي نَفْسِي نَفْسِي نَفْسِي، اذْهَبُوا إِلَى غَيْرِي اذْهَبُوا إِلَى إِبْرَاهِيمَ، فَيَأْتُونَ إِبْرَاهِيمَ فَيَقُولُونَ: يَا إِبْرَاهِيمُ أَنْتَ نَبِيُّ اللهِ وَخَلِيلُهُ مِنْ أَهْلِ الْأَرْضِ، اشْفَعْ لَنَا إِلَى رَبِّكَ أَلَا تَرَى مَا نَحْنُ فِيهِ، أَلَا تَرَى مَا قَدْ بَلَغَنَا؟ فَيَقُولُ: إِنَّ رَبِّي قَدْ غَضِبَ الْيَوْمَ غَضَبًا لَمْ يَغْضَبْ قَبْلَهُ مِثْلَهُ، وَلَنْ يَغْضَبَ بَعْدَهُ مِثْلَهُ فَذَكَرَ كَذَبَاتِهِ نَفْسِي نَفْسِي نَفْسِي، اذْهَبُوا إِلَى غَيْرِي اذْهَبُوا إِلَى مُوسَى، فَيَأْتُونَ مُوسَى عَلَيْهِ السَّلَامُ فَيَقُولُونَ: يَا مُوسَى أَنْتَ رَسُولُ اللهِ اصْطَفَاكَ اللهُ بِرِسَالَاتِهِ وَبِكَلَامِهِ عَلَى النَّاسِ، اشْفَعْ لَنَا إِلَى رَبِّكَ أَلَا تَرَى مَا نَحْنُ فِيهِ، أَلَا تَرَى مَا قَدْ بَلَغَنَا؟ فَيَقُولُ لَهُمْ مُوسَى: إِنَّ رَبِّي قَدْ غَضِبَ الْيَوْمَ غَضَبًا لَمْ يَغْضَبْ قَبْلَهُ مِثْلَهُ، وَلَنْ يَغْضَبَ بَعْدَهُ مِثْلَهُ، وَإِنِّي قَدْ قَتَلْتُ نَفْسًا لَمْ أُومَرْ بِقَتْلِهَا، نَفْسِي نَفْسِي نَفْسِي، اذْهَبُوا إِلَى غَيْرِي اذْهَبُوا إِلَى عِيسَى، فَيَأْتُونَ عِيسَى فَيَقُولُونَ: يَاعِيسَى أَنْتَ رَسُولُ اللهِ وَكَلِمَتُهُ أَلْقَاهَا إِلَى مَرْيَمَ وَرُوحٌ مِنْهُ، وَكَلَّمْتَ النَّاسَ فِي الْمَهْدِ صَبِيًّا، فَاشْفَعْ لَنَا إِلَى رَبِّكَ أَلَا تَرَى مَا نَحْنُ فِيهِ، أَلَا تَرَى مَا قَدْ بَلَغَنَا؟ فَيَقُولُ لَهُمْ عِيسَى: إِنَّ رَبِّي قَدْ غَضِبَ الْيَوْمَ غَضَبًا لَمْ يَغْضَبْ قَبْلَهُ مِثْلَهُ، وَلَنْ يَغْضَبَ بَعْدَهُ مِثْلَهُ، وَلَمْ يَذْكُرْ ذَنْبًا، نَفْسِي نَفْسِي نَفْسِي، اذْهَبُوا إِلَى غَيْرِي اذْهَبُوا إِلَى مُحَمَّدٍ، فَيَأْتُونَ مُحَمَّدًا فَيَقُولُونَ: يَا مُحَمَّدُ أَنْتَ رَسُولُ اللهِ وَخَاتَمُ الْأَنْبِيَاءِ، وَقَدْ غَفَرَ اللهُ لَكَ مَا تَقَدَّمَ مِنْ ذَنْبِكَ وَمَا تَأَخَّرَ، فَاشْفَعْ لَنَا إِلَى رَبِّكَ

أَلَا تَرَى مَا نَحْنُ فِيهِ، أَلَا تَرَى مَا قَدْ بَلَغَنَا؟ فَأَقُومُ فَآتِي تَحْتَ الْعَرْشِ، فَأَقَعُ سَاجِدًا لِرَبِّي عَزَّ وَجَلَّ، ثُمَّ يَفْتَحُ اللهُ عَلَيَّ وَيُلْهِمُنِي مِنْ مَحَامِدِهِ وَحُسْنِ الثَّنَاءِ عَلَيْهِ مَا لَمْ يَفْتَحْهُ عَلَى أَحَدٍ قَبْلِي، فَيُقَالُ: يَا مُحَمَّدُ ارْفَعْ رَأْسَكَ وَسَلْ تُعْطَهُ، وَاشْفَعْ تُشَفَّعْ، فَأَرْفَعُ رَأْسِي فَأَقُولُ: أُمَّتِي يَا رَبِّ، أُمَّتِي يَا رَبِّ، أُمَّتِي يَا رَبِّ، فَيُقَالُ: يَا مُحَمَّدُ أَدْخِلْ مِنْ أُمَّتِكَ مَنْ لَا حِسَابَ عَلَيْهِ مِنَ الْبَابِ الْأَيْمَنِ مِنْ أَبْوَابِ الْجَنَّةِ، وَهُمْ شُرَكَاءُ النَّاسِ فِيمَا سِوَى ذَلِكَ مِنَ الْأَبْوَابِ، ثُمَّ قَالَ: وَالَّذِي نَفْسُ مُحَمَّدٍ بِيَدِهِ إِنَّ مَا بَيْنَ الْمِصْرَاعَيْنِ مِنْ مَصَارِيعِ الْجَنَّةِ كَمَا بَيْنَ مَكَّةَ وَهَجَرَ، أَوْ كَمَا بَيْنَ مَكَّةَ وَبُصْرَى»

(I will be the leader of mankind on the Day of Resurrection. Do you know why it will be so Allah will gather the first and the last in one place, and they will hear a voice calling out, and they will all be seen. The sun will come close until their anguish and distress becomes unbearable, and some will say to others, "Do you not see how much you are suffering Why do you not find someone to intercede for you with your Lord" And some of the people will say to others, "How about Adam" So they will go to Adam and say, "O Adam, you are the father of mankind, Allah created you with His Hand and breathed into you of His spirit, and commanded the angels to prostrate to you. Intercede for us with your Lord, do you not see the state we are in, how bad it is" Adam will say, "My Lord is angry today in a way that He has never been angry before and He will never be this angry again. He forbade me to approach the Tree and I disobeyed Him. Myself, myself, myself (i.e., I am only concerned about myself). Go to someone else. Go to Nuh." So they will go to Nuh and say, "O Nuh, you are the first of the Messengers sent to the people of earth, and Allah called you a grateful servant. Intercede for us with your Lord, do you not see the state we are in, how bad it is" Nuh will say, "My Lord is angry today in a way that He has never been angry before and He will never be this angry again. There is a prayer that I prayed against my people. Myself, myself, myself (i.e., I am only concerned about myself). Go to someone else. Go to Ibrahim. " So they will go to Ibrahim and say, "O Ibrahim, you are the Prophet of Allah and His close Friend among the people of earth. Intercede for us with your Lord, do you not see the state we are in, how bad it is" Ibrahim will say, "My Lord is angry today in a way that He has never been angry before and He will never be this angry again." And he mentioned some untruths he had told. "Myself, myself, myself (i.e., I am only concerned about myself). Go to someone else. Go to Musa."

So they will go to Musa and say, "O Musa, you are the Messenger of Allah, Allah chose you above others by selecting you to convey His Message and by speaking to you directly. Intercede for us with your Lord, do you not see the state we are in, how bad it is" Musa will say, "My Lord is angry today in a way that He has never been angry before and He will never be this angry again. I killed a soul whom I had not been commanded to kill. Myself, myself, myself (i.e., I am only concerned about myself). Go to someone else. Go to `Isa." So they will go to `Isa and say, `O `Isa, you are the Messenger of Allah and His Word which He bestowed upon Maryam and a spirit created by Him. You spoke to the people as an infant in the cradle. Intercede for us with your Lord, do you not see the state we are in, how bad it is" `Isa will say, "My Lord is angry today in a way that He has never been angry before and He will never be this angry again." And he will not mention any sin. "Myself, myself, myself (i.e., I am only concerned about myself). Go to someone else. Go to Muhammad." So they will go to Muhammad and will say, "O Muhammad, you are the Messenger of Allah and the Last of the Prophets, Allah forgave all your past and future sins. Intercede for us with your Lord, do you not see the state we are in, how bad it is" I will stand up and come before the Throne, and will fall prostrating to my Lord, may He be glorified and exalted. Then Allah will inspire me to speak and I will speak beautiful words of praise such as no one has ever been inspired with before. It will be said, "O Muhammad, raise your head and ask, it will be granted to you. Intercede, and your intercession will be heard." So I will raise my head and say, "My Ummah, O Lord, my Ummah, O Lord, my Ummah, O Lord." It will be said, "O Muhammad, admit those who will not be brought to account from among your Ummah through the right-hand gate of Paradise. Then the rest of your Ummah will share the other gates with the rest of the people.") Then he said, ("By the One in Whose Hand is the soul of Muhammad, the distance between two of the gateposts of Paradise is like the distance between Makkah and Hajar, or between Makkah and Busra.) It was also reported in the Two Sahihs.

Surah: 17 Ayah: 80 & Ayah: 81

وَقُل رَّبِّ أَدْخِلْنِي مُدْخَلَ صِدْقٍ وَأَخْرِجْنِي مُخْرَجَ صِدْقٍ وَاجْعَل لِّي مِن لَّدُنكَ سُلْطَانًا نَّصِيرًا ۝

80. And say (O Muhammad (peace be upon him)) My Lord! Let my entry (to the city of Al-Madinah) be good, and (likewise) my exit (from the city of Makkah) be good. And grant me from You an authority to help me (or a firm sign or a proof).

وَقُلْ جَاءَ الْحَقُّ وَزَهَقَ الْبَاطِلُ إِنَّ الْبَاطِلَ كَانَ زَهُوقًا ۝

81. And say: "Truth (i.e. Islâmic Monotheism or this Qur'ân or Jihâd against polytheists) has come and Bâtil (falsehood, i.e. Satan or polytheism) has vanished. Surely! Bâtil is ever bound to vanish."

Transliteration

80. Waqul rabbi adkhilnee mudkhala sidqin waakhrijnee mukhraja sidqin waijAAal lee min ladunka sultanan naseeran 81. Waqul jaa alhaqqu wazahaqa albatilu inna albatila kana zahooqan

Tafsir Ibn Kathir

The Command to emigrate

Imam Ahmad recorded that Ibn `Abbas said: The Prophet was in Makkah, then he was commanded to emigrate, and Allah revealed the words:

(And say: "My Lord! Let my entry be good, and (likewise) my exit be good. And grant me from You a helping authority.") At-Tirmidhi said, "This is Hasan Sahih." Al-Hasan Al-Basri commented on this Ayah, "When the disbelievers of Makkah conspired to kill the Messenger of Allah , or expel him or imprison him, Allah wanted him to fight the people of Makkah, and commanded him to go to Al-Madinah. What Allah said was:

(And say: "My Lord! Let my entry be good, and (likewise) my exit be good...")

(And say: "My Lord! Let my entry be good...") means, my entry to Al-Madinah.

(and (likewise) my exit be good,) means, my exit from Makkah. This was also the view of `Abdur-Rahman bin Zayd bin Aslam.

(And grant me from You a helping authority.) Al-Hasan Al-Basri explained this Ayah; "His Lord promised to take away the kingdom and glory of Persia and give it to him, and the kingdom and glory of Byzantium and give it to him." Qatadah said, "The Prophet of Allah knew that that he could not achieve this without authority or power, so he asked for authority to help him support the Book of Allah, the Laws of Allah, the obligations of Allah and to establish the religion of Allah. Authority is a mercy from Allah which He places among His servants, otherwise some of them would attack others, and the strong would consume the weak." Alongside the truth, he also needed power and authority in order to suppress those who opposed and resisted him, hence Allah said:

(Indeed We have sent Our Messengers with clear proofs,) until His saying,

(And We brought forth iron) (57:25)

A Threat to the Disbelievers of the Quraysh

(And say: "Truth has come and falsehood has vanished...") This is a threat and a warning to the disbelievers of the Quraysh, for there has come to them from Allah the truth of which there can be no doubt and which they have no power to resist. This is what Allah has sent to them of the Qur'an, faith and beneficial knowledge. Their falsehood has perished or vanished and been destroyed, it cannot remain or stand firm in the face of the truth.

Nay, We fling the truth against the falsehood, so it destroys it, and behold, it disappears. Al-Bukhari recorded that `Abdullah bin Mas`ud said: The Prophet entered Makkah (at the Con- quest), and around the House (the Ka`bah) were three hundred and sixty idols. He started to strike them with a stick in his hand, saying,

(Truth has come and falsehood has vanished. Surely falsehood is ever bound to vanish.) (17:81)

(Truth has come, and falsehood can neither create anything nor resurrect (anything).) (34:49)

Surah: 17 Ayah: 82

وَنُنَزِّلُ مِنَ ٱلْقُرْءَانِ مَا هُوَ شِفَآءٌ وَرَحْمَةٌ لِّلْمُؤْمِنِينَ وَلَا يَزِيدُ ٱلظَّٰلِمِينَ إِلَّا خَسَارًا

82. And We send down from the Qur'ân that which is a healing and a mercy to those who believe (in Islâmic Monotheism and act on it), and it increases the Zâlimûn (polytheists and wrong-doers) nothing but loss.

Transliteration

82. Wanunazzilu mina alqur-ani ma huwa shifaon warahmatun lilmu/mineena wala yazeedu alththalimeena illa khasaran

Tafsir Ibn Kathir

The Qur'an is a Cure and a Mercy

Allah tells us that His Book, which He has revealed to His Messenger Muhammad, the Qur'an to which falsehood cannot come, from before it or behind it, (it is) sent down by the All-Wise, Worthy of all praise, is a cure and a mercy for the believers, meaning that it takes away whatever is in their hearts of doubt, hypocrisy, Shirk, confusion and inclination towards falsehood. The Qur'an cures all of that. It is also a mercy through which one attains faith and wisdom and seeks goodness. This is only for those who believe in it and accept it as truthful, it is a cure and a mercy only for such people. As for the disbeliever who is wronging himself by his disbelief, when he hears the Qur'an, it only makes him further from the truth and increases him in his disbelief. The problem lies with the disbeliever himself, not with the Qur'an, as Allah says:

(Say: "It is for those who believe, a guide and a cure. And as for those who disbelieve, there is heaviness in their ears, and it is blindness for them. They are those who are called from a place far away (so they neither listen nor understand).") (41:44)

(And whenever there comes down a Surah, some of them (hypocrites) say: "Which of you has had his faith increased by it" As for those who believe, it has increased their faith, and they rejoice. But as for those in whose hearts is a disease, it will add suspicion and doubt to their suspicion, disbelief and doubt; and they die while they are disbelievers.) (9:124-125) And there are many other similar Ayat.

(And We send down of the Qur'an that which is a cure and a mercy to the believers,) Qatadah said, "When the believer hears it, he benefits from it and memorizes it and understands it."

(and it increases the wrongdoers in nothing but loss.) They do not benefit from it or memorize it or understand it, for Allah has made this Qur'an a cure and a mercy for the believers.

Surah: 17 Ayah: 83 & Ayah: 84

وَإِذَآ أَنْعَمْنَا عَلَى ٱلْإِنسَٰنِ أَعْرَضَ وَنَـَٔا بِجَانِبِهِۦ وَإِذَا مَسَّهُ ٱلشَّرُّ كَانَ يَـُٔوسًا ۝

83. And when We bestow Our Grace on man (the disbeliever), he turns away and becomes arrogant, far away from the Right Path. And when evil touches him, he is in great despair.

قُلْ كُلٌّ يَعْمَلُ عَلَىٰ شَاكِلَتِهِۦ فَرَبُّكُمْ أَعْلَمُ بِمَنْ هُوَ أَهْدَىٰ سَبِيلًا ۝

84. Say (O Muhammad (peace be upon him) to mankind): "Each one does according to Shakilatihi (i.e. his way or his religion or his intentions), and your Lord knows best of him whose path (religion) is right."

Transliteration

83. Wa-itha anAAamna AAala al-insani aAArada wanaa bijanibihi wa-itha massahu alshsharru kana yaoosan 84. Qul kullun yaAAmalu AAala shakilatihi farabbukum aAAlamu biman huwa ahda sabeelan

Tafsir Ibn Kathir

Turning away from Allah at Times of Ease and despairing at Times of Calamity

Allah tells us about the weakness that is inherent in man, except for those whom He protects at both times of ease and calamity. If Allah blesses a man with wealth, good health, ease, provision and help, and he gets what he wants, he turns away from the obedience and worship of Allah, and becomes arrogant. Mujahid said, "(It means) he goes away from Us." I say, this is like the Ayah:

(But when We have removed his harm from him, he passes on as if he had never invoked Us for a harm that touched him!) (10:12) and;

(But when He brings you safe to land, you turn away.) When man is stricken with evil, which means disasters, accidents and calamities,

(he is in great despair.), meaning that he thinks he will never have anything good again. As Allah says,

(And if We give man a taste of mercy from Us, and remove it from him, verily, He is despairing, ungrateful. But if We let him taste good after evil has touched him, he is sure to say: "Ills have departed from me." Surely, he is exultant, and boastful. Except those who show patience and do righteous good deeds: those, theirs will be forgiveness and a great reward.) (11:9-11)

(Say: "Each one does according to Shakilatihi...") Ibn `Abbas said, "According to his inclinations." Mujahid said, "According to his inclinations and his nature." Qatadah said, "According to his intentions." Ibn Zayd said, "According to his religion." All these suggestions are close in meaning. This Ayah - and Allah knows best - is a threat and a warning to the idolators, like the Ayah:

(And say to those who do not believe: "Act according to your ability and way") (11:121) So Allah says:

(Say: "Each one does according to Shakilatihi, and your Lord knows best of him whose path is right.") meaning either us or you. Everyone will be rewarded in accordance with his deeds, for nothing whatsoever is hidden from Allah.

Surah: 17 Ayah: 85

وَيَسْأَلُونَكَ عَنِ ٱلرُّوحِ قُلِ ٱلرُّوحُ مِنْ أَمْرِ رَبِّى وَمَآ أُوتِيتُم مِّنَ ٱلْعِلْمِ إِلَّا قَلِيلًا ﴿٨٥﴾

85. And they ask you (O Muhammad (peace be upon him)) concerning the Rûh (the Spirit); Say: "The Rûh (the Spirit): it is one of the things, the knowledge of which is only with my Lord. And of knowledge, you (mankind) have been given only a little."

Transliteration

85. Wayas-aloonaka AAani alrroohi quli alrroohu min amri rabbee wama ooteetum mina alAAilmi illa qaleelan

Tafsir Ibn Kathir

The Ruh (spirit)

Al-Bukhari recorded in his Tafsir of this Ayah that `Abdullah bin Mas`ud said, "While I was walking with the Prophet on a farm, and he was resting on a palm-leaf stalk, some Jews passed by. Some of them said to the others, `Ask him about the Ruh.' Some of them said, `What urges you to ask him about that' Others said, `Do not ask him, lest he gives you a reply which you do not like.' But they said, `Ask him.' So they asked him about the Ruh. The Prophet kept quiet and did not give them an answer, and I knew that he was receiving revelation, so I stayed where I was. When the revelation was complete, the Prophet said:

(And they ask you concerning the Ruh (the spirit). Say: "The Ruh (the spirit) is one of the things, the knowledge of which is only with my Lord...") This context would seem to imply that this Ayah was revealed in Al-Madinah, and that it was revealed when the Jews asked him this question in Al-Madinah, although the entire Surah was revealed in Makkah. This may be answered with the suggestion that this Ayah may have been revealed to him in Al-Madinah a second time, after having previously been revealed in Makkah, or that he was divinely inspired to respond to their question with a previously-revealed Ayah, namely the Ayah in question. Ibn Jarir recorded that `Ikrimah said, "The People of the Book asked the Messenger of Allah about the Ruh, and Allah revealed:

(And they ask you concerning the Ruh...) They said, `You claim that we have only a little knowledge, but we have been given the Tawrah, which is the Hikmah,

(and he, to whom Hikmah is granted, is indeed granted abundant good.)' (2:269) Then the Ayah

(And if all the trees on the earth were pens and the sea (were ink wherewith to write), with seven seas behind it to add to its (supply),) (31:27) was revealed. He said, "Whatever knowledge you have been given, if Allah saves you from the Fire thereby, then it is great and good, but in comparison to the knowledge of Allah, it is very little."

(And they ask you concerning the Ruh.) Al-`Awfi reported that Ibn `Abbas said, "This was when the Jews said to the Prophet , `Tell us about the Ruh and how the Ruh will be punished that is in the body - for the Ruh is something about which only Allah knows, and there was no revelation concerning it.' He did not answer them at all, then Jibril came to him and said:

(Say: "The Ruh (the spirit) is one of the things, the knowledge of which is only with my Lord. And of knowledge, you (mankind) have been given only a little.") So the Prophet told them about that, and they said, `Who told you this' He said,

》جَاءَنِي بِهِ جِبْرِيلُ مِنْ عِنْدِ اللهِ《

(Jibril brought it to me from Allah.) They said, `By Allah, no one has told you that except our enemy (i.e., Jibril).' Then Allah revealed:

(Say: "Whoever is an enemy to Jibril (let him die in his fury), for indeed he has brought it (this Qur'an) down to your heart by Allah's permission, confirming what came before it.)" (2:97)

The Ruh and the Nafs

As-Suhayili mentioned the dispute among the scholars over whether the Ruh is the same as the Nafs, or something different. He stated that it is light and soft, like air, flowing through the body like water through the veins of a tree. He states that the Ruh which the angel breathes into the fetus is the Nafs, provided that it joins the body and acquires certain qualities because of it, whether good or bad. So then it is either a soul in (complete) rest and satisfaction (89:27) or inclined to evil (12:53), just as water is the life of the tree, then by mixing with it, it produces something else, so that if it mixes with grapes and the grapes are then squeezed, it becomes juice or wine. Then it is no longer called water, except in a metaphorical sense. Thus we should understand the connection between Nafs and Ruh; the Ruh is not called Nafs except when it joins the body and is affected by it. So in conclusion we may say: the Ruh is the origin and essence, and the Nafs consists of the Ruh and its connection to the body. So they are the same in one sense but not in another. This is a good explanation, and Allah knows best. I say: people speak about the essence of the Ruh and its rulings, and many books have been written on this topic. One of the best of those who spoke of this was Al-Hafiz Ibn Mandah in a book which we have heard about the Ruh.

Surah: 17 Ayah: 86, Ayah: 87, Ayah: 88 & Ayah: 89

وَلَئِن شِئْنَا لَنَذْهَبَنَّ بِالَّذِىٓ أَوْحَيْنَآ إِلَيْكَ ثُمَّ لَا تَجِدُ لَكَ بِهِۦ عَلَيْنَا وَكِيلًا ﴿٨٦﴾

86. And if We willed We could surely take away that which We have revealed to you by inspiration (i.e. this Qur'ân). Then you would find no protector for you against Us in that respect.

إِلَّا رَحْمَةً مِّن رَّبِّكَ إِنَّ فَضْلَهُۥ كَانَ عَلَيْكَ كَبِيرًا ﴿٨٧﴾

87. Except as a Mercy from your Lord. Verily! His Grace unto you (O Muhammad (peace be upon him)) is ever great.

قُل لَّئِنِ ٱجْتَمَعَتِ ٱلْإِنسُ وَٱلْجِنُّ عَلَىٰٓ أَن يَأْتُوا۟ بِمِثْلِ هَـٰذَا ٱلْقُرْءَانِ لَا يَأْتُونَ بِمِثْلِهِۦ وَلَوْ كَانَ بَعْضُهُمْ لِبَعْضٍ ظَهِيرًا ﴿٨٨﴾

88. Say: "If the mankind and the jinn were together to produce the like of this Qur'ân, they could not produce the like thereof, even if they helped one another."

وَلَقَدْ صَرَّفْنَا لِلنَّاسِ فِى هَـٰذَا ٱلْقُرْءَانِ مِن كُلِّ مَثَلٍ فَأَبَىٰٓ أَكْثَرُ ٱلنَّاسِ إِلَّا كُفُورًا ﴿٨٩﴾

89. And indeed We have fully explained to mankind, in this Qur'ân, every kind of similitude, but most of mankind refuse (the truth and accept nothing) but disbelief.

Transliteration

86. Wala-in shi/na lanathhabanna biallathee awhayna ilayka thumma la tajidu laka bihi AAalayna wakeelan 87. Illa rahmatan min rabbika inna fadlahu kana AAalayka kabeeran 88. Qul la-ini ijtamaAAati al-insu waaljinnu AAala an ya/too bimithli hatha alqur-ani la ya/toona bimithlihi walaw kana baAAduhum libaAAdin thaheeran 89. Walaqad sarrafna lilnnasi fee hatha alqur-ani min kulli mathalin faaba aktharu alnnasi illa kufooran

Tafsir Ibn Kathir

If Allah willed, He could take away the Qur'an

Allah mentions the blessing and great bounty that He has bestowed upon His servant and Messenger Muhammad by revealing to Him the Noble Qur'an to which falsehood cannot come, from before it or behind it, (it is) sent down by the All-Wise, Worthy of all praise. Ibn Mas`ud said, "A red wind will come to the people, meaning at the end of time, from the direction of Syria, and there will be nothing left in a man's Mushaf (copy of the Qur'an) or in his heart, not even one Ayah." Then Ibn Mas`ud recited:

(And if We willed, We could surely take away that which We have revealed to you.)

Challenging by the Qur'an

Then Allah points out the great virtue of the Qur'an, and says that even if mankind and the Jinn were all to come together and agree to produce something like that which was revealed to His Messenger, they would never be able to do it, even if they were to cooperate and support and help one another. This is something which is impossible. How could the words of created beings be like the Words of the Creator Who has no equal and peer, for there is none like unto Him

(And indeed We have fully explained to man- kind,) meaning, `We have furnished them with evidence and defini- tive proof, and We have shown them the truth and explained it in detail, yet despite that most of mankind insist on disbelief, i.e., denying and rejecting the truth.'

Surah: 17 Ayah: 90, Ayah: 91, Ayah: 92 & Ayah: 93

وَقَالُوا۟ لَن نُّؤْمِنَ لَكَ حَتَّىٰ تَفْجُرَ لَنَا مِنَ ٱلْأَرْضِ يَنۢبُوعًا ۝

90. And they say: "We shall not believe in you (O Muhammad (peace be upon him)) until you cause a spring to gush forth from the earth for us;

أَوْ تَكُونَ لَكَ جَنَّةٌ مِّن نَّخِيلٍ وَعِنَبٍ فَتُفَجِّرَ ٱلْأَنْهَٰرَ خِلَٰلَهَا تَفْجِيرًا ۝

91. "Or you have a garden of date-palms and grapes, and cause rivers to gush forth in their midst abundantly;

أَوْ تُسْقِطَ ٱلسَّمَآءَ كَمَا زَعَمْتَ عَلَيْنَا كِسَفًا أَوْ تَأْتِىَ بِٱللَّهِ وَٱلْمَلَٰٓئِكَةِ قَبِيلًا ۝

92. "Or you cause the heaven to fall upon us in pieces, as you have pretended, or you bring Allâh and the angels before (us) face to face;

أَوْ يَكُونَ لَكَ بَيْتٌ مِّن زُخْرُفٍ أَوْ تَرْقَىٰ فِى ٱلسَّمَآءِ وَلَن نُّؤْمِنَ لِرُقِيِّكَ حَتَّىٰ تُنَزِّلَ عَلَيْنَا كِتَٰبًا نَّقْرَؤُهُۥ ۗ قُلْ سُبْحَانَ رَبِّى هَلْ كُنتُ إِلَّا بَشَرًا رَّسُولًا ۝

93. "Or you have a house of Zukhruf (like silver and pure gold), or you ascend up into the sky, and even then we will put no faith in your ascension until you bring

down for us a Book that we would read." Say (O Muhammad (peace be upon him)) "Glorified (and Exalted) is my Lord (Allâh) above all that evil they (polytheists) associate with Him! Am I anything but a man, sent as a Messenger?"

Transliteration

90. Waqaloo lan nu/mina laka hatta tafjura lana mina al-ardi yanbooAAan 91. Aw takoona laka jannatun min nakheelin waAAinabin fatufajjira al-anhara khilalaha tafjeeran 92. Aw tusqita alssamaa kama zaAAamta AAalayna kisafan aw ta/tiya biAllahi waalmala-ikati qabeelan 93. Aw yakoona laka baytun min zukhrufin aw tarqa fee alssama-i walan nu/mina liruqiyyika hatta tunazzila AAalayna kitaban naqraohu qul subhana rabbee hal kuntu illa basharan rasoolan

Tafsir Ibn Kathir

The Demand of Quraysh for a specific Sign, and the Rejection of that

Ibn Jarir recorded from Muhammad bin Ishaq, "An old man from among the people of Egypt who came to us forty-odd years ago told me, from `Ikrimah, from Ibn `Abbas, that `Utbah and Shaybah -- the two sons of Rabi'ah, Abu Sufyan bin Harb, a man from Bani `Abd Ad-Dar, Abu Al-Bakhtari -- the brother of Bani Asad, Al-Aswad bin Al-Muttalib bin Asad, Zam`ah bin Al-Aswad, Al-Walid bin Al-Mughirah, Abu Jahl bin Hisham, `Abdullah bin Abi Umayyah, Umayyah bin Khalaf, Al-`As bin Wa'il, and Nabih and Munabbih - the two sons of Al-Hajjaj As-Sahmin, gathered all of them or some of them behind the Ka`bah after sunset. Some of them said to others, `Send for Muhammad and talk with him and argue with him, so that nobody will think we are to blame.' So they sent for him saying, `The nobles of your people have gathered for you to speak to them.' So the Messenger of Allah came quickly, thinking that maybe they were going to change their minds, for he was very keen that they should be guided, and it upset him to see their stubbornness. So he came and sat with them, and they said, `O Muhammad, we have sent for you so that nobody will think we are to blame. By Allah we do not know any man among the Arabs who has brought to his people what you have brought to your people. You have slandered our forefathers, criticized our religion, insulted our reason, slandered our gods and caused division. There is no objectionable thing that you have not brought between us. If you are preaching these things because you want wealth, we will collect some of our wealth together for you and make you the wealthiest man among us.

Untitled

If you are looking for position, we will make you our leader. If you are looking for kingship, we will make you our king. If what has come to you is a type of Jinn that has possessed you, then we can spend our money looking for the medicine that will rid you of it so that no one will think we are to blame.' The Messenger of Allah said:

«مَا بِي مَا تَقُولُونَ، مَا جِئْتُكُمْ بِمَا جِئْتُكُمْ بِهِ أَطْلُبُ أَمْوَالَكُمْ، وَلَا الشَّرَفَ فِيكُمْ، وَلَا الْمُلْكَ عَلَيْكُمْ، وَلَكِنَّ اللَّهَ بَعَثَنِي إِلَيْكُمْ رَسُولًا وَأَنْزَلَ عَلَيَّ كِتَابًا، وَأَمَرَنِي أَنْ أَكُونَ لَكُمْ بَشِيرًا وَنَذِيرًا، فَبَلَّغْتُكُمْ رِسَالَاتِ رَبِّي وَنَصَحْتُ لَكُمْ، فَإِنْ تَقْبَلُوا مِنِّي مَا جِئْتُكُمْ بِهِ فَهُوَ حَظُّكُمْ فِي الدُّنْيَا وَالْآخِرَةِ، وَإِنْ تَرُدُّوهُ عَلَيَّ أَصْبِرْ لِأَمْرِ اللَّهِ حَتَّى يَحْكُمَ اللَّهُ بَيْنِي وَبَيْنَكُمْ»

(My case is not as you say. I have not brought what I have brought to you because I want your wealth or to be your leader or king. But Allah has sent me to you as a Messenger and has revealed to me a Book and has commanded me to bring you good news and a warning. So, I have conveyed to you the Messages of my Lord and have advised you accordingly. If you accept what I have brought to you, then this is your good fortune in this world and the Hereafter, but if you reject it, I shall wait patiently for the command of Allah until Allah judges between me and you.) or words to that effect. They said, `O Muhammad, if you do not accept what we have offered you, then you know that there is no other people whose country is smaller, whose wealth is less and whose life is harder than ours, so ask your Lord Who has sent you with what He has sent you, to move away these mountains for us that are constricting us, to make our land wider and cause rivers to gush forth in it like the rivers of Syria and Iraq, and to resurrect for us those of our forefathers who have passed away.

Untitled

Let there be among those whom He resurrects Qusayy bin Kilab, for he was a truthful old man, and we will ask them whether what you are saying is true or false. If you do what we are asking, and they (the people who are resurrected) say that you are telling the truth, then we will believe you and acknowledge your status with Allah and believe that He has sent you as a Messenger as you say.' The Messenger of Allah said to them:

«مَا بِهَذَا بُعِثْتُ، إِنَّمَا جِئْتُكُمْ مِنْ عِنْدِ اللَّهِ بِمَا بَعَثَنِي بِهِ، فَقَدْ بَلَّغْتُكُمْ مَا أُرْسِلْتُ بِهِ إِلَيْكُمْ، فَإِنْ تَقْبَلُوهُ فَهُوَ حَظُّكُمْ فِي الدُّنْيَا وَالْآخِرَةِ، وَإِنْ تَرُدُّوهُ عَلَيَّ أَصْبِرْ لِأَمْرِ اللَّهِ حَتَّى يَحْكُمَ اللَّهُ بَيْنِي وَبَيْنَكُمْ»

(I was not sent for this purpose. I have brought to you from Allah that with which He has sent me, and I have conveyed to you the Message with which I was sent to you. If you accept what I have brought to you, then this is your good fortune in this world and the Hereafter, but if you reject it, I shall wait patiently for the command of Allah until Allah judges between me and you.) They said, `If you will not do this for us, then at least do something for yourself. Ask your Lord to send an angel to confirm that what you are saying is the truth and to speak up on your behalf. Ask Him to give you gardens and treasures and palaces of gold and silver, and to make you independent so that you will not have to do what we see you doing, for you stand in the marketplaces seeking provision just as we do. Then we will know the virtue of your position with your Lord and whether you are a Messenger as you claim.' The Messenger of Allah said to them:

»مَا أَنَا بِفَاعِلٍ، مَا أَنَا بِالَّذِي يَسْأَلُ رَبَّهُ هَذَا، وَمَا بُعِثْتُ إِلَيْكُمْ بِهَذَا، وَلَكِنَّ اللهَ بَعَثَنِي بَشِيرًا وَنَذِيرًا، فَإِنْ تَقْبَلُوا مَا جِئْتُكُمْ بِهِ، فَهُوَ حَظُّكُمْ فِي الدُّنْيَا وَالْآخِرَةِ، وَإِنْ تَرُدُّوهُ عَلَيَّ أَصْبِرْ لِأَمْرِ اللهِ حَتَّى يَحْكُمَ اللهُ بَيْنِي وَبَيْنَكَ«

(I will not do that, and I will not ask my Lord for this. I was not sent to you for this reason. But Allah has sent me to you to bring you good news and a warning. If you accept what I have brought to you, then this is your good fortune in this world and the Hereafter, but if you reject it, I shall wait patiently for the command of Allah until Allah judges between me and you.) They said, `Then cause the sky to fall upon us, as you claim that if your Lord wills, He can do that. We will not believe in you until you do this.' The Messenger of Allah said to them:

»ذَلِكَ إِلَى اللهِ، إِنْ شَاءَ فَعَلَ بِكُمْ ذَلِكَ«

(That is for Allah to decide. If He wills, He will do that to you.) They said, `O Muhammad, did your Lord not know that we would sit with you and ask you what we have asked and make the requests that we have made He should have told you beforehand and taught you how to reply to us, and informed you what He would do to us if we do not accept what you have brought to us. We have heard that the one who is teaching you this, is a man in Al-Yamamah called Ar-Rahman. By Allah, we will never believe in Ar-Rahman. We are warning you, O Muhammad, that we will not let you do what you want to do until you or we are destroyed.' One of them said, `We worship the angels who are the daughters of Allah.' Another said, `We will never believe in you until you bring Allah and the angels before (us) face to face.' When they said this, the Messenger of Allah got up and left them. `Abdullah bin Abi Umayyah bin Al-Mughirah bin `Abdullah bin `Umar bin

Makhzum, the son of his paternal aunt `Atikah, the daughter of `Abdul-Muttalib, also got up and followed him. He said to him, `O Muhammad, your people have offered you what they have offered you, and you did not accept it. Then they asked for things for themselves so that they would know your position with Allah, and you did not do that for them. Then they asked you to hasten on the punishments with which you are scaring them. By Allah, I will never believe in you unless you take a ladder to heaven and ascend it while I am watching, then you bring with you an open book and four angels to testify that you are as you say. By Allah, even if you did that, I think that I would not believe you.' Then he turned away from the Messenger of Allah , and the Messenger of Allah went home to his family, grieving over having missed out on what he had hoped for when his people had called him, because he saw that they were resisting him even more.''

The Reason why the Idolators' Demands were refused

In the case of this gathering where the Quraysh came together to speak with the Messenger of Allah , if Allah knew that they were making these requests in order to be guided, they would have been granted, but He knew that they were making these demands out of disbelief and stubbornness. It was said to the Messenger of Allah , "If you wish, We will give them what they are asking, but if they then disbelieve, I will punish them with a punishment that I have never imposed upon anyone else in the universe; or if you wish, I will open for them the gate of repentance and mercy." He said:

«بَلْ تَفْتَحُ عَلَيْهِمْ بَابَ التَّوْبَةِ وَالرَّحْمَةِ»

(Rather, You open for them the gate of repentance and mercy.) This is like the Ayah:

(And nothing stops Us from sending the Ayat but that the people of old denied them. And We sent the she-camel to Thamud as a clear sign, but they did her wrong. And We sent not the signs except to warn, and to make them afraid (of destruction).) (17:59) And Allah says:

(And they say: "Why does this Messenger eat food, and walk about in the markets (as we). Why is not an angel sent down to him to be a warner with him Or (why) has not a treasure been granted to him, or why has he not a garden whereof he may eat'' And the wrongdoers say: "You follow none but a man bewitched.'' See how they coin similitudes for you, so they have gone astray, and they cannot find a path. Blessed be He Who, if He wills, will assign you better than that - Gardens under which rivers flow and will assign you palaces. Nay, they deny the Hour, and for those who deny the Hour, We have prepared a flaming Fire.) (25:7-11) Allah's saying,

(until you cause a spring to gush forth from the earth for us) refers to a spring of flowing water. They asked him to bring forth springs of fresh water in the land of Al-Hijaz, here and there. This is easy for Allah, may He be glorified and exalted; if He

Chapter 17: Al-Israa (The Night Journey or Bani Isra'il), Verses 001-111

willed, He could do that. He could have responded to all their demands, but He knew that they would not be guided by that, as He says:

(Truly, those, against whom the Word (wrath) of your Lord has been justified, will not believe. Even if every sign should come to them, until they see the painful torment.) (10:96-97) And Allah says:

(And even if We had sent down unto them angels, and the dead had spoken unto them, and We had gathered together all things before their very eyes, they would not have believed) (6:111) His saying;

(Or you cause the heaven to fall upon us in pieces, as you have pretended,) means, `you promised us that on the Day of Resurrection the heavens will be split asunder, being broken and torn up, with parts of it falling down, so do that in this world and make it fall in pieces.' This is like when they said:

(O Allah! If this (the Qur'an) is indeed the truth from You, then rain down stones on us from the sky.) (8:32) Similarly, the people of Shu`ayb asked him:

(So cause a piece of the heaven to fall on us, if you are of the truthful!) (26:187) So Allah punished them with the punishment of the day of Shadow (a gloomy cloud), which was the torment of a Great Day. (26:189) As for the Prophet of Repentance and Mercy, who was sent as a mercy to the worlds, he asked Allah to delay their punishment, in the hope that Allah would bring forth from their offspring people who would worship Allah Alone, with no partner or associate. This is what indeed did happen, for among those who are mentioned above were some who later embraced Islam and became good and sincere Muslims, even `Abdullah bin Abi Umayyah, who followed the Prophet (out of that meeting) and spoke to him as he did. He became a sincere Muslim and turned to Allah in repentance.

(Or you have a house of Zukhruf.) Ibn `Abbas, Mujahid and Qatadah said, "This is gold." This was also what was said in the recitation of Ibn Mas`ud, "Or you have a house of gold."

(or you ascend up into the sky,) meaning, you climb up on a ladder while we are watching you.

(and even then we will put no faith in your ascension until you bring down for us a Book that we would read.) Mujahid said, "This means a book in which there would be one page for each person, on which would be the words: `This is a book from Allah to so-and-so the son of so-and-so, which he would find by his head when he woke up in the morning."

(Say: "Glorified be my Lord! Am I anything but a man, sent as a Messenger") meaning, `Glorified, exalted and sanctified be He above the notion that anyone would come before Him concerning any matter pertaining to His authority and sovereignty. He is the One Who does what He wills. If He willed, he could have given you what you asked for, or if He willed, he could have refrained. I am only a Messenger to you, sent to convey the Messages of my Lord and advise you. I have done that, and the response to what you have asked is to be decided by Allah, may He be glorified.'

Surah: 17 Ayah: 94 & Ayah: 95

وَمَا مَنَعَ ٱلنَّاسَ أَن يُؤْمِنُوٓا۟ إِذْ جَآءَهُمُ ٱلْهُدَىٰٓ إِلَّآ أَن قَالُوٓا۟ أَبَعَثَ ٱللَّهُ بَشَرًا رَّسُولًا ۝

94. And nothing prevented men from believing when the guidance came to them, except that they said: "Has Allâh sent a man as (His) Messenger?"

قُل لَّوْ كَانَ فِى ٱلْأَرْضِ مَلَٰٓئِكَةٌ يَمْشُونَ مُطْمَئِنِّينَ لَنَزَّلْنَا عَلَيْهِم مِّنَ ٱلسَّمَآءِ مَلَكًا رَّسُولًا ۝

95. Say: "If there were on the earth, angels walking about in peace and security, We should certainly have sent down for them from the heaven an angel as a Messenger."

Transliteration

94. Wama manaAAa alnnasa an yu/minoo ith jaahumu alhuda illa an qaloo abaAAatha Allahu basharan rasoolan 95. Say: "If there were on the earth, angels walking about in peace and security, We should certainly have sent down for them from the heaven an angel as a Messenger."

Tafsir Ibn Kathir

The refusal of the Idolators to believe because the Messenger was a Human -- and its refutation

(And nothing prevented men) means, most of them,

(from believing) and following the Messengers, except the fact that they found it strange that human beings would be sent as Messengers, as Allah says:

(Is it a wonder for mankind that We have sent Our revelation to a man from among themselves (saying): "Warn mankind, and give good news to those who believe that they shall have with their Lord the rewards of their good deeds") (10:2) And Allah says:

(That was because there came to them their Messengers with clear proofs, but they said: "Shall mere men guide us") (64:6) Fira`wn and his people said:

(They said: "Shall we believe in two men like ourselves, and their people are obedient to us with humility!") (23: 47) Similarly, the nations said to their Messengers:

("You are no more than human beings like us! You wish to turn us away from what our fathers used to worship. Then bring us a clear authority") (14:10) And there are many other similar Ayat. Then Allah says, pointing out His kindness and mercy towards His servants, that He sends to them Messengers of their own kind so that they will understand what he says and will be able to speak to him directly. If He sent to mankind a Messenger from among the angels, they would not be able to deal with him face to face and learn from him, as Allah says:

(Indeed, Allah conferred a great favor on the believers when He sent among them a Messenger from among themselves) (3:164)

(Verily, there has come unto you a Messenger from among yourselves) (10:128)

(Similarly, We have sent among you a Messenger of your own, reciting to you Our verses (the Qur'an) and purifying you, and teaching you the Book and the Hikmah, and teaching you that which you used not to know. Therefore remember Me. I will remember you, and be grateful to Me and never be ungrateful to Me.) (2:151-152)
Allah says here:

(Say: "If there were on the earth, angels walking about in peace and security,) meaning, just as you do,

(We should certainly have sent down for them from the heaven an angel as a Messenger). meaning, `one of their own kind. But as you are human, We have sent to you Messengers from yourselves, as a kindness and a mercy.'

Surah: 17 Ayah: 96

قُل كَفَىٰ بِٱللَّهِ شَهِيدًۢا بَيۡنِى وَبَيۡنَكُمۡ إِنَّهُۥ كَانَ بِعِبَادِهِۦ خَبِيرًۢا بَصِيرًا ۝

96. Say: "Sufficient is Allâh for a witness between me and you. Verily! He is Ever the All-Knower, the All-Seer of His slaves."

Transliteration

96. Qul kafa biAllahi shaheedan baynee wabaynakum innahu kana biAAibadihi khabeeran baseeran

Tafsir Ibn Kathir

Allah tells His Prophet how to prove that what he has brought is true, saying to him to tell them: "He (Allah) is a witness over me and over you. He knows what I have brought to you. If I were lying to you, He would take revenge on me in the severest manner," as Allah says:

(And if he had forged a false saying concerning Us, We surely would have seized him by his right hand, And then We certainly would have cut off his life artery.) (69:44-46)
Allah said;

(Verily, He is Ever the All-Knower, the All-Seer of His servants.) meaning, He knows best who among them deserves blessings, good treatment and guidance, and who deserves to be doomed and led astray. He says:

Surah: 17 Ayah: 97

وَمَن يَهْدِ ٱللَّهُ فَهُوَ ٱلْمُهْتَدِ ۖ وَمَن يُضْلِلْ فَلَن تَجِدَ لَهُمْ أَوْلِيَآءَ مِن دُونِهِۦ ۖ وَنَحْشُرُهُمْ يَوْمَ ٱلْقِيَـٰمَةِ عَلَىٰ وُجُوهِهِمْ عُمْيًا وَبُكْمًا وَصُمًّا ۖ مَّأْوَىٰهُمْ جَهَنَّمُ ۖ كُلَّمَا خَبَتْ زِدْنَـٰهُمْ سَعِيرًا ۩

97. And he whom Allâh guides, he is led aright; but he whom He sends astray, for such you will find no Auliyâ' (helpers and protectors), besides Him, and We shall gather them together on the Day of Resurrection on their faces, blind, dumb and deaf; their abode will be Hell; whenever it abates, We shall increase for them the fierceness of the Fire.

Transliteration

97. Waman yahdi Allahu fahuwa almuhtadi waman yudlil falan tajida lahum awliyaa min doonihi wanahshuruhum yawma alqiyamati AAala wujoohihim AAumyan wabukman wasumman ma/wahum jahannamu kullama khabat zidnahum saAAeeran

Tafsir Ibn Kathir

Guidance and Misguidance are in the Hands of Allah

Allah tells us how He deals with His creation and how His rulings are carried out. He tells us that there is none who can put back His judgement, for whomever He guides cannot be led astray,

(and whomever He leaves astray can never find helpers other than Him) to guide him. As Allah says:

(He whom Allah guides, he is the rightly-guided; but he whom He sends astray, for him you will find no Wali (guiding friend) to lead him) (18:17)

The Punishment of the People of Misguidance

(and We shall gather them together on the Day of Resurrection on their faces,) Imam Ahmad recorded from Anas bin Malik that the Prophet was asked, "O Messenger of Allah, how will the people be gathered on their faces" He said,

«الَّذِي أَمْشَاهُمْ عَلَى أَرْجُلِهِمْ قَادِرٌ عَلَى أَنْ يُمْشِيَهُمْ عَلَى وُجُوهِهِم»

(The One Who made them walk on their feet is able to make them walk on their faces.) It was also reported (by Al-Bukhari and Muslim) in the Two Sahihs.

(blind) means, unable to see.

(dumb) means, unable to speak.

(deaf) means, unable to hear. They will be in this state as a punishment for the way they were in this world, blind, dumb and deaf to the truth. This will be their recompense when they are gathered on the Day of Resurrection, at the time when they need these faculties most of all.

(their abode) means, their destination.

(will be Hell; whenever it abates,) Ibn `Abbas said, "(This means) calms down," Mujahid said, (It means) is extinguished,"

(We shall increase for them the fierceness of the Fire.) meaning, increasing its flames and heat and coals, as Allah says:

(So taste you (the results of your evil actions). No increase shall We give you, except in torment.) (78:30)

Surah: 17 Ayah: 98 & Ayah: 99

ذَٰلِكَ جَزَآؤُهُم بِأَنَّهُمْ كَفَرُوا۟ بِـَٔايَٰتِنَا وَقَالُوٓا۟ أَءِذَا كُنَّا عِظَٰمًا وَرُفَٰتًا أَءِنَّا لَمَبْعُوثُونَ خَلْقًا جَدِيدًا ۝

98. That is their recompense, because they denied Our Ayât (proofs, evidences, verses, lessons, signs, revelations, etc.) and said: "When we are bones and fragments, shall we really be raised up as a new creation?"

۞ أَوَلَمْ يَرَوْا۟ أَنَّ ٱللَّهَ ٱلَّذِى خَلَقَ ٱلسَّمَٰوَٰتِ وَٱلْأَرْضَ قَادِرٌ عَلَىٰٓ أَن يَخْلُقَ مِثْلَهُمْ وَجَعَلَ لَهُمْ أَجَلًا لَّا رَيْبَ فِيهِ فَأَبَى ٱلظَّٰلِمُونَ إِلَّا كُفُورًا ۝

99. See they not that Allâh, Who created the heavens and the earth, is Able to create the like of them. And He has decreed for them an appointed term, whereof there is not doubt. But the Zâlimûn (polytheists and wrong-doers) refuse (the truth - the Message of Islâmic Monotheism, and accept nothing) but disbelief.

Transliteration

98. Thalika jazaohum bi-annahum kafaroo bi-ayatina waqaloo a-itha kunna AAithaman warufatan ainna lamabAAoothoona khalqan jadeedan 99. Awa lam yaraw anna Allaha allathee khalaqa alssamawati waal-arda qadirun AAala an yakhluqa mithlahum wajaAAala lahum ajalan la rayba feehi faaba alththalimoona illa kufooran

Tafsir Ibn Kathir

Allah says: `This punishment, being resurrected blind, dumb and deaf, is what they deserve, because they disbelieved,

(Our Ayat), i.e., Our proof and evidence, and did not think that the resurrection could ever happen.'

(and said: "When we are bones and fragments...") meaning, when we have disintegrated and our bodies have rotted away,

(shall we really be raised up as a new creation) meaning, after we have disintegrated and disappeared and been absorbed into the earth, will we come back a second time Allah established proof against them and told them that He is able to do that, for He created the heavens and the earth, so raising them up again is easier for Him than that, as He says:

(The creation of the heavens and the earth is indeed greater than the creation of mankind;) (40:57)

(Do they not see that Allah, Who created the heavens and the earth, and was not wearied by their creation, is able to give life to the dead) (46: 33)

(Is not He Who created the heavens and the earth, able to create the like of them Yes, indeed! He is the All-Knowing Supreme Creator. Verily, His command, when He intends a thing, is only that He says to it, "Be!" and it is!) (36:81-82) And Allah says here:

(See they not that Allah, Who created the heavens and the earth, is able to create the like of them.) meaning, on the Day of Resurrection, He will recreate and restore their bodies, as He created them in the first place.

(And He has decreed for them an appointed term, whereof there is no doubt.) means, He has set a time for them to be re-created and brought forth from their graves, an appointed time which must surely come to pass. As Allah says:

(And We delay it only for a term (already) fixed.) (11:104)

(But the wrongdoers refuse) -- after the proof has been established against them,

((and accept nothing) but disbelief.) means, they persist in their falsehood and misguidance.

Surah: 17 Ayah: 100

قُل لَّوْ أَنتُمْ تَمْلِكُونَ خَزَآئِنَ رَحْمَةِ رَبِّى إِذًا لَّأَمْسَكْتُمْ خَشْيَةَ ٱلْإِنفَاقِ وَكَانَ ٱلْإِنسَـٰنُ قَتُورًا ۝

100. Say (to the disbelievers): "If you possessed the treasure of the Mercy of my Lord (wealth, money, provision.), then you would surely hold back (from spending) for fear of (being exhausted), and man is ever miserly!"

Transliteration

100. Qul law antum tamlikoona khaza-ina rahmati rabbee ithan laamsaktum khashyata al-infaqi wakana al-insanu qatooran

Chapter 17: Al-Israa (The Night Journey or Bani Isra'il), Verses 001-111

Tafsir Ibn Kathir

Holding back is Part of Man's Nature

Allah says to His Messenger : "Tell them, O Muhammad, even if you had authority over the treasures of Allah, you would refrain from spending for fear of exhausting it." Ibn `Abbas and Qatadah said, "This means for fear of poverty," lest it run out, despite the fact that it can never be exhausted or come to an end. This is because it is part of your nature. So Allah says:

(and man is ever miserly.) Ibn `Abbas and Qatadah said: "(This means) stingy and holding back." Allah says:

(Or have they a share in the dominion Then in that case they would not give mankind even a Naqira.) (4:53), meaning that even if they had a share in the authority of Allah, they would not have given anything to anyone, not even the amount of a Naqira (speck on the back of a date stone). Allah describes man as he really is, except for those whom Allah helps and guides. Miserliness, discontent and impatience are human characteristics, as Allah says:

(Verily, man was created very impatient; irritable when evil touches him; and stingy when good touches him. Except those who are devoted to Salah (prayers).) (70:19-22). And there are many other such references in the Qur'an. This is an indication of the generosity and kindness of Allah. In the Two Sahihs it says:

«يَدُ اللهِ مَلْأَى لَا يَغِيضُهَا نَفَقَةٌ سَحَّاءُ اللَّيْلَ وَالنَّهَارَ، أَرَأَيْتُمْ مَا أَنْفَقَ مُنْذُ خَلَقَ السَّمَوَاتِ وَالْأَرْضَ، فَإِنَّهُ لَمْ يَغِضْ مَا فِي يَمِينِهِ»

(Allah's Hand is full and never decreases because of His giving night and day. Do you not see how much He has given since He created the heavens and the earth, yet that which is in His right hand never decreases.)

Surah: 17 Ayah: 101, Ayah: 102, Ayah: 103 & Ayah: 104

وَلَقَدْ ءَاتَيْنَا مُوسَىٰ تِسْعَ ءَايَٰتٍۭ بَيِّنَٰتٍ فَسْـَٔلْ بَنِىٓ إِسْرَٰٓءِيلَ إِذْ جَآءَهُمْ فَقَالَ لَهُۥ فِرْعَوْنُ إِنِّى لَأَظُنُّكَ يَٰمُوسَىٰ مَسْحُورًا ﴿١٠١﴾

101. And indeed We gave to Mûsa (Moses) nine clear signs. Ask then the Children of Israel, when he came to them, then Fir'aun (Pharaoh) said to him: "O Mûsa (Moses)! I think you are indeed bewitched."

قَالَ لَقَدْ عَلِمْتَ مَآ أَنزَلَ هَٰٓؤُلَآءِ إِلَّا رَبُّ ٱلسَّمَٰوَٰتِ وَٱلْأَرْضِ بَصَآئِرَ وَإِنِّى لَأَظُنُّكَ يَٰفِرْعَوْنُ مَثْبُورًا ﴿١٠٢﴾

102. (Mûsa (Moses)) said: "Verily, you know that these signs have been sent down by none but the Lord of the heavens and the earth as clear (evidences i.e. proofs of Allâh's Oneness and His Omnipotence.). And I think you are, indeed, O Fir'aun (Pharaoh) doomed to destruction (away from all good)!"

فَأَرَادَ أَن يَسْتَفِزَّهُم مِّنَ ٱلْأَرْضِ فَأَغْرَقْنَـٰهُ وَمَن مَّعَهُۥ جَمِيعًۭا ۝

103. So he resolved to turn them out of the land (of Egypt). But We drowned him and all who were with him.

وَقُلْنَا مِنۢ بَعْدِهِۦ لِبَنِىٓ إِسْرَٰٓءِيلَ ٱسْكُنُوا۟ ٱلْأَرْضَ فَإِذَا جَآءَ وَعْدُ ٱلْءَاخِرَةِ جِئْنَا بِكُمْ لَفِيفًۭا ۝

104. And We said to the Children of Israel after him: "Dwell in the land, then, when the final and the last promise comes near (i.e. the Day of Resurrection or the descent of Christ ('Iesa (Jesus), son of Maryam (Mary) (peace be upon them) on the earth). We shall bring you altogether as mixed crowd (gathered out of various nations). (Tafsir Al-Qurtubî)

Transliteration

101. Walaqad atayna moosa tisAAa ayatin bayyinatin fais-al banee isra-eela ith jaahum faqala lahu firAAawnu innee laathunnuka ya moosa mashooran   102. Qala laqad AAalimta ma anzala haola-i illa rabbu alssamawati waal-ardi basa-ira wa-innee laathunnuka ya firAAawnu mathbooran   103. Faarada an yastafizzahum mina al-ardi faaghraqnahu waman maAAahu jameeAAan   104. Waqulna min baAAdihi libanee isra-eela oskunoo al-arda fa-itha jaa waAAdu al-akhirati ji/na bikum lafeefan

Tafsir Ibn Kathir

The Nine Signs of Musa

Allah tells us that He sent Musa with nine clear signs, which provided definitive proof that his prophethood was real and that what he was conveying from the One Who had sent him to Fira`wn was true. These clear signs were: his staff, his hand, the years of famine, the sea, the flood, the locusts, the lice, the frogs and the blood. This was the view of Ibn `Abbas. Muhammad bin Ka`b said, "They were his hand and his staff, the five signs mentioned in Al-A`raf, and destruction of wealth and the rock." Ibn `Abbas, Mujahid, `Ikrimah, Ash-Sha`bi and Qatadah said: "They are his hand, his staff, the years of famine, the failure of the crops, the flood, the locusts, the lice, the frogs and the blood."

(Yet they remained arrogant, and they were of those people who were criminals,) (7:133) meaning, despite all these signs and their witnessing of them, they disbelieved them and belied them wrongfully and arrogantly, although they were themselves were convinced of them, so they did not have any effect on them. By the same token, (Allah tells His Messenger here,) `if We were to respond to what these people are asking you for, who have said that they will not believe in you until you cause springs to gush forth throughout the land for them, they would not respond or believe except if Allah willed.' As Fira`wn said to Musa, even though he had witnessed the signs which he brought,

("O Musa! I think you are indeed bewitched. ") It was said that this meant he thought he was a sorcerer, but Allah knows best. These nine signs which were mentioned by the Imams (scholars) quoted above are what is referred to here, and in the Ayah :

("And throw down your stick!" But when he saw it moving as if it were a snake, he turned in flight, and did not look back. (It was said:) "O Musa ! Fear not.") until His saying,

(among the nine signs (you will take) to Fir`awn and his people. Verily, they are a people who are rebellious.) (27:10-12) These Ayat include mention of the stick and the hand, and the rest of the nine signs are mentioned in detail in Surat Al-A`raf. Musa was also given many other signs, such as striking the rock with his staff and water flowing from it, their being shaded with clouds, manna and quails, and other signs which were bestowed upon the Children of Israel after they had left the land of Egypt. But here Allah mentions the nine signs which were witnessed by his people in Egypt. These became evidence against them, because they stubbornly rejected them out of disbelief. So Musa said to Fira`wn:

("Verily, you know that these signs have been sent down by none but the Lord of the heavens and the earth.) meaning, as proof and evidence of the truth of what I have brought to you.

(And I think you are indeed, O Fir`awn, doomed to destruction!) i.e., bound to be destroyed. This was the view of Mujahid and Qatadah. Ibn `Abbas said: "It means cursed." Ibn `Abbas and Ad-Dahhak said:

(doomed to destruction.) means defeated. As Mujahid said, "doomed" includes all of these meanings.

The Destruction of Fir`awn and His People

(So he resolved to turn them out of the land.) means, he wanted to expel them and drive them out.

(But We drowned him and all who were with him. And We said to the Children of Israel after him: "Dwell in the land...") This is good news for Muhammad , a foretelling of the conquest of Makkah, even though this Surah was revealed in Makkah before the Hijrah. Similarly, the people of Makkah wanted to expel the Prophet from the city, as Allah says in two Ayat:

(And verily, they were about to frighten you so much as to drive you out from the land...) (17:76-77) Hence Allah caused His Messenger to inherit Makkah, so he entered it by force, according to the better-known of the two opinions, and he defeated its people then out of kindness and generosity, he let them go, just as Allah caused the Children of Israel, who had been oppressed, to inherit the land, east and west, and to inherit the land of Fir`awn's people, with its farmland, crops and treasures. As Allah said,

(thus We caused the Children of Israel to inherit them.) (26:59). Here Allah says:

(And We said to the Children of Israel after him: "Dwell in the land, then, when the final and the last promise comes near, We shall bring you altogether as mixed crowd.") meaning, all of you, you and your enemies. Ibn `Abbas, Qatadah and Ad-Dahhak said, "It means all together."

Surah: 17 Ayah: 105 & Ayah: 106

وَبِٱلْحَقِّ أَنزَلْنَٰهُ وَبِٱلْحَقِّ نَزَلَ ۗ وَمَآ أَرْسَلْنَٰكَ إِلَّا مُبَشِّرًا وَنَذِيرًا ۝

105. And with truth We have sent it down (i.e. the Qur'ân), and with truth it has descended. And We have sent you (O Muhammad (peace be upon him)) as nothing but a bearer of glad tidings (of Paradise for those who follow your Message of Islâmic Monotheism), and a warner (of Hell-fire for those who refuse to follow your Message of Islâmic Monotheism).

وَقُرْءَانًا فَرَقْنَٰهُ لِتَقْرَأَهُ عَلَى ٱلنَّاسِ عَلَىٰ مُكْثٍ وَنَزَّلْنَٰهُ تَنزِيلًا ۝

106. And (it is) a Qur'ân which We have divided (into parts), in order that you might recite it to men at intervals. And We have revealed it by stages (in 23 years).

Transliteration

105. Wabialhaqqi anzalnahu wabialhaqqi nazala wama arsalnaka illa mubashshiran wanatheeran 106. Waqur-anan faraqnahu litaqraahu AAala alnnasi AAala mukthin wanazzalnahu tanzeelan

Tafsir Ibn Kathir

The Revelation of the Qur'an in Stages

Allah tells us that His Book, the Glorious Qur'an, has been sent with truth, i.e., it contains the truth, as Allah says:

(But Allah bears witness to that which He has sent down unto you; He has sent it down with His knowledge, and the angels bear witness) (4:166) meaning, it contains the knowledge which Allah wanted to teach to you, with His rulings, commands and prohibitions.

(and with truth it has descended.) means, "It has been sent down to you, O Muhammad, preserved and protected, not contaminated or mixed with anything else, with nothing added or taken away. It has come to you with the truth, brought down by one mighty in power, trustworthy and strong, one who is obeyed by the higher group (angels).'

(And We have sent you) O Muhammad

(as nothing but a bearer of glad tidings and a warner). a bearer of glad tidings for the believers who obey you and a warner to the disbelievers who disobey you.

(And (it is) a Qur'an which We have divided), The word translated here as "We have divided" may be read in two ways. If it is read as "Faraqnahu", with no Shaddah, the meaning is: `We have made it depart from Al-Lawh Al-Mahfuz to Bayt Al-`Izzah in the lowest heaven, then it was revealed in stages to the Messenger of Allah, according to events, over a period of twenty-three years.' This was narrated by `Ikrimah from Ibn `Abbas. It was also narrated that Ibn `Abbas read it as "Farraqnahu", with a Shaddah, meaning, `We revealed it Ayah by Ayah , and have explained it and made it clear.' Hence Allah says:

(in order that you might recite it to men), meaning, convey it to the people and recite it to them,

(at intervals.) meaning slowly.

(And We have revealed it by stages.) means, little by little.

Surah: 17 Ayah: 107, Ayah: 108 & Ayah: 109

قُلْ ءَامِنُوا۟ بِهِۦٓ أَوْ لَا تُؤْمِنُوٓا۟ إِنَّ ٱلَّذِينَ أُوتُوا۟ ٱلْعِلْمَ مِن قَبْلِهِۦٓ إِذَا يُتْلَىٰ عَلَيْهِمْ يَخِرُّونَ لِلْأَذْقَانِ سُجَّدًا ﴿١٠٧﴾

107. Say (O Muhammad (peace be upon him) to them): "Believe in it (the Qur'ân) or do not believe (in it). Verily those who were given knowledge before it (the Jews and the Christians like 'Abdullâh bin Salâm and Salmân Al-Farisî), when it is recited to them, fall down on their faces in humble prostration."

وَيَقُولُونَ سُبْحَٰنَ رَبِّنَآ إِن كَانَ وَعْدُ رَبِّنَا لَمَفْعُولًا ﴿١٠٨﴾

108. And they say: "Glory is to our Lord! Truly, the Promise of our Lord must be fulfilled."

وَيَخِرُّونَ لِلْأَذْقَانِ يَبْكُونَ وَيَزِيدُهُمْ خُشُوعًا ﴿١٠٩﴾

109. And they fall down on their faces weeping and it increases their humility.

Transliteration

107. Qul aminoo bihi aw la tu/minoo inna allatheena ootoo alAAilma min qablihi itha yutla AAalayhim yakhirroona lil-athqani sujjadan 108. Wayaqooloona subhana rabbina in kana waAAdu rabbina lamafAAoolan 109. Wayakhirroona lil-athqani yabkoona wayazeeduhum khushooAAan

Tafsir Ibn Kathir

Those Who were given Knowledge before truly admit the Qur'an

Allah says to His Prophet Muhammad :

(Say) O Muhammad to these disbelievers concerning what you have brought to them of this Glorious Qur'an:

("Believe in it (the Qur'an) or do not believe (in it).) meaning, it is all the same whether you believe in it or not, for it is true in and of itself. It was revealed by Allah, Who mentioned it previously in the Books that He revealed to other Messengers. Hence He says:

(Verily, those who were given knowledge before it,) meaning righteous people among the People of the Book, who adhered to their Books and appreciated them without distorting them.

(when it is recited to them,) means, when this Qur'an is recited to them,

(fall down on their chins (faces) in humble prostration.) means, to Allah, in gratitude for the blessing He has bestowed on them by considering them fit to live until they met this Messenger to whom this Book was revealed. Hence they say:

(Glory be to our Lord!), meaning, they extol and glorify their Lord for His perfect power and for not delaying the fulfillment of the promise which He made through His earlier Prophets, that He would send Muhammad . Hence they said:

(Glory be to our Lord! Truly, the promise of our Lord must be fulfilled.)

(And they fall down on their chins (faces) weeping) means, in submission to Allah, may He be glorified, and in expression of their belief and faith in His Book and His Messenger .

(and it increases their humility.) means, it increases them in faith and submission. As Allah says:

(While as for those who accept guidance, He increases their guidance and bestows on them their Taqwa.) (47:17).

(And they fall down) is a description rather than an action (i.e., this is a further description of their humility as referred to in Ayah 107; it does not imply that they prostrate twice).

Surah: 17 Ayah: 110 & Ayah: 111

قُلِ ٱدْعُواْ ٱللَّهَ أَوِ ٱدْعُواْ ٱلرَّحْمَـٰنَ أَيًّا مَّا تَدْعُواْ فَلَهُ ٱلْأَسْمَآءُ ٱلْحُسْنَىٰ وَلَا تَجْهَرْ بِصَلَاتِكَ وَلَا تُخَافِتْ بِهَا وَٱبْتَغِ بَيْنَ ذَٰلِكَ سَبِيلًا ۝

110. Say (O Muhammad (peace be upon him)) "Invoke Allâh or invoke the Most Gracious (Allâh), by whatever name you invoke Him (it is the same), for to Him belong the Best Names. And offer your Salât (prayer) neither aloud nor in a low voice, but follow a way between.

وَقُلِ ٱلْحَمْدُ لِلَّهِ ٱلَّذِى لَمْ يَتَّخِذْ وَلَدًا وَلَمْ يَكُن لَّهُ شَرِيكٌ فِى ٱلْمُلْكِ وَلَمْ يَكُن لَّهُ, وَلِىٌّ مِّنَ ٱلذُّلِّ وَكَبِّرْهُ تَكْبِيرًۢا ۝

111. And say: "All the praises and thanks be to Allâh, Who has not begotten a son (nor an offspring), and Who has no partner in (His) Dominion, nor He is low to have a Walî (helper, protector or supporter). And magnify Him with all the magnificence, (allâhu-Akbar (Allâh is the Most Great))"

Transliteration

110. Quli odAAoo Allaha awi odAAoo alrrahmana ayyan ma tadAAoo falahu al-asmao alhusna wala tajhar bisalatika wala tukhafit biha waibtaghi bayna thalika sabeelan
111. Waquli alhamdu lillahi allathee lam yattakhith waladan walam yakun lahu shareekun fee almulki walam yakun lahu waliyyun mina alththulli wakabbirhu takbeeran

Tafsir Ibn Kathir

To Allah belong the Most Beautiful Names

Allah says:

(Say) O Muhammad, to these idolators who deny that Allah possesses the attribute of mercy and refuse to call Him Ar-Rahman,

("Invoke Allah or invoke Ar-Rahman (the Most Gracious), by whatever name you invoke Him (it is the same), for to Him belong the Best Names.) meaning, there is no difference between calling on Him as Allah or calling on Him as Ar-Rahman, because He has the Most Beautiful Names, as He says:

(He is Allah, beside Whom none has the right to be worshipped but He the All-Knower of the unseen and the seen. He is the Most Gracious, the Most Merciful.) (59:22) Until His saying;

(To Him belong the Best Names. All that is in the heavens and the earth glorify Him.) (59:24) Makhul reported that one of the idolators heard the Prophet saying when he was prostrating: "O Most Gracious, O Most Merciful." The idolator said, he claims to pray to One, but he is praying to two! Then Allah revealed this Ayah. This was also narrated from Ibn `Abbas, and by Ibn Jarir.

The Command to recite neither loudly nor softly

(And offer your Salah neither aloud) Imam Ahmad reported that Ibn `Abbas said: "This Ayah was revealed when the Messenger of Allah was preaching underground in Makkah."

(And offer your Salah neither aloud nor in a low voice,) Ibn `Abbas said: "When he prayed with his Companions, he would recite Qur'an loudly, and when the idolators heard that, they insulted the Qur'an, and the One Who had revealed it and the one who had brought it. So Allah said to His Prophet :

(And offer your Salah (prayer) neither aloud) means, do not recite it aloud, lest the idolators hear you and insult the Qur'an,

(nor in a low voice,) means, nor recite it so quietly that your companions cannot hear the Qur'an and learn it from you.

(but follow a way between.)" This was also reported in the Two Sahihs. Ad-Dahhak also narrated something similar from Ibn `Abbas, and added: "When he migrated to Al-Madinah, this no longer applied, and he recited as he wished." Muhammad bin Ishaq said that Ibn `Abbas said, "When the Messenger of Allah recited Qur'an quietly while he was praying, the (idolators) would disperse and refuse to listen to him; if one of them wanted to hear some of what he was reciting in his prayer, he would try to listen without anyone seeing him, because he was afraid of them. If he realized that anybody knew he was listening, he would go away lest they harm him, so he would stop listening. If the Prophet lowered his voice, those who wanted to listen to his recitation could not hear anything, so Allah revealed, (And offer your Salah neither aloud) meaning, do not recite aloud, lest those who want to listen disperse for fear of attracting unwelcome attention, (nor in a low voice,) but do not make your voice so soft that the one who is trying to listen without being seen cannot hear anything at all. Perhaps he will pay attention to some of what he hears and benefit from it. (but follow a way between.)" This was the view of `Ikrimah, Al-Hasan Al-Basri and Qatadah that this Ayah was revealed concerning recitation in prayer. It was narrated from Ibn Mas`ud: "Do not make it so soft that no one can hear it except yourself."

Declaration of Tawhid

(And say: "All the praises and thanks be to Allah, Who has not begotten a son...") because Allah has stated that the Most Beautiful Names belong to Him, and has declared Himself to be above having any faults or defects. (And say: "All the praises and thanks be to Allah, Who has not begotten a son, and Who has no partner in (His) dominion...") indeed, He is Allah, (the) One, the Self-Sufficient Master, Who begets not, nor was He begotten, and there is none co-equal or comparable unto Him.

(nor He is low to have a supporter.) means, He is not so humble or weak that He needs to have a helper or supporter or adviser, rather He Alone, with no partner or associate, may He be exalted, is the Creator of all things and is the One Who is running and controlling them by His will, with no partner or associate.

(nor He is low to have a supporter).) Mujahid said: He does not form an alliance with anyone, nor does He seek the support or help of anyone.

(And magnify Him with all magnificence.) means, glorify and extol Him far above whatever the transgressors and aggressors say. Ibn Jarir recorded that Al-Qurazi used to say about this Ayah,

(And say: "All the praises and thanks be to Allah, Who has not begotten a son...") that the Jews and Christians said that Allah has taken a son; the Arabs said, "At Your service, You have no partner except the partner You have, and You possess him and whatever he owns;" and the Sabians and Magians said, "If it were not for the supporters of Allah, He would be weak." Then Allah revealed this Ayah :

(And say: "All the praises and thanks be to Allah, Who has not begotten a son, and Who has no partner in (His) dominion, nor is He low to have a supporter. And magnify Him with all magnificence.") End of Tafsir Surah Subhan (Surat Al-Isra'). And to Allah be the praise and blessings.

INTRODUCTION TO CHAPTER (SURAH) 18: AL-KAHF (THE CAVE)

Ibn kathir's Introduction

What has been mentioned about the Virtues of this Surah and the first and last ten Ayat, which provide protection from the Dajjal

Imam Ahmad recorded that Al-Bara' said: "A man recited Al-Kahf and there was an animal in the house which began acting in a nervous manner. He looked, and saw a fog or cloud overhead. He mentioned this to the Prophet, who said:

«اقْرَأْ فُلَانُ، فَإِنَّهَا السَّكِينَةُ تَنْزِلُ عِنْدَ الْقُرْآنِ أَوْ تَنَزَّلَتْ لِلْقُرْآن»

(Keep on reciting so and so, for this is the tranquillity which descends when one reads Qur'an or because of reading Qur'an;) This was also recorded in the Two Sahihs. This man who recited it was Usayd bin Al-Hudayr, as we have previously mentioned in our Tafsir of Surat Al-Baqarah. Imam Ahmad recorded from Abu Ad-Darda' that the Prophet said:

«مَنْ حَفِظَ عَشْرَ آيَاتٍ مِنْ أَوَّلِ سُورَةِ الْكَهْفِ عُصِمَ مِنَ الدَّجَّال»

(Whoever memorizes ten Ayat from the beginning of Surat Al-Kahf will be protected from the Dajjal.) This was also recorded by Muslim, Abu Dawud, An-Nasa'i and At-Tirmidhi. According to the version recorded by At-Tirmidhi,

«مَنْ حَفِظَ ثَلَاثَ آيَاتٍ مِنْ أَوَّلِ الْكَهْف»

(Whoever memorizes three Ayat from the beginning of Al-Kahf.) He said, it is "Hasan Sahih." In his Mustadrak, Al-Hakim recorded from Abu Sa`id that the Prophet said:

«مَنْ قَرَأَ سُورَةَ الْكَهْفِ فِي يَوْمِ الْجُمْعَةِ أَضَاءَ لَهُ مِنَ النُّورِ مَا بَيْنَهُ وَبَيْنَ الْجُمُعَتَيْنِ»

(Whoever recites Surat Al-Kahf on Friday, it will illuminate him with light from one Friday to the next.) Then he said: "This Hadith has a Sahih chain, but they (Al-Bukhari and Muslim) did not record it." Al-Hafiz Abu Bakr Al-Bayhaqi also recorded it in his Sunan from Al-Hakim, then he narrated with his own chain that the Prophet said:

«مَنْ قَرَأَ سُورَةَ الْكَهْفِ كَمَا نَزَلَتْ، كَانَتْ لَهُ نُورًا يَوْمَ الْقِيَامَةِ»

(Whoever recites Surat Al-Kahf as it was revealed, it will be a light for him on the Day of Resurrection.)

CHAPTER 18: AL-KAHF (THE CAVE), VERSES 001–074

(بِسْمِ اللَّهِ الرَّحْمَنِ الرَّحِيمِ)

In the Name of Allah, the Most Gracious, the Most Merciful.

Surah: 18 Ayah: 1, Ayah: 2, Ayah: 3, Ayah: 4 & Ayah: 5

ٱلْحَمْدُ لِلَّهِ ٱلَّذِى أَنزَلَ عَلَىٰ عَبْدِهِ ٱلْكِتَٰبَ وَلَمْ يَجْعَل لَّهُۥ عِوَجَا ۜ ۝

1. All the praises and thanks are to Allâh, Who has sent down to His slave (Muhammad (peace be upon him)) the Book (the Qur'ân), and has not placed therein any crookedness.

قَيِّمًا لِّيُنذِرَ بَأْسًا شَدِيدًا مِّن لَّدُنْهُ وَيُبَشِّرَ ٱلْمُؤْمِنِينَ ٱلَّذِينَ يَعْمَلُونَ ٱلصَّٰلِحَٰتِ أَنَّ لَهُمْ أَجْرًا حَسَنًا ۝

2. (He has made it) straight to give warning (to the disbelievers) of a severe punishment from Him, and to give glad tidings to the believers (in the Oneness of Allâh - Islâmic Monotheism), who do righteous deeds, that they shall have a fair reward (i.e. Paradise).

مَّٰكِثِينَ فِيهِ أَبَدًا ۝

3. They shall abide therein for ever.

وَيُنذِرَ ٱلَّذِينَ قَالُوا۟ ٱتَّخَذَ ٱللَّهُ وَلَدًا ۝

4. And to warn those (Jews, Christians, and pagans) who say, "Allâh has begotten a son (or offspring or children)."

مَّا لَهُم بِهِۦ مِنْ عِلْمٍ وَلَا لِءَابَآئِهِمْ ۚ كَبُرَتْ كَلِمَةً تَخْرُجُ مِنْ أَفْوَٰهِهِمْ ۚ إِن يَقُولُونَ إِلَّا كَذِبًا ۝

5. No knowledge have they of such a thing, nor had their fathers. Mighty is the word that comes out of their mouths (i.e. He begot sons and daughters). They utter nothing but a lie.

Transliteration

1. Alhamdu lillahi allathee anzala AAala AAabdihi alkitaba walam yajAAal lahu AAiwajan   2. Qayyiman liyunthira ba/san shadeedan min ladunhu wayubashshira almu/mineena allatheena yaAAmaloona alssalihati anna lahum ajran hasanan   3. Makitheena feehi abadan   4. Wayunthira allatheena qaloo ittakhatha Allahu waladan   5. Ma lahum bihi min AAilmin wala li-aba-ihim kaburat kalimatan takhruju min afwahihim in yaqooloona illa kathiban

Tafsir Ibn Kathir

The Revelation of the Qur'an brings both Good News and a Warning

In the beginning of this Tafsir, we mentioned that Allah, praises His Holy Self at the beginning and end of matters, for He is the One to be praised in all circumstances, all praise and thanks be to Him, in the beginning and in the end. He praises Himself for revealing His Mighty Book to His Noble Messenger Muhammad , which is the greatest blessing that Allah has granted the people of this earth. Through the Qur'an, He brings them out of the darkness into light. He has made it a Book that is straight, neither distorted nor confusion therein. It clearly guides to a straight path, plain and manifest, giving a warning to the disbelievers and good news to the believers. This is why Allah says:

(and has not placed therein any crookedness.) meaning, there is nothing twisted or confusing about it. But He has made it balanced and straightforward as He said;

((He has made it) straight), meaning straightforward,

(to give warning of a severe punishment from Him,) meaning, to those who oppose His Prophet and disbelieve in His Book, He issues a warning of severe punishment hastened in this world and postponed to the world Hereafter.

(from Him) means, from Allah. For none can punish as He punishes and none is stronger or more reliable than Him.

(and to give good news to the believers,) means, those who believe in this Qur'an and confirm their faith by righteous actions.

(that they shall have a fair reward.) means, a beautiful reward from Allah.

(They shall abide therein) means, in what Allah rewards them with, and that is Paradise, where they will live forever.

(forever.) means, for always, never ending or ceasing to be.

(And to warn those who say, "Allah has begotten a child.") Ibn Ishaq said: "These are the pagan Arabs, who said, `We worship the angels who are the daughters of Allah.'"

(No knowledge have they of such a thing,) meaning, this thing that they have fabricated and made up.

(nor had their fathers.) meaning, their predecessors.

(Mighty is the word) This highlights the seriousness and enormity of the lie they have made up. Allah says:

(Mighty is the word that comes out of their mouths.) meaning, it has no basis apart from what they say, and they have no evidence for it apart from their own lies and fabrications. Hence Allah says:

(They utter nothing but a lie.)

Reason why this Surah was revealed

Muhammad bin Ishaq mentioned the reason why this Surah was revealed. He said that an old man from among the people of Egypt who came to them some forty-odd years ago told him, from `Ikrimah that Ibn `Abbas said: "The Quraysh sent An-Nadr bin Al-Harith and `Uqbah bin Abi Mu`it to the Jewish rabbis in Al-Madinah, and told them: `Ask them (the rabbis) about Muhammad, and describe him to them, and tell them what he is saying. They are the people of the first Book, and they have more knowledge of the Prophets than we do.' So they set out and when they reached Al-Madinah, they asked the Jewish rabbis about the Messenger of Allah . They described him to them and told them some of what he had said. They said, `You are the people of the Tawrah and we have come to you so that you can tell us about this companion of ours.' They (the rabbis) said, `Ask him about three things which we will tell you to ask, and if he answers them then he is a Prophet who has been sent (by Allah); if he does not, then he is saying things that are not true, in which case how you will deal with him will be up to you. Ask him about some young men in ancient times, what was their story For theirs is a strange and wondrous tale. Ask him about a man who travelled a great deal and reached the east and the west of the earth. What was his story And ask him about the Ruh (soul or spirit) -- what is it If he tells you about these things, then he is a Prophet, so follow him, but if he does not tell you, then he is a man who is making things up, so deal with him as you see fit.' So An-Nadr and `Uqbah left and came back to the Quraysh, and said: `O people of Quraysh, we have come to you with a decisive solution which will put an end to the problem between you and Muhammad. The Jewish rabbis told us to ask him about some matters,' and they told the Quraysh what they were. Then they came to the Messenger of Allah and said, `O Muhammad, tell us,' and they asked him about the things they had been told to ask. The Messenger of Allah said,

«أُخْبِرُكُمْ غَدًا عَمَّا سَأَلْتُمْ عَنْهُ»

(I will tell you tomorrow about what you have asked me.) but he did not say `If Allah wills.' So they went away, and the Messenger of Allah stayed for fifteen days without any revelation from Allah concerning that, and Jibril, peace be upon him, did not come to him either. The people of Makkah started to doubt him, and said, `Muhammad promised to tell us the next day, and now fifteen days have gone by and he has not told us anything in response to the questions we asked.' The Messenger of Allah felt sad because of the delay in revelation, and was grieved by what the people of Makkah were saying about him. Then Jibril came to him from Allah with the Surah about the companions of Al-Kahf, which also contained a rebuke for feeling sad about the idolators. The Surah also told him about the things they had asked him about, the young men and the traveler. The question about the Ruh was answered in the Ayah;

(And they ask you concerning the Ruh (the spirit); say: "The Ruh...") (17:85).

Surah: 18 Ayah: 6, Ayah: 7 & Ayah: 8

فَلَعَلَّكَ بَاخِعٌ نَفْسَكَ عَلَىٰ ءَاثَارِهِمْ إِن لَّمْ يُؤْمِنُوا۟ بِهَـٰذَا ٱلْحَدِيثِ أَسَفًا ۝

6. Perhaps, you, would kill yourself (O Muhammad (peace be upon him)) in grief, over their footsteps (for their turning away from you), because they believe not in this narration (the Qur'ân).

إِنَّا جَعَلْنَا مَا عَلَى ٱلْأَرْضِ زِينَةً لَّهَا لِنَبْلُوَهُمْ أَيُّهُمْ أَحْسَنُ عَمَلًا ۝

7. Verily! We have made that which is on earth as an adornment for it, in order that We may test them (mankind) as to which of them are best in deeds. (i.e. those who do good deeds in the most perfect manner, that means to do them (deeds) totally for Allâh's sake and in accordance to the legal ways of the Prophet (peace be upon him))

وَإِنَّا لَجَـٰعِلُونَ مَا عَلَيْهَا صَعِيدًا جُرُزًا ۝

8. And verily! We shall make all that is on it (the earth) a bare dry soil (without any vegetation or trees.).

Transliteration

6. FalaAAallaka bakhiAAun nafsaka AAala atharihim in lam yu/minoo bihatha alhadeethi asafan 7. Inna jaAAalna ma AAala al-ardi zeenatan laha linabluwahum ayyuhum ahsanu AAamalan 8. Wa-inna lajaAAiloona ma AAalayha saAAeedan juruzan

Tafsir Ibn Kathir

Do not feel sorry because the Idolators do not believe. Allah consoles His Messenger for his sorrow over the idolators because they would not believe and keep away from him. He also said:

(So destroy not yourself in sorrow for them.) (35:8)

(And grieve not over them.) (16:127)

(It may be that you are going to kill yourself with grief, that they do not become believers.) (26:3) meaning, maybe you will destroy yourself with your grief over them. Allah says:

(Perhaps, you would kill yourself in grief, over their footsteps, because they believe not in this narration.) meaning the Qur'an.

(in grief) Allah is saying, `do not destroy yourself with regret.' Qatadah said: "killing yourself with anger and grief over them." Mujahid said: "with anxiety." These are synonymous, so the meaning is: `Do not feel sorry for them, just convey the Message of Allah to them. Whoever goes the right way, then he goes the right way only for the benefit of himself. And whoever goes astray, then he strays at his own loss, so do not destroy yourself in sorrow for them.'

This World is the Place of Trial. Then Allah tells us that He has made this world a temporary abode, adorned with transient beauty, and He made it a place of trial, not a place of settlement.

So He says:

(Verily, we have made that which is on earth an adornment for it, in order that We may test which of them are best in deeds.) Abu Maslamah narrated from Abu Nadrah from Abu Sa`id that the Messenger of Allah said:

»إِنَّ الدُّنْيَا حُلْوَةٌ خَضِرَةٌ، وَإِنَّ اللهَ مُسْتَخْلِفُكُمْ فِيهَا فَنَاظِرٌ مَاذَا تَعْمَلُونَ، فَاتَّقُوا الدُّنْيَا، وَاتَّقُوا النِّسَاءَ، فَإِنَّ أَوَّلَ فِتْنَةِ بَنِي إِسْرَائِيلَ كَانَتْ فِي النِّسَاءِ«

(This world is sweet and green, and Allah makes you generations succeeding one another, so He is watching what you will do. Beware of (the beguilements of) this world and beware of women, for the first affliction that Children of Israel suffered from was that of women.) Then Allah tells us that this world will pass away and come to an end, as He says:

(And verily, We shall make all that is on it bare, dry soil.) means, `after having adorned it, We will destroy it and make everything on it bare and dry, with no vegetation or any other benefit.' Al-`Awfi reported from Ibn `Abbas that this means everything on it would be wiped out and destroyed. Mujahid said: "a dry and barren plain." Qatadah said, "A plain on which there are no trees or vegetation."

Surah: 18 Ayah: 9, Ayah: 10, Ayah: 11 & Ayah: 12

أَمْ حَسِبْتَ أَنَّ أَصْحَبَ ٱلْكَهْفِ وَٱلرَّقِيمِ كَانُوا۟ مِنْ ءَايَتِنَا عَجَبًا ۝

9. Do you think that the people of the Cave and the Inscription (the news or the names of the people of the Cave) were a wonder among Our Signs?

إِذْ أَوَى ٱلْفِتْيَةُ إِلَى ٱلْكَهْفِ فَقَالُوا۟ رَبَّنَآ ءَاتِنَا مِن لَّدُنكَ رَحْمَةً وَهَيِّئْ لَنَا مِنْ أَمْرِنَا رَشَدًا ۝

10. (Remember) when the young men fled for refuge (from their disbelieving folk) to the Cave. They said: "Our Lord! Bestow on us mercy from Yourself, and facilitate for us our affair in the right way!"

فَضَرَبْنَا عَلَىٰٓ ءَاذَانِهِمْ فِى ٱلْكَهْفِ سِنِينَ عَدَدًا ۝

11. Therefore We covered up their (sense of) hearing (causing them to go in deep sleep) in the Cave for a number of years.

ثُمَّ بَعَثْنَهُمْ لِنَعْلَمَ أَىُّ ٱلْحِزْبَيْنِ أَحْصَىٰ لِمَا لَبِثُوٓا۟ أَمَدًا ۝

12. Then We raised them up (from their sleep), that We might test which of the two parties was best at calculating the time period that they had tarried.

Transliteration

9. Am hasibta anna as-haba alkahfi waalrraqeemi kanoo min ayatina AAajaban 10. Ith awa alfityatu ila alkahfi faqaloo rabbana atina min ladunka rahmatan wahayyi/ lana min amrina rashadan 11. Fadarabna AAala athanihim fee alkahfi sineena AAadadan 12. Thumma baAAathnahum linaAAlama ayyu alhizbayni ahsa lima labithoo amadan

Tafsir Ibn Kathir

The Story of the People of Al-Kahf. Here Allah tells us about the story of the people of Al-Kahf in brief and general terms, then He explains it in more detail. He says:

(Do you think) -- O Muhammad --

(that the people of Al-Kahf and Ar-Raqim were a wonder among Our signs) meaning, their case was not something amazing compared to Our power and ability, for the creation of the heavens and earth, the alternation of night and day and the subjugation of the sun, moon and heavenly bodies, and other mighty signs indicate the great power of Allah and show that He is able to do whatever He wills. He is not incapable of doing more amazing things than the story of the people of the Cave. Similarly, Ibn Jurayj reported Mujahid saying about,

(Do you think that the people of Al-Kahf and Ar-Raqim were a wonder among Our signs) "Among Our signs are things that are more amazing than this." Al-`Awfi reported that Ibn `Abbas said:

(Do you think that the people of Al-Kahf and Ar-Raqim were a wonder among Our signs) "What I have given to you of knowledge, the Sunnah and the Book is far better than the story of the people of Al-Kahf and Ar-Raqim." Muhammad bin Ishaq said: "(It means) I have not shown My creatures a proof more amazing than the story of the people of the Al-Kahf and Ar-Raqim." iAl-Kahf refers to a cave in a mountain, which is where the young men sought refuge. With regard to the word Ar-Raqim, Al-`Awfi reported from Ibn `Abbas that it is a valley near Aylah. This was also said (in another narration) by `Atiyah Al-`Awfi and Qatadah. Ad-Dahhak said: "As for Al-Kahf, it is a cave in the valley, and Ar-Raqim is the name of the valley." Mujahid said, "Ar-Raqim refers to their buildings." Others said it refers to the valley in which their cave was. `Abdur-Razzaq recorded that Ibn `Abbas said about Ar-Raqim: "Ka`b used to say that it was the town." Ibn Jurayj reported that Ibn `Abbas said, "Ar-Raqim is the mountain in which the cave was." Sa`id bin Jubayr said, "Ar-Raqim is a tablet of stone on which they wrote the story of the people of the Cave, then they placed it at the entrance to the Cave."

((Remember) when the young men fled for refuge to Al-Kahf. They said: "Our Lord! Bestow on us mercy from Yourself, and facilitate for us our affair in the right way!") Here Allah tells us about those young men who fled from their people for the sake of their religion, fearing persecution. So they fled taking refuge in the cave of a mountain, where they hid from their people. When they entered the cave, they asked Allah to show mercy and kindness towards them,

(Our Lord! Bestow on us mercy from Yourself,) meaning, `give us Your mercy and conceal us from our people.'

(and facilitate for us our affair in the right way.) means, direct our matter well, i.e., grant us a good end. As was reported in the Hadith:

《وَمَا قَضَيْتَ لَنَا مِنْ قَضَاءٍ فَاجْعَلْ عَاقِبَتَهُ رَشَدًا》

(Whatever You have decreed for us, make its consequences good).

(Therefore, We covered up their hearing in the cave for a number of years.) meaning, `We caused them to sleep when they entered the cave, and they slept for many years.'

(Then We raised them up) from that slumber, and one of them went out with his Dirhams (silver coins) to buy them some food, as it will be discussed in more detail below. Allah says:

(Then We raised them up, that We might test which of the two parties) meaning, the two parties who disputed about them,

(was best at calculating the time period that they tarried.) It was said that this refers to how long they stayed in the cave.

Surah: 18 Ayah: 13, Ayah: 14, Ayah: 15 & Ayah: 16

نَحْنُ نَقُصُّ عَلَيْكَ نَبَأَهُم بِٱلْحَقِّ إِنَّهُمْ فِتْيَةٌ ءَامَنُواْ بِرَبِّهِمْ وَزِدْنَٰهُمْ هُدًى ۝

13. We narrate unto you (O Muhammad (peace be upon him)) their story with truth: Truly! They were young men who believed in their Lord (Allâh), and We increased them in guidance.

وَرَبَطْنَا عَلَىٰ قُلُوبِهِمْ إِذْ قَامُواْ فَقَالُواْ رَبُّنَا رَبُّ ٱلسَّمَٰوَٰتِ وَٱلْأَرْضِ لَن نَّدْعُوَاْ مِن دُونِهِۦٓ إِلَٰهًا لَّقَدْ قُلْنَآ إِذًا شَطَطًا ۝

14. And We made their hearts firm and strong (with the light of Faith in Allâh and bestowed upon them patience to bear the separation of their kith and kin and dwellings) when they stood up and said: "Our Lord is the Lord of the heavens and the earth, never shall we call upon any ilâh (god) other than Him; if we did, we should indeed have uttered an enormity in disbelief.

هَٰٓؤُلَآءِ قَوْمُنَا ٱتَّخَذُواْ مِن دُونِهِۦٓ ءَالِهَةً لَّوْلَا يَأْتُونَ عَلَيْهِم بِسُلْطَٰنٍۭ بَيِّنٍ فَمَنْ أَظْلَمُ مِمَّنِ ٱفْتَرَىٰ عَلَى ٱللَّهِ كَذِبًا ۝

15. "These our people have taken for worship âlihah (gods) other than Him (Allâh). Why do they not bring for them a clear authority? And who does more wrong than he who invents a lie against Allâh.

وَإِذِ ٱعْتَزَلْتُمُوهُمْ وَمَا يَعْبُدُونَ إِلَّا ٱللَّهَ فَأْوُۥٓاْ إِلَى ٱلْكَهْفِ يَنشُرْ لَكُمْ رَبُّكُم مِّن رَّحْمَتِهِۦ وَيُهَيِّئْ لَكُم مِّنْ أَمْرِكُم مِّرْفَقًا ۝

16. (The young men said to one another): "And when you withdraw from them, and that which they worship, except Allâh, then seek refuge in the Cave; your Lord will open a way for you from His Mercy and will make easy for you your affair (i.e. will give you what you will need of provision, dwelling)."

Transliteration

13. Nahnu naqussu AAalayka nabaahum bialhaqqi innahum fityatun amanoo birabbihim wazidnahum hudan 14. Warabatna AAala quloobihim ith qamoo faqaloo rabbuna rabbu alssamawati waal-ardi lan nadAAuwa min doonihi ilahan laqad qulna ithan shatatan 15. Haola-i qawmuna ittakhathoo min doonihi alihatan lawla ya/toona AAalayhim bisultanin bayyinin faman athlamu mimmani iftara AAala Allahi kathiban

16. Wa-ithi iAAtazaltumoohum wama yaAAbudoona illa Allaha fa/woo ila alkahfi yanshur lakum rabbukum min rahmatihi wayuhayyi/ lakum min amrikum mirfaqan

Tafsir Ibn Kathir

Their Belief in Allah and their Retreat from their People

From here Allah begins to explain the story in detail. He states that they were boys or young men, and that they were more accepting of the truth and more guided than the elders who had become stubbornly set in their ways and clung to the religion of falsehood. For the same reason, most of those who responded to Allah and His Messenger were young people. As for the elders of Quraysh, most of them kept to their religion and only a few of them became Muslims. So Allah tells us that the people of the cave were young men. Mujahid said, "I was informed that some of them wore some kind of earrings, then Allah guided them and inspired them to fear Him, so they recognized His Oneness, and bore witness that there is no god besides Him."

(and We increased them in guidance.) From this and other similar Ayat, several scholars, such as Al-Bukhari and others, understood that faith may increase, that it may vary in degrees, and that it may fluctuate. Allah says:

(and We increased them in guidance.) as He said elsewhere:

(While as for those who accept guidance, He increases their guidance and bestows on them their Taqwa.) (47:17)

(As for those who believe, it has increased their faith, and they rejoice.) (9:124),

(...that they may grow more in faith along with their (present) faith.) (48:4) There are other Ayat indicating the same thing. It has been mentioned that they were followers of the religion of Al-Masih `Isa, `Isa bin Maryam, but Allah knows best. It seems that they lived before the time of Christianity altogether, because if they had been Christians, the Jewish rabbis would not have cared about preserving because of their differences. We have mentioned above the report from Ibn `Abbas that the Quraysh sent a message to the Jewish rabbis in Al-Madinah to ask them for things with which they could test the Messenger of Allah , and they told them to ask him about these young men, and about Dhul-Qarnayn (the man who traveled much) and about the Ruh. This indicates that this story was something recorded in the books of the People of the Book, and that it came before Christianity. And Allah knows best.

(And We made their hearts firm and strong when they stood up and said: "Our Lord is the Lord of the heavens and the earth,) Here Allah is saying: `We gave them the patience to go against their people and their city, and to leave behind the life of luxury and ease that they had been living.' Several of the earlier and later Tafsir scholars have mentioned that they were sons of the kings and leaders of Byzantium, and that they went out one day to one of the festivals of their people. They used to gather once a year outside the city, and they would worship idols and offer sacrifices to them. They had an arrogant, tyrannical king who was called Decianus, who commanded and encouraged the people to do that. When the people went out to attend this gathering, these young men went out with their fathers and their people, and when they saw their people's actions with clear insight, they realized that the prostrations and sacrifices the people were offering to their idols should only be dedicated to Allah, Who created the heavens and the earth. Each of them started to withdraw from his people and keep aloof from them. The first one of them to move away on his own went and sat in the shade of a tree, then another came and sat with him, then another came and sat with them, then four more followed suit one by one. None of them knew the others, but they were brought together by the One Who instilled faith in their hearts. As it says in the Hadith recorded by Al-Bukhari with an incomplete chain of narrators from `A'ishah (may Allah be pleased with her), the Messenger of Allah said:

«الْأَرْوَاحُ جُنُودٌ مُجَنَّدَةٌ، فَمَا تَعَارَفَ مِنْهَا ائْتَلَفَ وَمَا تَنَاكَرَ مِنْهَا اخْتَلَفَ»

(Souls are like recruited soldiers. Those that recognize one another will come together, and those that do not recognize one another will turn away from each another). Muslim also recorded this in his Sahih from the Hadith of Suhayl from his father from Abu Hurayrah from the Messenger of Allah . People say that similar qualities or characteristics are what bring people together. So each of the young men was trying to conceal what he really believed from the others, out of fear of them, not knowing that they were like him. Then one of them said, "O people, you know by Allah that only one thing is making you leave your people and isolate yourselves from them, so let each one of you say what it is in his case." Another said, "As for me, by Allah I saw what my people are doing and I realized that it was false, and that the only One Who deserves to be worshipped Alone with out partner or associate is Allah Who created everything, the heavens, the earth and everything in between." Another said, "By Allah, the same thing happened to me." The others said the same, and they all agreed and became brothers in faith. They adopted a particular location as a place of worship and began worshipping Allah there, but their people found out about them and told their king about them. The king ordered them to appear before him, and asked them about their beliefs. They told him the truth and called him to Allah, as Allah says about them:

(And We made their hearts firm and strong when they stood up and said: "Our Lord is the Lord of the heavens and the earth, never shall we call upon any god other than Him...") "Never" (Lan) implies an absolute and eternal negation, meaning, `this will never happen, and if we were to do that it would be false.' So Allah says about them:

(...if we did, we should indeed have uttered an enormity in disbelief.) meaning, untruth and utter falsehood.

(These, our people, have taken for worship gods other than Him (Allah). Why do they not bring for them a clear authority) meaning, why do they not produce some clear evidence and genuine proof for their behavior

(And who does more wrong than he who invents a lie against Allah.) They said: `but by saying that they are lying transgressors.' It was said that when they called their king to believe in Allah, he refused, and warned and threatened them. He commanded them to be stripped of their clothing bearing the adornments of their people, then he gave them some time to think about the situation, hoping that they would return to their former religion. This was a way that Allah showed kindness for them, because during that time they managed to escape from him and flee from persecution for the sake of their religion. This is what is prescribed in the Shari`ah during times of trial and persecution -- a person who fears for his religion should flee from his persecutors, as was reported in the Hadith:

﴿يُوشِكُ أَنْ يَكُونَ خَيْرُ مَالِ أَحَدِكُمْ غَنَمًا يَتْبَعُ بِهَا شَعَفَ الْجِبَالِ وَمَوَاقِعَ الْقَطْرِ يَفِرُّ بِدِينِهِ مِنَ الْفِتَنِ﴾

(Soon there will come a time when the best wealth any of you can have will be sheep, which he can follow to the tops of the mountains and places where rain falls, (fleeing) for the sake of his religion from persecution.) In such cases, it is allowed to seclude oneself from people, but this is not prescribed in any other case, because by such seclusion one loses the benefits of congregational and Friday prayers. These young men were determined to flee from their people, and Allah decreed that for them, as He says about them,

(And when you withdraw from them, and that which they worship, except Allah,) meaning, when you depart from them and follow a different religion, opposing their worship of others besides Allah, then separate from them in a physical sense too,

(then seek refuge in the cave; your Lord will open a way for you from His mercy) meaning, He will bestow His mercy upon you, by which He will conceal you from your people.

(and will make easy for you your affair.) means, He will give you what you need. So they left and fled to the cave where they sought refuge. Then their people noticed they were missing, and the king looked for them, and it was said when he could not find them that Allah concealed them from him so that he could not find any trace of them or any information about them, as Allah concealed His Prophet Muhammad and his Companion (Abu Bakr) As-Siddiq, when they sought refuge in the cave of Thawr. The Quraysh idolators came in pursuit, but they did not find him even though they passed right by him. When the Messenger of Allah noticed that As-Siddiq was anxious and said, "O Messenger of Allah, if one of them looks down at the place of his feet, he will see us," he told him:

﴿يَا أَبَا بَكْرٍ مَا ظَنُّكَ بِاثْنَيْنِ اللهُ ثَالِثُهُمَا؟﴾

(O Abu Bakr, what do you think of two who have Allah as their third) And Allah said:

(If you help him not, for Allah did indeed help him when the disbelievers drove him out, the second of the two; when they were in the cave, he said to his companion: "Do not grieve, surely, Allah is with us." Then Allah sent down His tranquillity upon him, and strengthened him with forces which you saw not, and made the word of those who disbelieved the lower, while the Word of Allah became the higher; and Allah is All-Mighty, All-Wise.) (9:40) -The story of this cave (Thawr) is far greater and more wondrous than that of the people of the Cave.

Surah: 18 Ayah: 17

وَتَرَى ٱلشَّمْسَ إِذَا طَلَعَت تَّزَٰوَرُ عَن كَهْفِهِمْ ذَاتَ ٱلْيَمِينِ وَإِذَا غَرَبَت تَّقْرِضُهُمْ ذَاتَ ٱلشِّمَالِ وَهُمْ فِى فَجْوَةٍ مِّنْهُ ۚ ذَٰلِكَ مِنْ ءَايَٰتِ ٱللَّهِ ۗ مَن يَهْدِ ٱللَّهُ فَهُوَ ٱلْمُهْتَدِ ۖ وَمَن يُضْلِلْ فَلَن تَجِدَ لَهُۥ وَلِيًّا مُّرْشِدًا ۝

17. And you might have seen the sun, when it rose, declining to the right from their Cave, and when it set, turning away from them to the left, while they lay in the midst of the Cave. That is (one) of the Ayât (proofs, evidences, signs) of Allâh. He whom Allâh guides, is rightly guided; but he whom He sends astray, for him you will find no Walî (guiding friend) to lead him (to the right Path).

Transliteration

17. Watara alshshamsa itha talaAAat tazawaru AAan kahfihim thata alyameeni wa-itha gharabat taqriduhum thata alshshimali wahum fee fajwatin minhu thalika min ayati Allahi man yahdi Allahu fahuwa almuhtadi waman yudlil falan tajida lahu waliyyan murshidan

Tafsir Ibn Kathir

The Location of the Cave. This indicates that the entrance to the cave faced north, because Allah tells us that when the sun was rising, sunlight entered the cave

(the right), meaning that the shade decreased towards the right, as Ibn `Abbas, Sa`id bin Jubayr and Qatadah said:

(declining) means leaning. Every time the sun rises on the horizon, its rays decline until there is nothing left in such a place when it reaches its zenith. So Allah said,

(and when it set, turning away from them to the left,) meaning, it entered their cave from the left of its entrance, which means from the west. This proves what we say, and it is clear to anyone who thinks about the matter and has some knowledge of astronomy and the paths of the sun, moon and stars. If the entrance of the cave faced east, nothing would have entered it when the sun set, and if it faced the direction of the Qiblah (in this case, south), nothing would have entered it at the time of sunrise or sunset, and the shadows would have leaned neither to the right nor the left. If it had faced west, nothing would have entered it at the time of sunrise, until after the sun had passed its zenith, and would have stayed until sunset. This supports what we have said, and to Allah is the praise. Ibn `Abbas, Mujahid and Qatadah said that "turning away from them" means that it would shine on them and then leave them. Allah has told us this, and He wants us to understand it and ponder its meaning, but He did not tell us the location of this cave, i.e., in which country on earth it is, because there is no benefit for us in knowing that, and no legislative objective behind it. If there was any spiritual or religious interest that could be served by our knowing that, Allah and His Messenger would have taught us about it, as the Prophet said:

«مَا تَرَكْتُ شَيْئًا يُقَرِّبُكُمْ إِلَى الْجَنَّةِ وَيُبَاعِدُكُمْ مِنَ النَّارِ إِلَّا وَقَدْ أَعْلَمْتُكُمْ بِهِ»

(I have not left anything that will bring you closer to Paradise and keep you further away from Hell but I have certainly taught you about it.) So Allah has told us about the features of the cave, but He did not tell us where it is, and He said,

(And you might have seen the sun, when it rose, declining from their cave.) Malik narrated from Zayd bin Aslam, "Leaning."

(the right, and when it set, turning away from them to the left, while they lay in the midst of the cave.) meaning, the sun entered the cave without touching them, because if it had touched them, it would have burnt their bodies and clothes. This was the view of Ibn `Abbas.

(That is from the Ayat of Allah), how He guided them to this cave where He kept them alive, and the sun and wind entered the cave preserving their bodies. Allah says,

(That is from the Ayat of Allah.) Then He says:

(He whom Allah guides, he is the rightly-guided;) meaning that He is the One Who guided these young men to true guidance among their people, for the one whom Allah guides is truly guided, and the one whom Allah leaves astray will find no one to guide him.

Surah: 18 Ayah: 18

وَتَحْسَبُهُمْ أَيْقَاظًا وَهُمْ رُقُودٌ وَنُقَلِّبُهُمْ ذَاتَ ٱلْيَمِينِ وَذَاتَ ٱلشِّمَالِ وَكَلْبُهُم بَٰسِطٌ ذِرَاعَيْهِ بِٱلْوَصِيدِ لَوِ ٱطَّلَعْتَ عَلَيْهِمْ لَوَلَّيْتَ مِنْهُمْ فِرَارًا وَلَمُلِئْتَ مِنْهُمْ رُعْبًا ۞

18. And you would have thought them awake, while they were asleep. And We turned them on their right and on their left sides, and their dog stretching forth his two forelegs at the entrance (of the Cave or in the space near to the entrance of the Cave (as a guard at the gate)) Had you looked at them, you would certainly have turned back from them in flight, and would certainly have been filled with awe of them.

Transliteration

18. Watahsabuhum ayqathan wahum ruqoodun wanuqallibuhum thata alyameeni wathata alshshimali wakalbuhum basitun thiraAAayhi bialwaseedi lawi ittalaAAta AAalayhim lawallayta minhum firaran walamuli/ta minhum ruAAban

Tafsir Ibn Kathir

Their Sleep in the Cave

Some of the scholars mentioned that when Allah caused them to sleep, their eyelids did not close, lest disintegration took hold of them. If their eyes remained open to the air, this would be better for the sake of preservation. Allah says:

(And you would have thought them awake, whereas they were asleep.) It was mentioned that when the wolf sleeps, it closes one eye and keeps one eye open, then it switches eyes while asleep.

(And We turned them on their right and on their left sides,) Ibn `Abbas said: "If they did not turn over, the earth would have consumed them."

(and their dog stretching forth his two forelegs at the Wasid) Ibn `Abbas, Mujahid, Sa`id bin Jubayr and Qatadah said: "The Wasid means the threshold." Ibn `Abbas said: "By the door." It was said: "On the ground." The correct view is that it means on the threshold, i.e., at the door.

(Verily, it shall be closed upon them) (104:8) Their dog lay down at the door, as is the habit of dogs. Ibn Jurayj said, "He was guarding the door for them." It was his nature and habit to lie down at their door as if guarding them. He was sitting outside the door, because the angels do not enter a house in which there is a dog, as was reported in As-Sahih, nor do they enter a house in which there is an image, a person in a state of ritual impurity or a disbeliever, as was narrated in the Hasan Hadith. The blessing they enjoyed extended to their dog, so the sleep that overtook them overtook him too. This is the benefit of accompanying good people, and so this dog attained fame and stature. It was said that he was the hunting dog of one of the people which is the more appropriate view, or that he was the dog of the king's cook, who shared their religious views, and brought his dog with him. And Allah knows best. Allah says:

(Had you happened upon them, you would certainly have turned back from them in flight, and would certainly have been filled with awe of them.) meaning that Allah made them appear dreadful, so that no one could look at them without being filled with terror, because of the frightening appearance they had been given. This was so that no one would come near them or touch them until the appointed time when their sleep would come to an end as Allah willed, because of the wisdom, clear proof and great mercy involved in that.

Surah: 18 Ayah: 19 & Ayah: 20

وَكَذَٰلِكَ بَعَثْنَٰهُمْ لِيَتَسَآءَلُوا۟ بَيْنَهُمْ ۚ قَالَ قَآئِلٌ مِّنْهُمْ كَمْ لَبِثْتُمْ ۖ قَالُوا۟ لَبِثْنَا يَوْمًا أَوْ بَعْضَ يَوْمٍ ۚ قَالُوا۟ رَبُّكُمْ أَعْلَمُ بِمَا لَبِثْتُمْ فَٱبْعَثُوٓا۟ أَحَدَكُم بِوَرِقِكُمْ هَٰذِهِۦٓ إِلَى ٱلْمَدِينَةِ فَلْيَنظُرْ أَيُّهَآ أَزْكَىٰ طَعَامًا فَلْيَأْتِكُم بِرِزْقٍ مِّنْهُ وَلْيَتَلَطَّفْ وَلَا يُشْعِرَنَّ بِكُمْ أَحَدًا ۝

19. Likewise, We awakened them (from their long deep sleep) that they might question one another. A speaker from among them said: "How long have you stayed (here)?" They said: "We have stayed (perhaps) a day or part of a day." They said: "Your Lord (Alone) knows best how long you have stayed (here). So send one of you with this silver coin of yours to the town, and let him find out which is the good lawful food, and bring some of that to you. And let him be careful and let no man know of you.

إِنَّهُمْ إِن يَظْهَرُوا۟ عَلَيْكُمْ يَرْجُمُوكُمْ أَوْ يُعِيدُوكُمْ فِى مِلَّتِهِمْ وَلَن تُفْلِحُوٓا۟ إِذًا أَبَدًا

20. "For if they come to know of you, they will stone you (to death or abuse and harm you) or turn you back to their religion; and in that case you will never be successful."

Transliteration

19. Wakathalika baAAathnahum liyatasaaloo baynahum qala qa-ilun minhum kam labithtum qaloo labithna yawman aw baAAda yawmin qaloo rabbukum aAAlamu bima labithtum faibAAathoo ahadakum biwariqikum hathihi ila almadeenati falyanthur ayyuha azka taAAaman falya/tikum birizqin minhu walyatalattaf wala yushAAiranna bikum ahadan 20. Innahum in yaththaroo AAalaykum yarjumookum aw yuAAeedookum fee millatihim walan tuflihoo ithan abadan

Tafsir Ibn Kathir

Their awakening and sending One of Themselves to buy Food. Allah says: `just as We caused them to sleep, We resurrected them with their bodies, hair and skin intact, and nothing lacking in their form and appearance.' This was after three hundred and nine years. This is why they asked each other,

(How long have you stayed (here)) meaning, `how long have you slept'

(They said: "We have stayed a day or part of a day.") because they entered the cave at the beginning of the day, and they woke up at the end of the day, which is why they then said,

("...or a part of a day." They said: "Your Lord knows best how long you have stayed...") meaning, `Allah knows best about your situation.' It seems that they were not sure about how long they had slept, and Allah knows best. Then they turned their attention to more pressing matters, like their need for food and drink, so they said:

(So send one of you with this silver coin of yours) They had brought with them some Dirhams (silver coins) from their homes, to buy whatever they might need, and they had given some in charity and kept some, so they said:

(So send one of you with this silver coin of yours to the town,) meaning to their city, which they had left. The definite article indicates that they were referring to a known city.

(and let him find out which is the Azka food.) Azka means "purest", as Allah says elsewhere,

(And had it not been for the grace of Allah and His mercy on you, not one of you would ever have been pure (Zaka) from sins) (24:21) and

(Indeed whosoever purifies himself (Tazakka) shall achieve success.) (87:14) From the same root also comes the word Zakah, which makes one's wealth good and purifies it.

(And let him be careful) meaning when he goes out buying food and coming back. They were telling him to conceal himself as much as he could,

(and let no man know of you. For, if they come to know of you, they will stone you) means, `if they find out where you are,'

(they will stone you or turn you back to their religion;) They were referring to the followers of Decianus, who they were afraid might find out where they were, and punish them with all kinds of torture until they made them go back to their former religion, or until they died, for if they agreed to go back to their (old) religion, they would never attain success in this world or the Hereafter. So they said:

(and in that case you will never be successful.)

Surah: 18 Ayah: 21

وَكَذَٰلِكَ أَعْثَرْنَا عَلَيْهِمْ لِيَعْلَمُوٓا۟ أَنَّ وَعْدَ ٱللَّهِ حَقٌّ وَأَنَّ ٱلسَّاعَةَ لَا رَيْبَ فِيهَآ إِذْ يَتَنَٰزَعُونَ بَيْنَهُمْ أَمْرَهُمْ ۖ فَقَالُوا۟ ٱبْنُوا۟ عَلَيْهِم بُنْيَٰنًا ۖ رَّبُّهُمْ أَعْلَمُ بِهِمْ ۚ قَالَ ٱلَّذِينَ غَلَبُوا۟ عَلَىٰٓ أَمْرِهِمْ لَنَتَّخِذَنَّ عَلَيْهِم مَّسْجِدًا ۝

21. And thus We made their case known (to the people), that they might know that the Promise of Allâh is true, and that there can be no doubt about the Hour. (Remember) when they (the people of the city) disputed among themselves about their case, they said: "Construct a building over them; their Lord knows

best about them;" (then) those who won their point said (most probably the disbelievers): "We verily shall build a place of worship over them."

Transliteration

21. Wakathalika aAAtharna AAalayhim liyaAAlamoo anna waAAda Allahi haqqun waanna alsaAAata la rayba feeha ith yatanazaAAoona baynahum amrahum faqaloo ibnoo AAalayhim bunyanan rabbuhum aAAlamu bihim qala allatheena ghalaboo AAala amrihim lanattakhithanna AAalayhim masjidan

Tafsir Ibn Kathir

How the People of the City came to know about Them; building a Memorial over the Cave

(And thus We made their case known,) means, `We caused the people to find them.'

(that they might know that the promise of Allah is true, and that there can be no doubt about the Hour.) Several scholars of the Salaf mentioned that the people of that time were skeptical about the Resurrection. `Ikrimah said: "There was a group of them who said that the souls would be resurrected but not the bodies, so Allah resurrected the people of the Cave as a sign and proof of resurrection." They mentioned that when they wanted to send one of their members out to the city to buy them something to eat, he disguised himself and set out walking by a different route, until he reached the city, which they said was called Daqsus. He thought that it was not long since he left it, but in fact century after century, generation after generation, nation after nation had passed, and the country and its people had changed. He saw no local landmarks that he recognized, and he did not recognize any of the people, elite or commoners. He began to feel confused and said to himself, "Maybe I am crazy or deluded, maybe I am dreaming." Then he said, "By Allah, I am nothing of the sort, what I know I saw last night was different from this." Then he said, "I had better get out of here." Then he went to one of the men selling food, gave him the money he had and asked him to sell him some food. When the man saw the money he did not recognize it or its imprint, so he passed it to his neighbor and they all began to pass it around, saying, "Maybe this man found some treasure." They asked him who he was and where he got this money. Had he found a treasure Who was he He said, "I am from this land, I was living here yesterday and Decianus was the ruler." They accused him of being crazy and took him to the governor who questioned him about his circumstances, and he told him. He was confused about his situation. When he told them about it, they -- the king and the people of the city -- went with him to the cave, where he told them, "Let me go in first and let my companions know." It was said that the people did not know how he entered it, and that the people did not know about their story. It was also said that they did enter the cave and see them, and the king greeted them and embraced them. Apparently he was a Muslim, and his name was Tedosis. They rejoiced at meeting him and spoke with him, then they bid farewell to him and went back to sleep, then Allah caused them to die. And Allah knows best. A

(And thus We made their case known,) meaning, `just as We caused them to sleep then woke them up physically intact, We made their story known to the people of that time.'

(that they might know that the promise of Allah is true, and that there can be no doubt about the Hour. (Remember) when they (the people) disputed among themselves about their case,) meaning, about Resurrection. Some believed in it and some denied it, so Allah made their discovery of the people of the cave evidence either in their favor or against them.

(they said: "Construct a building over them; their Lord knows best about them,") meaning, seal the door of their cave over them, and leave them as they are.

(those who won their point said: "We verily, shall build a place of worship over them.") Those who said this were the people of power and influence, but were they good people or not There is some debate on this point, because the Prophet said:

«لَعَنَ اللهُ الْيَهُودَ وَالنَّصَارَى اتَّخَذُوا قُبُورَ أَنْبِيَائِهِمْ وَصَالِحِيهِمْ مَسَاجِدَ»

(Allah has cursed the Jews and the Christians who took the graves of their Prophets and righteous people as places of worship) Warning against what they did. We have reported about the Commander of the faithful `Umar bin Al-Khattab that when he found the grave of Danyal (Daniel) in Iraq during his period of rule, he gave orders that news of this grave should be withheld from the people, and that the inscription containing mention of battles etc., that they found there should be buried.

Surah: 18 Ayah: 22

سَيَقُولُونَ ثَلَاثَةٌ رَابِعُهُمْ كَلْبُهُمْ وَيَقُولُونَ خَمْسَةٌ سَادِسُهُمْ كَلْبُهُمْ رَجْمًا بِالْغَيْبِ وَيَقُولُونَ سَبْعَةٌ وَثَامِنُهُمْ كَلْبُهُمْ قُل رَّبِّي أَعْلَمُ بِعِدَّتِهِم مَّا يَعْلَمُهُمْ إِلَّا قَلِيلٌ فَلَا تُمَارِ فِيهِمْ إِلَّا مِرَاءً ظَاهِرًا وَلَا تَسْتَفْتِ فِيهِم مِّنْهُمْ أَحَدًا

22. (Some) say they were three, the dog being the fourth among them; and (others) say they were five, the dog being the sixth, - guessing at the unseen; (yet others) say they were seven, the dog being the eighth. Say (O Muhammad (peace be upon him)) "My Lord knows best their number; none knows them but a few." So debate not (about their number) except with the clear proof (which We have revealed to you). And consult not any of them (people of the Scripture - Jews and Christians) about (the affair of) the people of the Cave.

Transliteration

22. Sayaqooloona thalathatun rabiAAuhum kalbuhum wayaqooloona khamsatun sadisuhum kalbuhum rajman bialghaybi wayaqooloona sabAAatun wathaminuhum kalbuhum qul rabbee aAAlamu biAAiddatihim ma yaAAlamuhum illa qaleelun fala tumari feehim illa miraan thahiran wala tastafti feehim minhum ahadan

Tafsir Ibn Kathir

Their Number

Allah tells us that people disputed over the number of the people of the Cave. The Ayah mentions three views, proving that there was no fourth suggestion. Allah indicates that the first two opinions are invalid, by saying,

(guessing at the unseen), meaning that they spoke without knowledge, like a person who aims at an unknown target -- he is hardly likely to hit it, and if he does, it was not on purpose. Then Allah mentions the third opinion, and does not comment on it, or He affirms it by saying,

(and the dog being the eighth.) indicating that this is correct and this is what happened.

(Say: "My Lord knows best their number...") indicating that the best thing to do in matters like this is to refer knowledge to Allah, because there is no need to indulge in discussing such matters without knowledge. If we are given knowledge of a matter, then we may talk about it, otherwise we should refrain.

(none knows them but a few.) of mankind. Qatadah said that Ibn `Abbas said: "I am one of the few mentioned in this Ayah; they were seven. " Ibn Jurayj also narrated that `Ata' Al-Khurasani narrated from him, "I am one of those referred to in this Ayah," and he would say: "Their number was seven." Ibn Jarir recorded that Ibn `Abbas said:

(none knows them but a few.) "I am one of the few, and they were seven." The chains of these reports narrated from Ibn `Abbas, which say that they were seven, are Sahih, and this is in accordance with what we have stated above.

(So debate not except with the clear proof.) meaning, gently and politely, for there is not a great deal to be gained from knowing about that.

(And consult not any of them (about the people of the Cave).) meaning, `They do not have any knowledge about it except what they make up, guessing at the unseen; they have no evidence from an infallible source. But Allah has sent you, O Muhammad, with the truth in which there is no doubt or confusion, which is to be given priority over all previous books and sayings.'

Surah: 18 Ayah: 23 & Ayah: 24

وَلَا تَقُولَنَّ لِشَاْىْءٍ إِنِّى فَاعِلٌ ذَٰلِكَ غَدًا ﴿٢٣﴾

23. And never say of anything, "I shall do such and such thing tomorrow."

إِلَّآ أَن يَشَآءَ ٱللَّهُ وَٱذْكُر رَّبَّكَ إِذَا نَسِيتَ وَقُلْ عَسَىٰٓ أَن يَهْدِيَنِ رَبِّى لِأَقْرَبَ مِنْ هَـٰذَا رَشَدًا ﴿٢٤﴾

24. Except (with the saying), "If Allâh will!" And remember your Lord when you forget and say: "It may be that my Lord guides me unto a nearer way of truth than this."

Transliteration

23. Wala taqoolanna lishay-in innee faAAilun thalika ghadan 24. Illa an yashaa Allahu waothkur rabbaka itha naseeta waqul AAasa an yahdiyani rabbee li-aqraba min hatha rashadan

Tafsir Ibn Kathir

Saying "If Allah wills" when determining to do Something in the Future

Here Allah, may He be glorified, shows His Messenger the correct etiquette when determining to do something in the future; this should always be referred to the will of Allah, the Knower of the Unseen, Who knows what was and what is yet to be and what is not to be, and how it will be if it is to be. It was recorded in the Two Sahihs that Abu Hurayrah said that the Messenger of Allah said:

»قَالَ سُلَيْمَانُ بْنُ دَاوُدَ عَلَيْهِمَا السَّلَامُ: لَأَطُوفَنَّ اللَّيْلَةَ عَلَى سَبْعِينَ امْرَأَةً وَفِي رِوَايَةٍ: تِسْعِينَ امْرَأَةً، وَفِي رِوَايَةٍ: مِائَةِ امْرَأَةٍ تَلِدُ كُلُّ امْرَأَةٍ مِنْهُنَّ غُلَامًا يُقَاتِلُ فِي سَبِيلِ اللهِ، فَقِيلَ لَهُ وَفِي رِوَايَةٍ قَالَ لَهُ الْمَلَكُ: قُلْ إِنْ شَاءَ اللهُ، فَلَمْ يَقُلْ، فَطَافَ بِهِنَّ فَلَمْ تَلِدْ مِنْهُنَّ إِلَّا امْرَأَةٌ وَاحِدَةٌ نِصْفَ إِنْسَانٍ، فَقَالَ رَسُولُ اللهِ صلى الله عليه وسلّم: وَالَّذِي نَفْسِي بِيَدِهِ، لَوْ قَالَ إِنْ شَاءَ اللهُ لَمْ يَحْنَثْ، وَكَانَ دَرَكًا لِحَاجَتِهِ«

(Sulayman bin Dawud (peace be upon them both) said: "Tonight I will go around to seventy women (according to some reports, it was ninety or one hundred women) so that each one of them will give birth to a son who will fight for the sake of Allah." It was said to him, (according to one report, the angel said to him) "Say: `If Allah wills'", but he did not say it. He went around to the women but none of them gave birth except for one who gave birth to a half-formed child.) The Messenger of Allah said, (By the One in Whose hand is my soul, had he said, "If Allah wills," he would not have broken his oath, and that would have helped him to attain what he wanted.) According to another report, (

»وَلَقَاتَلُوا فِي سَبِيلِ اللهِ فُرْسَانًا أَجْمَعُونَ«

They would all have fought as horsemen in the cause of Allah.) At the beginning of this Surah we discussed the reason why this Ayah was revealed: when the Prophet was asked about the story of the people of the Cave, he said, "I will tell you tomorrow." Then the revelation was delayed for fifteen days. Since we discussed this at length at the beginning of the Surah, there is no need to repeat it here.

(And remember your Lord when you forget) It was said that this means, if you forget to say "If Allah wills", then say it when you remember. This was the view of Abu Al-`Aliyah and Al-Hasan Al-Basri. Hushaym reported from Al-A`mash from Mujahid that concerning a man who swears an oath, Ibn `Abbas said "He may say `If Allah wills' even if it is a year later." Ibn `Abbas used to interpret this Ayah:

(And remember your Lord when you forget) in this way. Al-A`mash was asked, "Did you hear this from Mujahid" He said, "Layth bin Abi Salim told it to me." The meaning of Ibn `Abbas' view, that a person may say "If Allah wills", even if it is a year later, is that if he forgets to say it when he makes the oath or when he speaks, and he remembers it later, even a year later, the Sunnah is that he should say it, so that he will still be following the Sunnah of saying "If Allah wills", even if that is after breaking his oath. This was also the view of Ibn Jarir, but he stated that this does not make up for breaking the oath or mean that one is no longer obliged to offer expiation. What Ibn Jarir said is correct, and it is more appropriate to understand the words of Ibn Abbas in this way. And Allah knows best.

(And never say of anything, "I shall do such and such thing tomorrow." Except (with the saying), "If Allah wills!" And remember your Lord when you forget) At-Tabarani recorded that Ibn `Abbas said that this meant saying, "If Allah wills."

(and say: "It may be that my Lord guides me to a nearer way of truth than this.") meaning, `if you (O Prophet) are asked about something you know nothing about, ask Allah about it, and turn to Him so that He may guide you to what is right.' And Allah knows best.

Surah: 18 Ayah: 25 & Ayah: 26

$$\text{وَلَبِثُوا۟ فِى كَهْفِهِمْ ثَلَـٰثَ مِا۟ئَةٍ سِنِينَ وَٱزْدَادُوا۟ تِسْعًا ۝}$$

25. And they stayed in their Cave three hundred (solar) years, and add nine (for lunar years). (Tafsir Al-Qurtubi)

$$\text{قُلِ ٱللَّهُ أَعْلَمُ بِمَا لَبِثُوا۟ ۖ لَهُۥ غَيْبُ ٱلسَّمَـٰوَٰتِ وَٱلْأَرْضِ ۖ أَبْصِرْ بِهِۦ وَأَسْمِعْ ۚ مَا لَهُم مِّن دُونِهِۦ مِن وَلِىٍّ وَلَا يُشْرِكُ فِى حُكْمِهِۦٓ أَحَدًا ۝}$$

26. Say: "Allâh knows best how long they stayed. With Him is (the knowledge of) the Unseen of the heavens and the earth. How clearly He sees, and hears (everything)! They have no Walî (Helper, Disposer of affairs, Protector) other than Him, and He makes none to share in His Decision and His Rule."

Transliteration

25. Walabithoo fee kahfihim thalatha mi-atin sineena waizdadoo tisAAan 26. Quli Allahu aAAlamu bima labithoo lahu ghaybu alssamawati waal-ardi absir bihi waasmiAA ma lahum min doonihi min waliyyin wala yushriku fee hukmihi ahadan

Tafsir Ibn Kathir

The Length of their Stay in the Cave

Here Allah tells His Messenger the length of time the people of the Cave spent in their cave, from the time when He caused them to sleep until the time when He resurrected them and caused the people of that era to find them. The length of time was three hundred plus nine years in lunar years, which is three hundred years in solar years. The difference between one hundred lunar years and one hundred solar years is three years, which is why after mentioning three hundred, Allah says, `adding nine.'

(Say: "Allah knows best how long they stayed...") `If you are asked about how long they stayed, and you have no knowledge of that and no revelation from Allah about it, then do not say anything. Rather say something like this:

(Allah knows best how long they stayed. With Him is (the knowledge of) the Unseen of the heavens and the earth.)" meaning, no one knows about that except Him, and whoever among His creatures He chooses to tell. What we have said here is the view of more than one of the scholars of Tafsir, such as Mujahid and others among the earlier and later generations.

(And they stayed in their cave three hundred years,) Qatadah said, this was the view of the People of the Book, and Allah refuted it by saying:

(Say: "Allah knows best how long they stayed...") meaning, that Allah knows better than what the people say. This was also the view of Mutarraf bin `Abdullah. However, this view is open to debate, because when the People of the Book said that they stayed in the cave for three hundred years, without the extra nine, they were referring to solar years, and if Allah was merely narrating what they had said, He would not have said,

(adding nine.) The apparent meaning of the Ayah is that Allah is stating the facts, not narrating what was said. This is the view of Ibn Jarir (may Allah have mercy on him). And Allah knows best.

(How clearly He sees, and hears (everything)!) He sees them and hears them. Ibn Jarir said, "The language used is an eloquent expression of praise." The phrase may be understood to mean, how much Allah sees of everything that exists and how much He hears of everything that is to be heard, for nothing is hidden from Him! It was narrated that Qatadah commented on this Ayah:

(How clearly He sees, and hears (everything)!) "No one hears or sees more than Allah."

(They have no protector other than Him, and He makes none to share in His decision and His rule.) meaning, He, may He be glorified, is the One Who has the power to create and to command, the One Whose ruling cannot be overturned; He has no adviser, supporter or partner, may He be exalted and hallowed.

Surah: 18 Ayah: 27 & Ayah: 28

وَٱتْلُ مَآ أُوحِىَ إِلَيْكَ مِن كِتَابِ رَبِّكَ ۖ لَا مُبَدِّلَ لِكَلِمَـٰتِهِۦ وَلَن تَجِدَ مِن دُونِهِۦ مُلْتَحَدًا ۝

27. And recite what has been revealed to you (O Muhammad (peace be upon him)) of the Book (the Qur'ân) of your Lord (i.e. recite it, understand and follow its teachings and act on its orders and preach it to men). None can change His Words, and none will you find as a refuge other than Him.

وَٱصْبِرْ نَفْسَكَ مَعَ ٱلَّذِينَ يَدْعُونَ رَبَّهُم بِٱلْغَدَوٰةِ وَٱلْعَشِىِّ يُرِيدُونَ وَجْهَهُۥ ۖ وَلَا تَعْدُ عَيْنَاكَ عَنْهُمْ تُرِيدُ زِينَةَ ٱلْحَيَوٰةِ ٱلدُّنْيَا ۖ وَلَا تُطِعْ مَنْ أَغْفَلْنَا قَلْبَهُۥ عَن ذِكْرِنَا وَٱتَّبَعَ هَوَىٰهُ وَكَانَ أَمْرُهُۥ فُرُطًا ۝

28. And keep yourself (O Muhammad (peace be upon him)) patiently with those who call on their Lord (i.e. your companions who remember their Lord with glorification, praising in prayers, and other righteous deeds) morning and afternoon, seeking His Face; and let not your eyes overlook them, desiring the pomp and glitter of the life of the world; and obey not him whose heart We have made heedless of Our Remembrance, and who follows his own lusts, and whose affair (deeds) has been lost.

Transliteration

27. Waotlu ma oohiya ilayka min kitabi rabbika la mubaddila likalimatihi walan tajida min doonihi multahadan   28. Waisbir nafsaka maAAa allatheena yadAAoona rabbahum bialghadati waalAAashiyyi yureedoona wajhahu wala taAAdu AAaynaka AAanhum tureedu zeenata alhayati alddunya wala tutiAA man aghfalna qalbahu AAan thikrina waittabaAAa hawahu wakana amruhu furutan

Tafsir Ibn Kathir

The Command to recite the Qur'an and to patiently keep Company with the Believers

Commanding His Messenger to recite His Holy Book and convey it to mankind, Allah says,

(None can change His Words,) meaning, no one can alter them, distort them or misinterpret them.

(and none will you find as a refuge other than Him.) It was reported that Mujahid said, "A shelter," and that Qatadah said, "A helper or supporter." Ibn Jarir said: "Allah is saying, `if you O Muhammad, do not recite what is revealed to you of the Book of your Lord, then you will have no refuge from Allah.'" As Allah says:

(O Messenger! Proclaim (the Message) which has been sent down to you from your Lord. And if you do not, then you have not conveyed His Message. Allah will protect you from mankind.)(5:67)

(Verily, He Who has given you the Qur'an, will surely bring you back to the place of return.) (28:85) meaning, `He will call you to account for the duty of conveying the Message which He entrusted you with. '

(And keep yourself patiently with those who call on their Lord morning and afternoon, seeking His Face;) meaning, sit with those who remember Allah, who say "La Ilaha Illallah", who praise Him, glorify Him, declare His greatness and call on Him, morning and evening, all the servants of Allah, whether rich or poor, strong or weak. It was said that this was revealed about the nobles of Quraysh when they asked the Prophet to sit with them on his own, and not to bring his weak Companions with him, such as Bilal, `Ammar, Suhayb, Khabbab and Ibn Mas`ud. They wanted him to sit with them on his own, but Allah forbade him from doing that, and said,

(And turn not away those who invoke their Lord, morning and afternoon.) Allah commanded him to patiently content himself with sitting with those people (the weak believers), and said:

(And keep yourself patiently with those who call on their Lord morning and afternoon...) Imam Muslim recorded in his Sahih that Sa`d bin Abi Waqqas who said: "There was a group of six of us with the Prophet . The idolators said, `Tell these people to leave so they will not offend us.' There was myself, Ibn Mas`ud, a man from Hudayl, Bilal and two other men whose names I have forgotten. Allah's Messenger thought to himself about whatever Allah willed he should think about, then Allah revealed:

(And turn not away those who invoke their Lord, morning and afternoon.) Only Muslim reported this; excluding Al-Bukhari.

(and let not your eyes overlook them, desiring the pomp and glitter of the life of the world;) Ibn `Abbas said, `(this means) do not favor others over them, meaning do not seek the people of nobility and wealth instead of them.'

(and obey not him whose heart We have made heedless of Our remembrance) means, those who are distracted by this world from being committed to the religion and from worshipping their Lord.

(and whose affair (deeds) has been lost.) means, his actions and deeds are a foolish waste of time. Do not obey him or admire his way or envy what he has. As Allah says elsewhere:

(And strain not your eyes in longing for the things We have given for enjoyment to various groups of them, the splendor of the life of this world, that We may test them thereby. But the provision of your Lord is better and more lasting.) (20:131)

Surah: 18 Ayah: 29

وَقُلِ ٱلْحَقُّ مِن رَّبِّكُمْ ۖ فَمَن شَآءَ فَلْيُؤْمِن وَمَن شَآءَ فَلْيَكْفُرْ ۚ إِنَّآ أَعْتَدْنَا لِلظَّٰلِمِينَ نَارًا أَحَاطَ بِهِمْ سُرَادِقُهَا ۚ وَإِن يَسْتَغِيثُوا۟ يُغَاثُوا۟ بِمَآءٍ كَٱلْمُهْلِ يَشْوِى ٱلْوُجُوهَ ۚ بِئْسَ ٱلشَّرَابُ وَسَآءَتْ مُرْتَفَقًا ﴿٢٩﴾

29. And say: "The truth is from your Lord." Then whosoever wills, let him believe; and whosoever wills, let him disbelieve. Verily, We have prepared for the Zâlimûn (polytheists and wrong-doers), a Fire whose walls will be surrounding them (disbelievers in the Oneness of Allâh). And if they ask for help (relief, water), they will be granted water like boiling oil, that will scald their faces. Terrible the drink, and an evil Murtafaq (dwelling, resting place.)!

Transliteration

29. Waquli alhaqqu min rabbikum faman shaa falyu/min waman shaa falyakfur inna aAAtadna lilththalimeena naran ahata bihim suradiquha wa-in yastagheethoo yughathoo bima-in kaalmuhli yashwee alwujooha bi/sa alshsharabu wasaat murtafaqan

Tafsir Ibn Kathir

The Truth is from Allah, and the Punishment of Those Who do not believe in it

Allah says to His Messenger Muhammad : "Say to the people, `What I have brought to you from your Lord is the truth, in which there is no confusion or doubt.'"

(Then whosoever wills, let him believe; and whosoever wills, let him disbelieve.) This is a type of threat and stern warning, after which Allah says,

(Verily, We have prepared), meaning made ready,

(for the wrongdoers,) meaning those who disbelieve in Allah, His Messenger and His Book,

(a Fire whose walls will be surrounding them.) Ibn Jurayj said that Ibn `Abbas said,

(a Fire whose walls will be surrounding them.) "A wall of fire."

(And if they ask for drink, they will be granted water like Al-Muhl, that will scald their faces.) Ibn `Abbas said; "Al-Muhl is thick water which is similar to the sediment in oil." Mujahid said, "It is like blood and pus." `Ikrimah said, "It is the thing that is heated to the ultimate temperature." Others said: "It is everything that is melted."

Qatadah said, "Ibn Mas`ud melted some gold in a grove, and when it became liquid and foam rose to the top, he said, this is the thing that is most like Al-Muhl." Ad-Dahhak said: "The water of Hell is black, and it itself is black and its people are black." There is nothing contradictory in these comments, for Al-Muhl includes all of these unpleasant characteristics, it is black, evil-smelling, thick and hot, as Allah said,

((it) will scald their faces.) meaning because of its heat. When the disbeliever wants to drink it and brings it close to his face, it will scald it so that the skin of his face falls off into it. Sa`id bin Jubayr said, "When the people of Hell get hungry, they will ask for relief from it, and they will be given the tree of Zaqqum from which they will eat. The tree will tear off the skin of their faces, and if anyone who knew them were to pass by, he would recognize the skin of their faces in the tree. Then they will feel thirsty, so they will ask for drink, and they will be granted water like Al-Muhl, that is what has been heated to the ultimate temperature. When it is brought near their mouths, the flesh of their faces from which the skin has been torn off will be baked." After describing this drink in these horrifying qualities, Allah says:

(Terrible is the drink,) meaning, how awful this drink is. Similarly, He says in another Ayah:

(and be given to drink boiling water so that it cuts up their bowels.) (47:15)

(They will be given to drink from a boiling spring.) (88:5)

(They will go between it (Hell) and the fierce boiling water.) (55:44)

(and an evil Murtafaq!) means, how evil a place is the Fire to dwell and rest and gather. As Allah says elsewhere:

(Evil indeed it (Hell) is as an abode and as a place to rest in.) (25:66)

Surah: 18 Ayah: 30 & Ayah: 31

إِنَّ ٱلَّذِينَ ءَامَنُوا۟ وَعَمِلُوا۟ ٱلصَّـٰلِحَـٰتِ إِنَّا لَا نُضِيعُ أَجْرَ مَنْ أَحْسَنَ عَمَلًا ۝

30. Verily! As for those who believed and did righteous deeds, certainly We shall not make the reward of anyone who does his (righteous) deeds in the most perfect manner to be lost.

أُو۟لَـٰٓئِكَ لَهُمْ جَنَّـٰتُ عَدْنٍ تَجْرِى مِن تَحْتِهِمُ ٱلْأَنْهَـٰرُ يُحَلَّوْنَ فِيهَا مِنْ أَسَاوِرَ مِن ذَهَبٍ وَيَلْبَسُونَ ثِيَابًا خُضْرًا مِّن سُندُسٍ وَإِسْتَبْرَقٍ مُّتَّكِـِٔينَ فِيهَا عَلَى ٱلْأَرَآئِكِ نِعْمَ ٱلثَّوَابُ وَحَسُنَتْ مُرْتَفَقًا ۝

31. These! For them will be 'Adn (Eden) Paradise (everlasting Gardens); wherein rivers flow underneath them; therein they will be adorned with bracelets of gold, and they will wear green garments of fine and thick silk. They will recline therein

on raised thrones. How good is the reward, and what an excellent Murtafaq (dwelling, resting place.)!

Transliteration

30. Inna allatheena amanoo waAAamiloo alssalihati inna la nudeeAAu ajra man ahsana AAamalan 31. Ola-ika lahum jannatu AAadnin tajree min tahtihimu al-anharu yuhallawna feeha min asawira min thahabin wayalbasoona thiyaban khudran min sundusin wa-istabraqin muttaki-eena feeha AAala alara- iki niAAma alththawabu wahasunat murtafaqan

Tafsir Ibn Kathir

The Reward of those Who believe and do Righteous Deeds

When Allah mentions the state of those who are doomed, He follows that by mentioning the blessed who believed in Allah and believed what His Messengers brought, those who did the righteous deeds that they commanded them to do. They will have Jannatu `Adn. `Adn means lasting.

(wherein rivers flow beneath them,) means, from beneath its rooms and dwellings. Fir`awn said:

(and these rivers flowing beneath me...) (43:51)

(they will be adorned) means, with jewelry.

(with bracelets of gold,) Allah says elsewhere:

(and pearls and their garments therein will be of silk) (22:23). This is explained in more detail here, where Allah says:

(and they will wear green garments of Sundus and Istabraq.) Sundus refers to a fine garment, like a shirt and the like, and Istabraq is thick and shiny velvet.

(They will be Muttaki'in therein on Ara'ik.) The word Muttaki'in implies lying down, or it was said that it means sitting with one's legs crossed, which is closer to the meaning here. In a Sahih Hadith, the Prophet said:

«أَمَّا أَنَا فَلَا آكُلُ مُتَّكِئًا»

(As for me, I do not eat sitting with legs crossed (Muttaki'an)). Ara'ik is the plural of Arikah, which is a bed under a canopy. And Allah knows best.

(How good is the reward, and what an excellent place of rest (Murtafaq)!) means, how blessed is Paradise as a reward for their good deeds. And what an excellent Murtafaq means, and how good a place to dwell and rest and stay. Previously, Allah had said of Hell,

(Terrible is the drink, and an evil place of rest (Murtafaq)!) (18:29). In a similar way, He contrasts the two (Paradise and Hell) in Surat Al-Furqan, where He says:

(Evil indeed it (Hell) is as an abode, and as a place to rest in.) (25:66). Then He mentions the qualities of the believers, then says:

(Those will be rewarded with the highest place because of their patience. Therein they shall be met with greetings and the word of peace and respect. Abiding therein excellent it is as an abode, and as a place to rest in.) (25:75-76)

Surah: 18 Ayah: 32, Ayah: 33, Ayah: 34, Ayah: 35 & Ayah: 36

وَٱضْرِبْ لَهُم مَّثَلًا رَّجُلَيْنِ جَعَلْنَا لِأَحَدِهِمَا جَنَّتَيْنِ مِنْ أَعْنَٰبٍ وَحَفَفْنَٰهُمَا بِنَخْلٍ وَجَعَلْنَا بَيْنَهُمَا زَرْعًا ۝

32. And put forward to them the example of two men; unto one of them We had given two gardens of grapes, and We had surrounded both with date-palms; and had put between them green crops (cultivated fields).

كِلْتَا ٱلْجَنَّتَيْنِ ءَاتَتْ أُكُلَهَا وَلَمْ تَظْلِم مِّنْهُ شَيْـًٔا ۚ وَفَجَّرْنَا خِلَٰلَهُمَا نَهَرًا ۝

33. Each of those two gardens brought forth its produce, and failed not in the least therein, and We caused a river to gush forth in the midst of them.

وَكَانَ لَهُۥ ثَمَرٌ فَقَالَ لِصَٰحِبِهِۦ وَهُوَ يُحَاوِرُهُۥٓ أَنَا۠ أَكْثَرُ مِنكَ مَالًا وَأَعَزُّ نَفَرًا ۝

34. And he had property (or fruit) and he said to his companion, in the course of mutual talk: I am more than you in wealth and stronger in respect of men." (See Tafsir Qurtubî).

وَدَخَلَ جَنَّتَهُۥ وَهُوَ ظَالِمٌ لِّنَفْسِهِۦ قَالَ مَآ أَظُنُّ أَن تَبِيدَ هَٰذِهِۦٓ أَبَدًا ۝

35. And he went into his garden while in a state (of pride and disbelief) unjust to himself. He said: "I think not that this will ever perish.

وَمَآ أَظُنُّ ٱلسَّاعَةَ قَآئِمَةً وَلَئِن رُّدِدتُّ إِلَىٰ رَبِّى لَأَجِدَنَّ خَيْرًا مِّنْهَا مُنقَلَبًا ۝

36. "And I think not the Hour will ever come, and if indeed I am brought back to my Lord, (on the Day of Resurrection), I surely shall find better than this when I return to Him."

Transliteration

32. Waidrib lahum mathalan rajulayni jaAAalna li-ahadihima jannatayni min aAAnabin wahafafnahuma binakhlin wajaAAalna baynahuma zarAAan 33. Kilta aljannatayni atat okulaha walam tathlim minhu shay-an wafajjarna khilalahuma naharan 34. Wakana lahu thamarun faqala lisahibihi wahuwa yuhawiruhu ana aktharu minka malan waaAAazzu nafaran 35. Wadakhala jannatahu wahuwa thalimun linafsihi qala ma

athunnu an tabeeda hathihi abadan 36. Wama athunnu alssaAAata qa-imatan wala-in rudidtu ila rabbee laajidanna khayran minha munqalaban

Tafsir Ibn Kathir

The Example of the Rich Idolators and the Poor Muslims

After mentioning the idolators who were too arrogant to sit with the poor and weak among Muslims, showing off before them with their wealth and noble lineage, Allah then gives a parable for them of two men, one of whom Allah gave two gardens of grapes, surrounded with palm trees and cultivated with crops throughout. All of the trees and plants were abundantly fruitful, providing readily accessible, good quality produce. Allah says:

(Each of those two gardens brought forth its produce,) meaning, produced its fruits,

(and failed not in the least therein,) meaning, nothing at all was diminishing.

(and We caused a river to gush forth in the midst of both.) means, rivers were flowing through them here and there.

(And he had Thamar,) It was said that what was meant here was wealth, and it was said that what was meant were fruits, which is the more apparent meaning here. This is also supported by the alternative recitation, Thumr, which is the plural of Thamrah (fruit) just as Khushb is the plural of Khashab (wood). Others recite it as Thamar.

(and he said) the owner of the two gardens

(to his companion in the course of discussion) means, while he was disputing with him and boasting to him and showing off,

(I am greater than you in wealth and have a mightier entourage.) meaning, `I have more servants, attendants and children.' Qatadah said, "This, by Allah, is the wish of the immoral to have a lot of wealth and a large entourage. R

(And he went into his garden having been unjust to himself.) meaning, in his disbelief, rebellion, arrogance and denial of the Hereafter.

(He said: "I do not think this will ever perish.") Thus he was allowing himself to be deceived because of the plants, fruits and trees that he saw, and the rivers flowing through the different parts of his gardens. He thought that it could never come to an end or cease or be destroyed. This was because of his lack of understanding and the weakness of his faith in Allah, and because he was enamored with this world and its adornments, and because he disbelieved in the Hereafter. So he said:

("And I do not think the Hour will ever come...") meaning, will ever happen

(and if indeed I am brought back to my Lord, I surely shall find better than this when I return to Him.) meaning, `if there is a Hereafter and a return to Allah, then I will have a better share than this with my Lord, for if it were not that I am dear to Him, He would not have given me all this.' As Allah says elsewhere:

(But if I am brought back to my Lord, surely there will be for me the best with Him.) (41:50)

(Have you seen him who disbelieved in Our Ayat and said: "I shall certainly be given wealth and children (if I will be alive again).")(19:77) He took it for granted that Allah would give him this, without any sound evidence for that. The reason why this Ayah was revea- led was because of Al-`As bin Wa'il, as we will explain in the appropriate place, if Allah wills. In Allah we put our trust.

Surah: 18 Ayah: 37, Ayah: 38, Ayah: 39, Ayah: 40 & Ayah: 41

قَالَ لَهُۥ صَاحِبُهُۥ وَهُوَ يُحَاوِرُهُۥٓ أَكَفَرْتَ بِٱلَّذِى خَلَقَكَ مِن تُرَابٍ ثُمَّ مِن نُّطْفَةٍ ثُمَّ سَوَّىٰكَ رَجُلًا ۝

37. His companion said to him during the talk with him: "Do you disbelieve in Him Who created you out of dust (i.e. your father Adam), then out of Nutfah (mixed semen drops of male and female discharge), then fashioned you into a man?

لَّٰكِنَّا۠ هُوَ ٱللَّهُ رَبِّى وَلَآ أُشْرِكُ بِرَبِّىٓ أَحَدًا ۝

38. "But as for my part, (I believe) that He is Allâh, my Lord and none shall I associate as partner with my Lord.

وَلَوْلَآ إِذْ دَخَلْتَ جَنَّتَكَ قُلْتَ مَا شَآءَ ٱللَّهُ لَا قُوَّةَ إِلَّا بِٱللَّهِ إِن تَرَنِ أَنَا۠ أَقَلَّ مِنكَ مَالًا وَوَلَدًا ۝

39. It was better for you to say, when you entered your garden: 'That which Allâh wills (will come to pass)! There is no power but with Allâh '. If you see me less than you in wealth, and children,

فَعَسَىٰ رَبِّىٓ أَن يُؤْتِيَنِ خَيْرًا مِّن جَنَّتِكَ وَيُرْسِلَ عَلَيْهَا حُسْبَانًا مِّنَ ٱلسَّمَآءِ فَتُصْبِحَ صَعِيدًا زَلَقًا ۝

40. "It may be that my Lord will give me something better than your garden, and will send on it Husbân (torment, bolt) from the sky, then it will be a slippery earth.

أَوْ يُصْبِحَ مَآؤُهَا غَوْرًا فَلَن تَسْتَطِيعَ لَهُۥ طَلَبًا ۝

41. "Or the water thereof (of the gardens) becomes deep-sunken (underground) so that you will never be able to seek it."

Transliteration

37. Qala lahu sahibuhu wahuwa yuhawiruhu akafarta biallathee khalaqaka min turabin thumma min nutfatin thumma sawwaka rajulan 38. Lakinna huwa Allahu rabbee wala

oshriku birabbee ahadan 39. Walawla ith dakhalta jannataka qulta ma shaa Allahu la quwwata illa biAllahi in tarani ana aqalla minka malan wawaladan 40. FaAAasa rabbee an yu/tiyani khayran min jannatika wayursila AAalayha husbanan mina alssama-i fatusbiha saAAeedan zalaqan 41. Aw yusbiha maoha ghawran falan tastateeAAa lahu talaban

Tafsir Ibn Kathir

The Response of the Poor Believer

Allah tells us how the rich man's believing companion replied to him, warning and rebuking him for his disbelief in Allah and allowing himself to be deceived.

(Do you disbelieve in Him Who created you out of dust...) This is a denunciation, pointing out the seriousness of his rejection of his Lord Who created and formed man out of dust -- that is, refering to Adam -- then made his offspring from despised liquid, as Allah says:

(How can you disbelieve in Allah Seeing that you were dead and He gave you life) (2:28) meaning, how can you reject your Lord and His clear signs to you, which every one recognizes in himself, for there is no one among His creatures who does not know that he was nothing, then he came to be, and his existence is not due to himself or any other creature. He knows that his existence is due to his Creator, beside Whom there is no other god, the Creator of all things. So the believer said:

(But as for my part, (I believe) that He is Allah, my Lord,) meaning, `I do not say what you say; rather I acknowledge the Oneness and Lordship of Allah,'

(and none shall I associate as partner with my Lord.) meaning, He is Allah, the One Who is to be worshipped Alone, with no partner or associate. Then he said:

(It was better for you to say, when you entered your garden, `That which Allah wills! There is no power but with Allah!' If you see me less than you in wealth, and children.) Here he was urging and encouraging him to say that, as if he was saying, "When you entered your garden and looked at it and liked it, why would'nt you praise Allah for the blessings He gave you and the wealth and children that He has given to you and not to others Why did you not say `That which Allah wills! There is no power but with Allah!"' One of the Salaf said, "Whoever is delighted with something in his circumstances or his wealth or his children, let him say, `That which Allah wills! There is no power but with Allah!"' This is based on this Ayah. It was reported in the Sahih from Abu Musa that the Messenger of Allah said:

«أَلَا أَدُلُّكَ عَلَى كَنْزٍ مِنْ كُنُوزِ الْجَنَّةِ؟ لَا حَوْلَ وَلَا قُوَّةَ إِلَّا بِالله»

(Shall I not tell you about some of the treasure of Paradise La hawla wa la quwwata illa billah (There is no power or might but with Allah).)

(It may be that my Lord will give me something better than your garden,) in the Hereafter (and will send on it) on your garden in this world, which you think will never come to an end or cease to be,

(Husban from the sky,) Ibn `Abbas, Ad-Dahhak and Qatadah said -- and Malik narrated that Az-Zuhri said -- a punishment from heaven. The apparent meaning is that it is a mighty rain which would disrupt his garden and uproot its plants and trees. As he said:

(then it will be as a barren slippery earth.) meaning, smooth mud in which one cannot get a foothold. Ibn `Abbas said, "Like land without vegetation, where nothing grows."

(Or the water thereof becomes Ghawran) means, it disappears into the earth, which is the opposite of flowing water that seeks the surface of the earth. So Gha'ir is to go lower. as Allah says:

(Say: "Tell me! If your water were Ghawran, who then can supply you with flowing water") (67: 30) meaning, water that flows in all directions. And here Allah says:

(Or the water thereof (of the gardens) becomes deep-sunken (underground) so that you will never be able to seek it.) Ghawr is from the same root as Gha'ir and has a similar meaning, but is more intensive.

Surah: 18 Ayah: 42, Ayah: 43 & Ayah: 44

وَأُحِيطَ بِثَمَرِهِ فَأَصْبَحَ يُقَلِّبُ كَفَّيْهِ عَلَىٰ مَآ أَنفَقَ فِيهَا وَهِىَ خَاوِيَةٌ عَلَىٰ عُرُوشِهَا وَيَقُولُ يَٰلَيْتَنِى لَمْ أُشْرِكْ بِرَبِّىٓ أَحَدًا ۞

42. So his fruits were encircled (with ruin). And he remained clapping his hands with sorrow over what he had spent upon it, while it was all destroyed on its trellises, and he could only say: "Would that I had ascribed no partners to my Lord!" (Tafsir Ibn Kathîr)

وَلَمْ تَكُن لَّهُۥ فِئَةٌ يَنصُرُونَهُۥ مِن دُونِ ٱللَّهِ وَمَا كَانَ مُنتَصِرًا ۞

43. And he had no group of men to help him against Allâh, nor could he defend (or save) himself.

هُنَالِكَ ٱلْوَلَٰيَةُ لِلَّهِ ٱلْحَقِّ هُوَ خَيْرٌ ثَوَابًا وَخَيْرٌ عُقْبًا ۞

44. There (on the Day of Resurrection), Al-Walâyah (the protection, power, authority and kingdom) will be for Allâh (Alone), the True God. He (Allâh) is the Best for reward and the Best for the final end. (Lâ ilâha illallâh - none has the right to be worshipped but Allâh).

Transliteration

42. Waoheeta bithamarihi faasbaha yuqallibu kaffayhi AAala ma anfaqa feeha wahiya khawiyatun AAala AAurooshiha wayaqoolu ya laytanee lam oshrik birabbee ahadan

43. Walam takun lahu fi-atun yansuroonahu min dooni Allahi wama kana muntasiran
44. Hunalika alwalayatu lillahi alhaqqi huwa khayrun thawaban wakhayrun AAuqban

Tafsir Ibn Kathir

The Evil Results of Kufr

Allah says:

(So his fruits were encircled), meaning his wealth, or according to the other opinion, his crops. What is meant is that what this disbeliever was afraid of and what the believer had terrified him actually had happened. A storm struck his garden, a garden which he had erroneously thought would last forever, distracting him from thoughts of Allah, may He be glorified.

(And he began Yuqallibu his hands over what he had spent upon it,) Qatadah said: "He was clasping his hands together in a gesture of regret and grief for the wealth he had lost."

(and he could only say: "Would that I had ascribed no partners to my Lord!" And he had no group of men) meaning a clan or children, as he had vainly boasted,

(to help him against Allah, nor could he defend himself. There, Al-Walayah will be for Allah, the True God.) Here there are differences in recitation. Some of the reciters pause at the word there,

(nor could he defend himself there.), i.e., at that time, when Allah sends the punishment upon him, there will be no one to save him. Then they start the next phrase with Al-Walayah;

(Al-Walayah will be for Allah, the True God.) Some of them pause at the phrase

(nor could he defend himself) and start the next phrase;

(There, Al-Walayah will be for Allah, the True God.) There is a further difference in the recitation of the word Al-Walayah. Some read it as Al-Walayah, which gives the meaning that all allegiance will be to Allah, i.e., on that Day everyone, believer or disbeliever, will return to Allah, for allegiance and submission to Him when the punishment comes to pass. This is like the Ayah:

(So when they saw Our punishment, they said: "We believe in Allah Alone and reject (all) that we used to associate with Him as partners.") (40:84) and Allah says concerning the Fir`awn;

(Till when drowning overtook him, he said: "I believe that none has the right to be worshipped but He in Whom the Children of Israel believe, and I am one of the Muslims." Now! While you refused to believe before and you were one of the mischief-makers.) (10:90-91) Some others read it as Al-Wilayah, meaning that on that Day the rule will belong to Allah, the True God. Some read Haqqu (True) refering to Al-Wilayah, as in the Ayah;

(The sovereignty on that Day will be the true (sovereignty), belonging to the Most Gracious (Allah), and it will be a hard Day for the disbelievers) (25:26). Others it read Haqqi referring to Allah, may He be glorified, as in the Ayah:

(Then they are returned to Allah, their True Protector.) (6:62) So Allah says:

(He (Allah) is the best to reward and the best for the final end.) for deeds that were done for the sake of Allah, their reward is good and their consequences are all good.

Surah: 18 Ayah: 45 & Ayah: 46

وَٱضْرِبْ لَهُم مَّثَلَ ٱلْحَيَوٰةِ ٱلدُّنْيَا كَمَآءٍ أَنزَلْنَٰهُ مِنَ ٱلسَّمَآءِ فَٱخْتَلَطَ بِهِۦ نَبَاتُ ٱلْأَرْضِ فَأَصْبَحَ هَشِيمًا تَذْرُوهُ ٱلرِّيَٰحُ ۗ وَكَانَ ٱللَّهُ عَلَىٰ كُلِّ شَىْءٍ مُّقْتَدِرًا

45. And put forward to them the example of the life of this world: it is like the water (rain) which We send down from the sky, and the vegetation of the earth mingles with it, and becomes fresh and green. But (later) it becomes dry and broken pieces, which the winds scatter. And Allâh is Able to do everything.

ٱلْمَالُ وَٱلْبَنُونَ زِينَةُ ٱلْحَيَوٰةِ ٱلدُّنْيَا ۖ وَٱلْبَٰقِيَٰتُ ٱلصَّٰلِحَٰتُ خَيْرٌ عِندَ رَبِّكَ ثَوَابًا وَخَيْرٌ أَمَلًا

46. Wealth and children are the adornment of the life of this world. But the good righteous deeds, that last, are better with your Lord for rewards and better in respect of hope.

Transliteration

45. Waidrib lahum mathala alhayati alddunya kama-in anzalnahu mina alssama-i faikhtalata bihi nabatu al-ardi faasbaha hasheeman tathroohu alrriyahu wakana Allahu AAala kulli shay-in muqtadiran 46. Almalu waalbanoona zeenatu alhayati alddunya waalbaqiyatu alssalihatu khayrun AAinda rabbika thawaban wakhayrun amalan

Tafsir Ibn Kathir

The Parable of the Worldly Life

Allah says:

(And mention) O Muhammad, to the people,

(the parable of the worldly life), its transient nature and how it will eventually cease and come to an end.

(it is like the water which We send down from the sky, and the vegetation of the earth mingles with it,) It mingles with the seeds that are in the earth, so they grow and become good, producing bright, fresh flowers, then after that, (it becomes dry and broken pieces,) withered up,

(which the winds scatter.) tossing them about right and left.

(And Allah is able to do everything) He has the power to do this and that. In the Qur'an Allah often gives parables like this of the life of this world, as He says in Surah Yunus,

(The parable of the worldly life is but that of water which We send down from the sky so by it arises the intermingled produce of the earth of which men and cattle eat. ..) (10:24) and in Surat Az-Zumar:

s(See you not that Allah sends down water from the sky, and causes it to penetrate the earth, then out from it comes crops of different colors.) (39:21) and in Surat Al-Hadid:

(Know that the life of this world is only play and amusement, pomp and mutual boasting among you, and rivalry in respect of wealth and children. (It is) like the parable of vegetation after rain, thereof the growth is pleasing to the tiller...) (57:20) and in the Sahih Hadith:

«الدُّنْيَا حُلْوَةٌ خَضِرَةٌ»

(This world is sweet and green.)

Between Wealth and Good Deeds

(Wealth and children are the adornment of the life of this world.) This is like the Ayah:

(Beautified for men is the love of things they covet; women, children, vaulted hoards of gold...) (3:14). Allah says:

(Your wealth and your children are only a trial, whereas Allah! With Him is a great reward (Paradise).) (64:15) turning towards Allah and worshipping Him is better for you than keeping busy with them, and accumulating wealth for them and going to extremes in feeling pity and compassion for them. Allah says:

(But the good righteous deeds that last, are better with your Lord for reward and better for hope.) Ibn `Abbas, Sa`id bin Jubayr and others among the Salaf said that the good righteous deeds that last are the five daily prayers. `Ata' bin Abi Rabah and Sa`id bin Jubayr narrated from Ibn `Abbas, "The good righteous deeds that last are `Subhan Allah (glory be to Allah)', `Al-Hamdu Lillah (praise be to Allah)', `La ilaha illallah (there is none worthy of worship except Allah)', and `Allahu Akbar (Allah is Most Great).'" The Commander of the faithful, `Uthman bin `Affan was questioned, "Which are the good righteous deeds that last" He replied, "They are: `La ilaha illallah, Subhan Allah, Al-Hamdu Lillah, Allahu Akbar and La hawla wa la quwwata illa billah hil-`Aliyil-`Azim (there is no strength and no power except with Allah the Exalted, the Almighty).'" This was recorded by Imam Ahmad. Imam Ahmad also recorded from a freed slave of the Messenger of Allah that he said:

> «بَخٍ بَخٍ لِخَمْسٍ مَا أَثْقَلَهُنَّ فِي الْمِيزَانِ: لَا إِلَهَ إِلَّا اللهُ وَاللهُ أَكْبَرُ، وَسُبْحَانَ اللهِ، وَالْحَمْدُ للهِ، وَالْوَلَدُ الصَّالِحُ يُتَوَفَّى فَيَحْتَسِبُهُ وَالِدُهُ وَقَالَ: بَخٍ بَخٍ لِخَمْسٍ مَنْ لَقِيَ اللهَ مُسْتَيْقِنًا بِهِنَّ دَخَلَ الْجَنَّةَ: يُؤْمِنُ بِاللهِ وَالْيَوْمِ الْآخِرِ، وَبِالْجَنَّةِ وَالنَّارِ، وَبِالْبَعْثِ بَعْدَ الْمَوْتِ، وَبِالْحِسَابِ»

(Well done! Well done for five things! (How heavy they will weigh in the balance! "La ilaha illallah, Allahu Akbar, Subhan Allah, and Al-Hamdu Lillah," and a righteous son who dies and his parents seek the reward of Allah.) And he said: (Well done! Well done for five things! Whoever meets Allah believing in them, he will enter Paradise; if he believes in Allah, the Last Day, Paradise and Hell, resurrection after death, and the Reckoning).

(the good righteous deeds that last,) `Ali bin Abi Talhah reported that Ibn `Abbas said, "This is the celebration of the remembrance of Allah, saying `La ilaha illallah, Allahu Akbar, Subhan Allah, Al-Hamdu Lillah, Tabarak Allah, La hawla wa la quwwata illa billah, Astaghfirallah, Sallallahu `ala Rasul-Allah', and fasting, prayer, Hajj, Sadaqah (charity), freeing slaves, Jihad, maintaining ties of kinship, and all other good deeds. These are the righteous good deeds that last, which will remain in Paradise for those who do them for as long as heaven and earth remain." Al-`Awfi reported from Ibn `Abbas: "They are good words." `Abdur-Rahman bin Zayd bin Aslam said, "They are all righteous deeds." This was also the view chosen by Ibn Jarir, may Allah have mercy on him.

Surah: 18 Ayah: 47, Ayah: 48 & Ayah: 49

وَيَوْمَ نُسَيِّرُ ٱلْجِبَالَ وَتَرَى ٱلْأَرْضَ بَارِزَةً وَحَشَرْنَـٰهُمْ فَلَمْ نُغَادِرْ مِنْهُمْ أَحَدًا ۝

47. And (remember) the Day We shall cause the mountains to pass away (like clouds of dust), and you will see the earth as a leveled plain, and we shall gather them all together so as to leave not one of them behind.

وَعُرِضُوا۟ عَلَىٰ رَبِّكَ صَفًّا لَّقَدْ جِئْتُمُونَا كَمَا خَلَقْنَـٰكُمْ أَوَّلَ مَرَّةٍۭ ۚ بَلْ زَعَمْتُمْ أَلَّن نَّجْعَلَ لَكُم مَّوْعِدًا ۝

48. And they will be set before your Lord in (lines as) rows, (and Allâh will say): "Now indeed, you have come to Us as We created you the first time. Nay, but you thought that We had appointed no meeting for you (with Us)."

$$\text{وَوُضِعَ ٱلْكِتَـٰبُ فَتَرَى ٱلْمُجْرِمِينَ مُشْفِقِينَ مِمَّا فِيهِ وَيَقُولُونَ يَـٰوَيْلَتَنَا مَالِ هَـٰذَا ٱلْكِتَـٰبِ لَا يُغَادِرُ صَغِيرَةً وَلَا كَبِيرَةً إِلَّآ أَحْصَىٰهَا ۚ وَوَجَدُوا۟ مَا عَمِلُوا۟ حَاضِرًا ۗ وَلَا يَظْلِمُ رَبُّكَ أَحَدًا ۝}$$

49. And the Book (one's Record) will be placed (in the right hand for a believer in the Oneness of Allâh, and in the left hand for a disbeliever in the Oneness of Allâh), and you will see the Mujrimûn (criminals, polytheists, sinners), fearful of that which is (recorded) therein. They will say: "Woe to us! What sort of Book is this that leaves neither a small thing nor a big thing, but has recorded it with numbers!" And they will find all that they did, placed before them, and your Lord treats no one with injustice.

Transliteration

47. Wayawma nusayyiru aljibala watara al-arda barizatan wahasharnahum falam nughadir minhum ahadan 48. WaAAuridoo AAala rabbika saffan laqad ji/tumoona kama khalaqnakum awwala marratin bal zaAAamtum allan najAAala lakum mawAAidan 49. WawudiAAa alkitabu fatara almujrimeena mushfiqeena mimma feehi wayaqooloona ya waylatana ma lihatha alkitabi la yughadiru sagheeratan wala kabeeratan illa ahsaha wawajadoo ma AAamiloo hadiran wala yathlimu rabbuka ahadan

Tafsir Ibn Kathir

The Major Terrors of the Hour

Allah tells us of the terrors of the Day of Resurrection, and the awesome things that will come to pass, as He says elsewhere:

(On the Day when the heaven will shake with a dreadful shaking, And the mountains pass moving away.) (52:9-10) meaning, they will move from their places and will vanish. As Allah says:

(And you will see the mountains and think them solid, but they shall pass away as the passing away of the clouds.) (27:88)

(And the mountains will be like carded wool.) (101:5)

(And they ask you about the mountains, say: "My Lord will pulverize them scattering (their dust). To leave them as a barren plain. You will not see in it crookness or curve.) (20:105-107) Allah tells us that He will cause the mountains to vanish and be levelled, and the earth will be left as a smooth plain, a level surface with nothing crooked or curved therein, no valleys or mountains. So Allah says:

(and you will see the earth as a levelled plain,) meaning clear and open, with no features that anyone may recognize and nothing for anyone to hide behind. All creatures will be visible to their Lord, and not one of them will be hidden from Him. Mujahid and Qatadah said,

Chapter 18: Al-Kahf (The Cave), Verses 001-074

(and you will see the earth as a levelled plain,) "No one will be hidden or absent." Qatadah said, "There will be no buildings and no trees."

(and we shall gather them, so that We will not leave one of them behind.) means, `We shall gather them all, the first of them and the last of them, and We shall not leave anyone behind, young or old.' As Allah says:

(Say: "(yes) verily, those of old, and those of later times. All will surely be gathered together for an appointed meeting of a known Day.) (56:49,50)

(That is a Day whereon mankind will be gathered together, and that is a Day when all will be present) (11:103).

(And they will be set before your Lord, aligned.) This may mean that all of creation will stand before Allah in one row, as Allah says:

(The Day that Ar-Ruh (Jibril) and the angels will stand aligned, they will not speak except him whom the Most Gracious (Allah) allows, and he will speak what is right) (78:38); or it may mean that they will stand in rows, as Allah says:

(And your Lord comes with the angels in rows.) (89:22)

(Now indeed, you have come to Us as We created you the first time.) This is a rebuke to those who denied the Hereafter, a reprimand before all creation. This is why Allah says to them:

(Nay, but you thought that We had appointed no meeting for you (with Us).), meaning, you did not think that this would happen to you or that it would come to pass.

(And the Book will be produced,) the Book of deeds, which contains a record of everything, major or minor, significant or insignificant, great or small.

(and you will see the criminals, fearful of that which is therein.) of their evil deeds and reprehensible actions.

(They will say, "Woe to us!") expressing words of regret for having wasted their lives.

(What sort of Book is this that leaves neither a small thing nor a large thing, but has recorded it with numbers!) it has left no sin, major or minor, and no action, no matter how small, but it has recorded it with the utmost precision and accuracy.

(And they will find all that they did, present,) everything, both good and evil, as Allah says,

(On the Day when every person will be confronted with all the good he has done) (3:30). Allah says:

(On that Day man will be informed of what he sent forward, and what he left behind.) (75:13) And Allah says:

(The Day when all the secrets will be exposed.) (86:9) meaning, everything that is hidden in people's hearts will become known. Imam Ahmad recorded from Anas that the Prophet said,

«لِكُلِّ غَادِرٍ لِوَاءٌ يَوْمَ الْقِيَامَةِ يُعْرَفُ بِهِ»

(Every traitor will have a banner on the Day of Resurrection, by which he will be known.) It was also narrated in the Two Sahihs, where one narration says,

«يُرْفَعُ لِكُلِّ غَادِرٍ لِوَاءٌ يَوْمَ الْقِيَامَةِ عِنْدَ اسْتِهِ بِقَدْرِ غَدْرَتِهِ، يُقَالُ: هَذِهِ غَدْرَةُ فُلَانِ بْنِ فُلَان»

(On the Day of Resurrection, for every traitor a banner will be erected by his backside, and it will be said, "This is the betrayer of so-and-so the son of so-and-so.")

(and your Lord treats no one with injustice.) means, He will judge between His creatures for all of their deeds, and He will not treat any of His creatures with injustice. He will overlook and forgive and have mercy, and He will punish whomever He wills by His power, wisdom and justice. He will fill Hell with the disbelievers and those who have been disobedient. Then He will rescue the disobedient, and leave the disbelievers there for eternity. He is the Judge Who never wrongs or oppresses. Allah says:

(Surely, Allah wrongs not even of the weight of a speck of dust, but if there is any good, He doubles it.) (4:40)

(And We shall set up Balances of justice on the Day of Resurrection, then none will be dealt with unjustly in anything.) Until His saying;

(to take account) (21:47) And there are many similar Ayat. Imam Ahmad recorded that `Abdullah bin Muhammad bin `Aqil heard Jabir bin `Abdullah say, "I was told about a Hadith which a man heard from the Prophet, so I bought a camel and put my saddle on it, then I traveled on it for a month until I came to Ash-Sham, where `Abdullah bin Unays was. I said to the doorkeeper, `Tell him that Jabir is at the door.' He said, `Jabir bin `Abdullah' I said, `Yes.' So he came out, still putting his garment on, and embraced me, and I embraced him, and said: `I heard a Hadith narrated by you, that you heard from the Messenger of Allah about reciprocal punishments. I was afraid that you or I would die before I could hear it.' He said, `I heard the Messenger of Allah say:

«يَحْشُرُ اللهُ عَزَّ وَجَلَّ النَّاسَ يَوْمَ الْقِيَامَةِ أَوْ قَالَ: الْعِبَادَ عُرَاةً غُرْلًا بُهْمًا»

(Allah will gather the people -- or His servants -- on the Day of Resurrection, naked, uncircumcised and Buhman.) I asked, `What is Buhman' He said,

لَيْسَ مَعَهُمْ شَيْءٌ، ثُمَّ يُنَادِيهِمْ بِصَوْتٍ يَسْمَعُهُ مَنْ بَعُدَ كَمَا يَسْمَعُهُ مَنْ قَرُبَ: أَنَا الْمَلِكُ، أَنَا الدَّيَّانُ، لَا يَنْبَغِي لِأَحَدٍ مِنْ أَهْلِ النَّارِ أَنْ يَدْخُلَ النَّارَ وَلَهُ عِنْدَ أَحَدٍ مِنْ أَهْلِ الْجَنَّةِ حَقٌّ حَتَّى أُقِصَّهُ مِنْهُ، وَلَا يَنْبَغِي لِأَحَدٍ مِنْ أَهْلِ الْجَنَّةِ أَنْ يَدْخُلَ الْجَنَّةَ وَلَهُ عِنْدَ رَجُلٍ مِنْ أَهْلِ النَّارِ حَقٌّ حَتَّى أُقِصَّهُ مِنْهُ حَتَّى اللَّطْمَةَ»

(They will have nothing with them. Then a voice will call out to them that will be heard by those far away just as easily as it will be heard by those near: "I am the Sovereign, I am the Judge. None of the people of Hell should enter Hell if he is owed something by one of the people of Paradise, until I have settled the matter, and none of the people of Paradise should enter Paradise if he is owed something by one of the people of Hell, until I settle the matter -- even if it is only the case of a slap.") We said, `How will that be, when we have come before Allah barefooted, naked, uncircumcised and having nothing with us' He said,

«بِالْحَسَنَاتِ وَالسَّيِّئَاتِ»

(By (merit for) good deeds, and (recompense) for evil deeds.) Shu`bah narrated from Al-`Awwam bin Muzahim from Abu `Uthman from `Uthman bin `Affan, may Allah be pleased with him, that the Messenger of Allah said:

«إِنَّ الْجَمَّاءَ لَتَقْتَصُّ مِنَ الْقَرْنَاءِ يَوْمَ الْقِيَامَةِ»

(The animal who lost a horn will settle the score with the one that has horns on the Day of Resurrection.) It was recorded by `Abdullah the son of Imam Ahmad, and there are corroborating narrations through other routes.

Surah: 18 Ayah: 50

وَإِذْ قُلْنَا لِلْمَلَٰٓئِكَةِ ٱسْجُدُوا۟ لِءَادَمَ فَسَجَدُوٓا۟ إِلَّآ إِبْلِيسَ كَانَ مِنَ ٱلْجِنِّ فَفَسَقَ عَنْ أَمْرِ رَبِّهِۦٓ ۗ أَفَتَتَّخِذُونَهُۥ وَذُرِّيَّتَهُۥٓ أَوْلِيَآءَ مِن دُونِى وَهُمْ لَكُمْ عَدُوٌّۢ ۚ بِئْسَ لِلظَّٰلِمِينَ بَدَلًا ۝

50. And (remember) when We said to the angels: "Prostrate yourselves to Adam." So they prostrated except Iblîs (Satan). He was one of the jinn; he disobeyed the Command of his Lord. Will you then take him (Iblîs) and his offspring as protectors and helpers rather than Me while they are enemies to you? What an evil is the exchange for the Zâlimûn (polytheists, and wrong-doers).

Transliteration

50. Wa-ith qulna lilmala-ikati osjudoo li-adama fasajadoo illa ibleesa kana mina aljinni fafasaqa AAan amri rabbihi afatattakhithoonahu wathurriyyatahu awliyaa min doonee wahum lakum AAaduwwun bi/sa lilththalimeena badalan

Tafsir Ibn Kathir

The Story of Adam and Iblis

Allah points out to the Children of Adam the enmity of Iblis towards them and their father before them, and rebukes those who follow him and go against their Creator and Master. It is He who created them from nothing and sustains and nourishes them by His kindness, yet they still took Iblis as their friend and declared their enmity towards Allah. So Allah says:

(And (remember) when We said to the angels), meaning all the angels, as was mentioned in the beginning of Surat Al-Baqarah.

(Prostrate yourselves unto Adam) a prostration of respect and honour, as Allah says:

(And (remember) when your Lord said to the angels, "I am going to create a human (Adam) from dried (sounding) clay of altered mud. So, when I have fashioned him completely and breathed into him the soul which I created for him, then fall (you) down prostrating yourselves unto him.) (15:28-29)

(So they prostrated themselves except Iblis. He was one of the Jinn;) meaning, his original nature betrayed him. He had been created from smokeless fire, whereas the angels had been created from light, as is stated in Sahih Muslim where it is reported that `A'ishah, may Allah be pleased with her, said that the Messenger of Allah said:

«خُلِقَتِ الْمَلَائِكَةُ مِنْ نُورٍ، وَخُلِقَ إِبْلِيسُ مِنْ مَارِجٍ مِنْ نَارٍ، وَخُلِقَ آدَمُ مِمَّا وُصِفَ لَكُم»

(The angels were created from light, Iblis was created from smokeless fire, and Adam was created from that which has been described to you.) When matters are crucial, every vessel leaks that which it contains and is betrayed by its true nature. Iblis used to do what the angels did and resembled them in their devotion and worship, so he was included when they were addressed, but he disobeyed and went against what he was told to do. So Allah points out here that he was one of the Jinn, i.e., he was created from fire, as He says elsewhere:

(I am better than he. You created me from fire, and You created him from clay.)(38:76) Al-Hasan Al-Basri said, "Iblis was not one of the angels, not even for a second. He was the origin of the Jinn just as Adam, upon him be peace, was the origin of mankind." This was narrated by Ibn Jarir with a Sahih chain.

(he disobeyed the command of his Lord.) meaning by stepping beyond the bounds of obedience to Allah. Fisq (disobeying) implies going out or stepping beyond. When the date emerges from its flower, the verb used in Arabic is Fasaqat; the same verb is used to describe a mouse coming out of its hole when it comes out to do damage. Then Allah says, rebuking those who follow and obey Iblis:

(Will you then take him and his offspring as protectors and helpers rather than Me) meaning, instead of Me. This is why Allah says:

(What an evil is the exchange for the wrongdoers.) This is like the Ayah in Surah Ya Sin where, after mentioning the Resurrection and its terrors, and the ultimate end of the blessed and the doomed, Allah then says:

((It will be said): "And O you the criminals! Get you apart this Day (from the believers).) until;

(Did you not then understand) (36:59-62)

Surah: 18 Ayah: 51

مَّآ أَشْهَدتُّهُمْ خَلْقَ ٱلسَّمَـٰوَٰتِ وَٱلْأَرْضِ وَلَا خَلْقَ أَنفُسِهِمْ وَمَا كُنتُ مُتَّخِذَ ٱلْمُضِلِّينَ عَضُدًا ﴿٥١﴾

51. I (Allâh) made them (Iblîs and his offspring) not to witness (nor took their help in) the creation of the heavens and the earth and not (even) their own creation, nor was I (Allâh) to take the misleaders as helpers.

Transliteration

51. Ma ashhadtuhum khalqa alssamawati waal-ardi wala khalqa anfusihim wama kuntu muttakhitha almudilleena AAadudan

Tafsir Ibn Kathir

The gods of the Idolators did not witness the Creation of anything, not even Themselves

Allah says: `These whom you take as helpers instead of Me are creatures just like you. They do not possess anything and did not witness the creation of heaven and earth, because they did not exist at that time.' Allah says, `I am the One Who independently and exclusively creates and controls all things, and I have no partner, associate or advisor in that.' As Allah says:

(Say: "Call upon those you claim besides Allah, they possess not even a speck of dust in the heavens or on the earth, nor have they any share in either, nor is there for Him any assistant among them. Intercession with Him profits not except for him whom He permits.) (34:22-23) Similarly Allah says here:

(nor did I take those who mislead as `Adudan.) Malik said: "Assistants."

Surah: 18 Ayah: 52 & Ayah: 53

وَيَوْمَ يَقُولُ نَادُواْ شُرَكَآءِىَ ٱلَّذِينَ زَعَمْتُمْ فَدَعَوْهُمْ فَلَمْ يَسْتَجِيبُواْ لَهُمْ وَجَعَلْنَا بَيْنَهُم مَّوْبِقًا ۝

52. And (remember) the Day He will say: "Call those (so-called) partners of Mine whom you pretended." Then they will cry unto them, but they will not answer them, and We shall put Maubiq (barrier) between them.

وَرَءَا ٱلْمُجْرِمُونَ ٱلنَّارَ فَظَنُّوٓاْ أَنَّهُم مُّوَاقِعُوهَا وَلَمْ يَجِدُواْ عَنْهَا مَصْرِفًا ۝

53. And the Mujrimûn (criminals, polytheists, sinners) shall see the Fire and apprehend that they have to fall therein. And they will find no way of escape from there.

Transliteration

52. Wayawma yaqoolu nadoo shuraka-iya allatheena zaAAamtum fadaAAawhum falam yastajeeboo lahum wajaAAalna baynahum mawbiqan 53. Waraa almujrimoona alnnara fathannoo annahum muwaqiAAooha walam yajidoo AAanha masrifan

Tafsir Ibn Kathir

Their Partners are not able to respond and the Criminals are brought to the Fire

Allah tells us how He will address the idolators on the Day of Resurrection before all of creation, rebuking and scolding them,

(Call those (so-called) partners of Mine whom you claimed.) meaning, in the world. Call them today to save you from the situation you are in! Allah says:

(And truly, you have come unto Us alone as We created you the first time. You have left what you were given behind your backs and We do see not with you your intercessors whom you claimed were your partners. Now all relations between you and them have been cut off, and all that you used to claim has vanished from you.) (6:94)

(Then they will cry unto them, but they will not answer them.) As Allah says:

(And it will be said (to them): "Call upon those partners of yours," then they will call upon them, but they will not answer them.) (28: 64) And the Ayah:

(And who is more astray than one who calls others besides Allah, such as will not answer him) (46:5) Until the end of the two Ayat;

(And they have taken gods besides Allah, that they may grant them honor. Nay, but they will deny their worship of them, and become opponents to them.) (19:81-82)

(and We shall put Mawbiq between them.) Ibn `Abbas, Qatadah and others said: "Destruction." The meaning is that Allah is stating that these idolators will have no way of reaching the gods they claimed in this world. He will separate them in the Hereafter and neither party will have any means of reaching the other. There will be devastation, great horrors and other terrible things in between them. `Abdullah bin `Amr understood the pronoun in the phrase "between them" to refer to the believers and the disbelievers, meaning that the people of guidance and the people of misguidance will be separated. This then is like the Ayat:

(And on the Day when the Hour will be established -- that Day shall (all men) be separated.) (30:14)

(On that Day men shall be divided.) (30:43),

((It will be said), "And O you the criminals! Get you apart this Day (from the believers).) (36:59)

(And on the Day when We shall gather them all together, then We shall say to those who joined partners, "Stop in your place! You and your partners." Then We shall separate between them...) until,

(And what they invented will vanish from them.) (10:28-30)

(And the criminals shall see the Fire and apprehend that they are to fall therein. And they will find no way of escape from it.) meaning when they see Hell with their own eyes, since it is being dragged forth by seventy thousand reins, each pulled by seventy thousand angels. When,

(the criminals shall see the Fire), they will realize that they cannot escape being thrown into it, and that will only intesify their anxiety and distress, because the anticipation and fear of punishment is in itself a real punishment.

(And they will find no way of escape from it.) means, they will have no way of fleeing, it will be inevitable.

Surah: 18 Ayah: 54

وَلَقَدْ صَرَّفْنَا فِى هَـٰذَا ٱلْقُرْءَانِ لِلنَّاسِ مِن كُلِّ مَثَلٍ وَكَانَ ٱلْإِنسَـٰنُ أَكْثَرَ شَىْءٍ جَدَلاً ۞

54. And indeed We have put forth every kind of example in this Qur'ân, for mankind. But, man is ever more quarrelsome than anything.

Transliteration

54. Walaqad sarrafna fee hatha alqur-ani lilnnasi min kulli mathalin wakana al-insanu akthara shay-in jadalan

Tafsir Ibn Kathir

Examples put forth in the Qur'an

Allah says, 'In this Qur'an, We have explained to mankind and given clear details of matters so that they will not stray from the truth or be misled from the path of guidance. Despite this explanation, man is very quarrelsome and opposes truth with falsehood,' except for those whom Allah guides to the path of salvation. Imam Ahmad recorded that `Ali bin Abi Talib said that the Messenger of Allah came to visit him and Fatimah, the daughter of Allah's Messenger at night, and said,

«أَلَا تُصَلِّيَانِ؟»

(Are you not going to pray) I said, "O Messenger of Allah, our souls are in the Hand of Allah. If He wills to wake us, He will wake us." When I said that, he went away without returning. Then I heard him as he was walking away, slapping his thigh and saying,

(But, man is ever more quarrelsome than anything.)" It was also recorded in the Two Sahihs.

Surah: 18 Ayah: 55 & Ayah: 56

وَمَا مَنَعَ ٱلنَّاسَ أَن يُؤْمِنُوٓاْ إِذْ جَآءَهُمُ ٱلْهُدَىٰ وَيَسْتَغْفِرُواْ رَبَّهُمْ إِلَّآ أَن تَأْتِيَهُمْ سُنَّةُ ٱلْأَوَّلِينَ أَوْ يَأْتِيَهُمُ ٱلْعَذَابُ قُبُلًا ۝

55. And nothing prevents men from believing, (now) when the guidance (the Qur'ân) has come to them, and from asking Forgiveness of their Lord, except that the ways of the ancients be repeated with them (i.e. their destruction decreed by Allâh), or the torment be brought to them face to face?

وَمَا نُرْسِلُ ٱلْمُرْسَلِينَ إِلَّا مُبَشِّرِينَ وَمُنذِرِينَ ۚ وَيُجَٰدِلُ ٱلَّذِينَ كَفَرُواْ بِٱلْبَٰطِلِ لِيُدْحِضُواْ بِهِ ٱلْحَقَّ ۖ وَٱتَّخَذُوٓاْ ءَايَٰتِى وَمَآ أُنذِرُواْ هُزُوًا ۝

56. And We send not the Messengers except as givers of glad tidings and warners. But those who disbelieve, dispute with false argument, in order to refute the truth thereby. And they treat My Ayât (proofs, evidences, verses, lessons, signs, revelations, etc.), and that with which they are warned, as a jest and mockery!

Transliteration

55. Wama manaAAa alnnasa an yu/minoo ith jaahumu alhuda wayastaghfiroo rabbahum illa an ta/tiyahum sunnatu al-awwaleena aw ya/tiyahum alAAathabu qubulan 56. Wama nursilu almursaleena illa mubashshireena wamunthireena wayujadilu allatheena kafaroo bialbatili liyudhidoo bihi alhaqqa waittakhathoo ayatee wama onthiroo huzuwan

Tafsir Ibn Kathir

The Rebellion of the Disbelievers

Allah tells us about the rebellion of the disbelievers in ancient times and in more recent times, and how they rejected the obvious truth even when they witnessed clear signs and proofs. Nothing stopped them from following the truth except their demand to witness with their own eyes the punishment which they were being warned about. As some of them said to their Prophet:

(So cause a piece of the heaven to fall on us, if you are of the truthful!) (26:187), Others said:

(Bring Allah's torment upon us if you are one of the truthful.) (29:29) The Quraysh said:

(O Allah! If this is indeed the truth from You, then rain down stones on us from the sky or bring upon us a painful torment.) (8:32)

(And they say: "O you to whom the Reminder has been sent down! Verily, you are a mad man! Why do you not bring angels to us if you are of the truthful") (15:6-7). There are other Ayat refering to the same thing. Then Allah says:

(except that the ways of the ancients be repeated with them,) meaning, their overwhelming punishment, destroying every last one of them.

(or the torment be brought to them face to face.) they see it with their own eyes, being directly confronted with it. Then Allah says:

(And We send not the Messengers except as bearers of good news and warners.) before the punishment they give good news to those who believe in them and follow them, and warnings to those who reject them and oppose them. Then Allah tells us about the disbelievers who argue:

(with falsehood, in order to refute the truth thereby.) they try to weaken the truth that the Messengers brought, but they cannot achieve that.

(And they take My Ayat and that which they are warned for jest!) they take the proof, evidence and miracles sent with the Messengers to warn them, and make them fear the punishment;

(as a jest and mockery) and they make fun of them, which is the worst type of disbelief.

Surah: 18 Ayah: 57, Ayah: 58 & Ayah: 59

وَمَنْ أَظْلَمُ مِمَّن ذُكِّرَ بِـَٔايَـٰتِ رَبِّهِۦ فَأَعْرَضَ عَنْهَا وَنَسِىَ مَا قَدَّمَتْ يَدَاهُ إِنَّا جَعَلْنَا عَلَىٰ قُلُوبِهِمْ أَكِنَّةً أَن يَفْقَهُوهُ وَفِىٓ ءَاذَانِهِمْ وَقْرًا وَإِن تَدْعُهُمْ إِلَى ٱلْهُدَىٰ فَلَن يَهْتَدُوٓا۟ إِذًا أَبَدًا ۝

57. And who does more wrong than he who is reminded of the Ayât (proofs, evidences, verses, lessons, signs, revelations, etc.) of his Lord, but turns away from them forgetting what (deeds) his hands have sent forth. Truly, We have set veils over their hearts lest they should understand this (the Qur'ân), and in their ears, deafness. And if you (O Muhammad (peace be upon him)) call them to guidance, even then they will never be guided.

وَرَبُّكَ ٱلْغَفُورُ ذُو ٱلرَّحْمَةِ لَوْ يُؤَاخِذُهُم بِمَا كَسَبُوا۟ لَعَجَّلَ لَهُمُ ٱلْعَذَابَ بَل لَّهُم مَّوْعِدٌ لَّن يَجِدُوا۟ مِن دُونِهِۦ مَوْئِلًا ۝

58. And your Lord is Most Forgiving, Owner of Mercy. Were He to call them to account for what they have earned, then surely, He would have hastened their punishment. But they have their appointed time, beyond which they will find no escape.

وَتِلْكَ ٱلْقُرَىٰٓ أَهْلَكْنَـٰهُمْ لَمَّا ظَلَمُوا۟ وَجَعَلْنَا لِمَهْلِكِهِم مَّوْعِدًا ۝

59. And these towns (population, - 'Ad, Thamûd) We destroyed when they did wrong. And We appointed a fixed time for their destruction.

Transliteration

57. Waman athlamu mimman thukkira bi-ayati rabbihi faaAArada AAanha wanasiya ma qaddamat yadahu inna jaAAalna AAala quloobihim akinnatan an yafqahoohu wafee athanihim waqran wa-in tadAAuhum ila alhuda falan yahtadoo ithan abadan
58. Warabbuka alghafooru thoo alrrahmati law yu-akhithuhum bima kasaboo laAAajjala lahumu alAAathaba bal lahum mawAAidun lan yajidoo min doonihi maw-ilan
59. Watilka alqura ahlaknahum lamma thalamoo wajaAAalna limahlikihim mawAAidan

Tafsir Ibn Kathir

The Worst People are Those Who turn away after being reminded

Allah says, `Who among My creatures does more wrong than one who is reminded of the signs of Allah then turns away from them,' i.e., ignores them and does not listen or pay attention to them.

(forgetting what his hands have sent forth.) means, bad deeds and evil actions.

(Truly, We have set over their hearts) means, the hearts of these people,

(Akinnah) means, coverings.

(lest they should understand this,) means, so that they will not understand this Qur'an and its clear Message

(and in their ears, deafness.) means that they will be deaf in an abstract way, to guidance.

(And if you call them to guidance, even then they will never be guided.)

(And your Lord is Most Forgiving, Owner of mercy.) means, `your Lord, O Muhammad, is forgiving and has great mercy.'

(Were He to call them to account for what they have earned, then surely, He would have hastened their punishment.) This is like the Ayah:

(And if Allah were to punish men for that which they earned, He would not leave a moving creature on the surface of the earth.) (35:45)

(But verily, your Lord is full of forgiveness for mankind in spite of their wrongdoing. And verily, your Lord is (also) severe in punishment) (13:6). And there are many Ayat which say the same thing. Then Allah tells us that He is patient, He conceals faults and forgives sins. He may guide some of them from wrongdoing to true guidance, and whoever continues in his evil ways, then there will come to him a Day when infants will turn grey and every pregnant female will shed her load. He says:

(But they have their appointed time, beyond which they will find no escape.) meaning, they will find no way out.

(And these towns, We destroyed them when they did wrong.) This refers to earlier nations in times past; `We destroyed them because of their stubborn disbelief.'

(And We appointed a fixed time for their destruction.) `We appointed for them a set time limit, not to be increased or decreased. The same applies to you, O ido- lators, so beware or what happened to them will happen to you too, for you have rejected the noblest Messenger and greatest Prophet, and you are not dearer to Us than them, so fear My punishment and wrath.'

Surah: 18 Ayah: 60, Ayah: 61, Ayah: 62, Ayah: 63, Ayah: 64 & Ayah: 65

وَإِذْ قَالَ مُوسَىٰ لِفَتَىٰهُ لَآ أَبْرَحُ حَتَّىٰٓ أَبْلُغَ مَجْمَعَ ٱلْبَحْرَيْنِ أَوْ أَمْضِىَ حُقُبًا

60. And (remember) when Mûsa (Moses) said to his boy-servant: "I will not give up (travelling) until I reach the junction of the two seas or (until) I spend years and years in travelling."

فَلَمَّا بَلَغَا مَجْمَعَ بَيْنِهِمَا نَسِيَا حُوتَهُمَا فَٱتَّخَذَ سَبِيلَهُۥ فِى ٱلْبَحْرِ سَرَبًا ﴿٦١﴾

61. But when they reached the junction of the two seas, they forgot their fish, and it took its way through the sea as in a tunnel.

فَلَمَّا جَاوَزَا قَالَ لِفَتَىٰهُ ءَاتِنَا غَدَآءَنَا لَقَدْ لَقِينَا مِن سَفَرِنَا هَـٰذَا نَصَبًا ﴿٦٢﴾

62. So when they had passed further on (beyond that fixed place), Mûsa (Moses) said to his boy-servant: "Bring us our morning meal; truly, we have suffered much fatigue in this, our journey."

قَالَ أَرَءَيْتَ إِذْ أَوَيْنَآ إِلَى ٱلصَّخْرَةِ فَإِنِّى نَسِيتُ ٱلْحُوتَ وَمَآ أَنسَىٰنِيهُ إِلَّا ٱلشَّيْطَـٰنُ أَنْ أَذْكُرَهُۥ وَٱتَّخَذَ سَبِيلَهُۥ فِى ٱلْبَحْرِ عَجَبًا ﴿٦٣﴾

63. He said: "Do you remember when we betook ourselves to the rock? I indeed forgot the fish; none but Shaitân (Satan) made me forget to remember it. It took its course into the sea in a strange (way)!"

قَالَ ذَٰلِكَ مَا كُنَّا نَبْغِ فَٱرْتَدَّا عَلَىٰٓ ءَاثَارِهِمَا قَصَصًا ﴿٦٤﴾

64. (Mûsa (Moses)) said: "That is what we have been seeking." So they went back retracing their footsteps.

فَوَجَدَا عَبْدًا مِّنْ عِبَادِنَآ ءَاتَيْنَـٰهُ رَحْمَةً مِّنْ عِندِنَا وَعَلَّمْنَـٰهُ مِن لَّدُنَّا عِلْمًا ﴿٦٥﴾

65. Then they found one of Our slaves, on whom We had bestowed mercy from Us, and whom We had taught knowledge from Us.

Transliteration

60. Wa-ith qala moosa lifatahu la abrahu hatta ablugha majmaAAa albahrayni aw amdiya huquban   61. Falamma balagha majmaAAa baynihima nasiya hootahuma faittakhatha sabeelahu fee albahri saraban   62. Falamma jawaza qala lifatahu atina ghadaana laqad laqeena min safarina hatha nasaban   63. Qala araayta ith awayna ila alssakhrati fa-innee naseetu alhoota wama ansaneehu illa alshshaytanu an athkurahu waittakhatha sabeelahu fee albahri AAajaban   64. Qala thalika ma kunna nabghi fairtadda AAala atharihima qasasan   65. Fawajada AAabdan min AAibadina ataynahu rahmatan min AAindina waAAallamnahu min ladunna AAilman

Tafsir Ibn Kathir

The Story of Musa and Al-Khidr

The reason for Musa's conversation with the boy-servant, Yusha` bin Nun, was that he had been told about one of the servants of Allah at the junction of the two seas, who had knowledge which Musa had not been granted, so he wanted to travel to meet him. So he said to that boy-servant of his:

Chapter 18: Al-Kahf (The Cave), Verses 001-074

(I will not give up) meaning, I will keep on traveling,

(until I reach the junction of the two seas) meaning, the place where the two seas met.

(or a Huqub passes.) meaning, even if I have to travel for a very long time. Ibn Jarir (may Allah have mercy on him) said, "Some of the scholars of the Arabic language said that Huqub means a year in the dialect of (the tribe of) Qays," then he narrated that `Abdullah bin `Amr said, "Huqub means eighty years." Mujahid said, "Seventy years." `Ali bin Abi Talhah reported that Ibn `Abbas said that it means a lifetime. Qatadah and Ibn Zayd said likewise.

(But when they reached the junction of the two seas, they forgot their fish,) He had been commanded to carry a salted fish with him, and it had been said to him, when you lose the fish, that will be a sign that you have reached the right place. So they set out and traveled until they reached the junction of the two seas, where there was a spring called `Ayn Al-Hayat (the Spring of Life). They went to sleep there, and the fish felt the drops of that water, so it came back to life. It was in a vessel with Yusha`, upon him be peace, and it jumped out of the vessel towards the sea. Yusha` woke up and the fish fell into the water and started to swim through the water, leaving a track or channel behind it. Allah said:

(and it took its way through the sea as in a tunnel.) meaning, like going through a tunnel on land. Ibn Jurayj said, "Ibn `Abbas said, `It left a trace as if it were a rock.'"

(So when they had passed further on,) means, past the place where they had forgotten the fish. Forgetfulness is attributed to them both even though it was actually Yusha` who forgot. This is like the Ayah:

(Out of them both come out pearl and coral.) (55:22), although they come from the salt water, according to one of the two opinions. When they had passed one stage beyond the place where they had forgotten the fish,

((Musa) said to his boy-servant: "Bring us our morning meal; truly, we have suffered in this, our journey) meaning, their journey beyond the place where they should have stopped.

(Nasaban) means, exhaustion.

(He said: "Do you remember when we betook ourselves to the rock I indeed forgot the fish; none but Shaytan made me forget to remember it...") Then he said,

(It took its course), meaning its path,

("...into the sea in a strange (way)!" (Musa) said: "That is what we have been seeking.") meaning, this is what we have been looking for.

(So they went back)

(their footsteps.)

(Then they found one of Our servants, on whom We had bestowed mercy from Us, and whom We had taught knowledge from Us.) This was Al-Khidr, peace be upon him, as is indicated by the authentic Hadiths narrated from the Messenger of Allah . Al-Bukhari recorded that Sa`id bin Jubayr said, "I said to Ibn `Abbas: `Nawf Al-Bikali claims that Musa, the companion of Al-Khidr was not the Musa of the Children of Israel.' Ibn `Abbas said, `The enemy of Allah has told a lie.' Ubayy bin Ka`b narrated that he heard the Messenger of Allah say,

(Musa got up to deliver a speech before the Children of Israel and he was asked, "Who is the most learned person among the people" Musa replied, "I am." Allah rebuked him because he did not refer the knowledge to Allah. So Allah revealed to him: "At the junction of the two seas there is a servant of Ours who is more learned than you." Musa asked, "O my Lord, how can I meet him" Allah said, "Take a fish and put it in a vessel and then set out, and where you lose the fish, you will find him." So Musa took a fish, put it in a vessel and set out, along with his boy-servant Yusha` bin Nun, peace be upon him, till they reached a rock (on which) they both lay down their heads and slept. The fish moved vigorously in the vessel and got out of it and fell into the sea and there it took its way through the sea (straight) as in a tunnel. Allah stopped the flow of water on both sides of the way created by the fish, and so that way was like a tunnel. When Musa got up, his companion forgot to tell him about the fish, and so they carried on their journey during the rest of the day and the whole night. The next morning Musa said to his boy-servant, ("Bring us our morning meal; truly, we have suffered much fatigue in this, our journey.")

Musa did not get tired till he had passed the place that Allah had ordered him to look for. His boy-servant then said to him, ("Do you remember when we betook ourselves to the rock I indeed forgot the fish; none but Shaytan made me forget to remember it. It took its course into the sea in a strange way.") There was a tunnel for the fish and Musa and his boy-servant were amazed. Musa said, ("That is what we have been seeking." So they went back retracing their footsteps.") So they went back retracing their steps until they reached the rock. There they found a man covered with a garment. Musa greeted him. Al-Khidr said, "Is there such a greeting in your land" Musa said, "I am Musa." He said, "Are you the Musa of the Children of Israel" Musa said, "Yes," and added, "I have come to you so that you may teach me something of that knowledge which you have been taught." Al-Khidr said, ("You will not be able to have patience with me.) O Musa! I have some of Allah's knowledge which He has bestowed upon me but you do not know it; and you too, have some of Allah's knowledge which He has bestowed upon you, but I do not know it."

Musa said, ("If Allah wills, you will find me patient, and I will not disobey you in aught.") Al-Khidr said to him, ("Then, if you follow me, ask me not about anything till I myself mention it to you.") So they set out walking along the shore, until a boat passed by and they asked the crew to let them go on board. The crew recognized Al-Khidr and allowed them to go on board free of charge. When they went on board, suddenly Musa saw that Al-Khidr had pulled out one of the planks of the ship with an adz. Musa said to him, "These people gave us a free ride, yet you have broken their boat so that its people will drown! Verily, you have done a terrible thing! ("Al-Khidr said, "Did I not tell you, that you would not be able to have patience with me") (Musa

Chapter 18: Al-Kahf (The Cave), Verses 001-074

said, "Call me not to account for what I forgot and be not hard upon me for my affair (with you). ")) The Messenger of Allah said,

(In the first instance, Musa asked Al-Khidr because he had forgotten his promise. Then a bird came and sat on the edge of the boat, dipping its beak once or twice in the sea. Al-Khidr said to Musa, "My knowledge and your knowledge, in comparison to Allah's knowledge, is like what this bird has taken out of the sea." Then they both disembarked from the boat, and while they were walking on the shore, Al-Khidr saw a boy playing with other boys. Al-Khidr took hold of the boy's head and pulled it off with his hands, killing him. Musa said to him, ("Have you killed an innocent person who had killed none! Verily, you have committed a thing Nukr!" He said, "Did I not tell you that you would not be able to have patience with me")

(The narrator) said, "The second blame was stronger than the first one". (Musa said, "If I ask you anything after this, keep me not in your company; you have received an excuse from me." Then they both proceeded until they came to the people of a town. They asked them for food but they refused to entertain them. (Then) they found there a wall on the point of falling down.) (Al-Khidr) set it up straight with his own hands. Musa said, "We came to these people, but they neither fed us nor received us as guests. (If you had wished, surely, you could have taken wages for it!" (Al-Khidr) said: "This is the parting between you and I. I will tell you the interpretation of (those) things over which you were unable to be patient.") The Messenger of Allah said:

》وَدِدْنَا أَنَّ مُوسَى كَانَ صَبَرَ حَتَّى يَقُصَّ اللهُ عَلَيْنَا مِنْ خَبَرِهِمَا《

(We wish that Musa was patient so that Allah would have told us more about both of them.) Sa`id bin Jubayr said: "Ibn `Abbas used to recite (Ayah no. 79) (There was a king before them who seized every good-conditioned ship by force) and (Ayah no 80) (As for the boy, he was a disbeliever and his parents were believers.) Then (in another narration) Al-Bukhari recorded a similar account which says:

(...then Musa set out and with him was his boy-servant Yusha` bin Nun, and they had the fish with them. When they reached the rock, they camped there, and Musa lay down his head and slept. At the base of the rock there was a spring called Al-Hayat; its water never touched a thing but it brought it to life. Some of its water touched the fish, so it began to move and jumped out of the vessel and into the sea. When he woke up, Musa said to his boy-servant: (Bring us our morning meal.)) Then he quoted the rest of the Hadith. Then a bird came and perched on the edge of the ship, and dipped its beak in the sea, and Al-Khidr said to Musa, "My knowledge and your knowledge and the knowledge of all of creation, in comparison to the knowledge of Allah, is like what this bird has taken from the sea." Then he mentioned the rest of the report.

Surah: 18 Ayah: 66, Ayah: 67, Ayah: 68, Ayah: 69 & Ayah: 70

قَالَ لَهُ مُوسَىٰ هَلْ أَتَّبِعُكَ عَلَىٰ أَن تُعَلِّمَنِ مِمَّا عُلِّمْتَ رُشْدًا ۝

66. Mûsa (Moses) said to him (Khidr): "May I follow you so that you teach me something of that knowledge (guidance and true path) which you have been taught (by Allâh)?"

$$قَالَ إِنَّكَ لَن تَسْتَطِيعَ مَعِىَ صَبْرًا ﴿٦٧﴾$$

67. He (Khidr) said: "Verily you will not be able to have patience with me!

$$وَكَيْفَ تَصْبِرُ عَلَىٰ مَا لَمْ تُحِطْ بِهِۦ خُبْرًا ﴿٦٨﴾$$

68. "And how can you have patience about a thing which you know not?"

$$قَالَ سَتَجِدُنِىٓ إِن شَآءَ ٱللَّهُ صَابِرًا وَلَآ أَعْصِى لَكَ أَمْرًا ﴿٦٩﴾$$

69. Mûsa (Moses) said: "If Allâh wills, you will find me patient, and I will not disobey you in aught."

$$قَالَ فَإِنِ ٱتَّبَعْتَنِى فَلَا تَسْـَٔلْنِى عَن شَىْءٍ حَتَّىٰٓ أُحْدِثَ لَكَ مِنْهُ ذِكْرًا ﴿٧٠﴾$$

70. He (Khidr) said: "Then, if you follow me, ask me not about anything till I myself mention it to you."

Transliteration

66. Qala lahu moosa hal attabiAAuka AAala an tuAAallimani mimma AAullimta rushdan 67. Qala innaka lan tastateeAAa maAAiya sabran 68. Wakayfa tasbiru AAala ma lam tuhit bihi khubran 69. Qala satajidunee in shaa Allahu sabiran wala aAAsee laka amran 70. Qala fa-ini ittabaAAtanee fala tas-alnee AAan shay-in hatta ohditha laka minhu thikran

Tafsir Ibn Kathir

Musa meeting with Al-Khidr and accompanying Him

Allah tells us what Musa said to that learned man, who was Al-Khidr. He was one to whom Allah had given knowledge that He had not given to Musa, just as He had given Musa knowledge that He had not given to Al-Khidr.

(Musa said to him: "May I follow you...") This is a question phrased in gentle terms, with no sense of force or coercion. This is the manner in which the seeker of knowledge should address the scholar.

(I follow you) means, I accompany you and spend time with you.

(so that you teach me something of that knowledge which you have been taught) meaning, teach me something from that which Allah has taught you so that I may be guided by it and learn something beneficial and do righteous deeds. At this point,

(He said) meaning, Al-Khidr said to Musa,

(Verily, you will not be able to have patience with me!) meaning, `You will not be able to accompany with me when you see me doing things that go against your law, because I have knowledge from Allah that He has not taught you, and you have knowledge from Allah that He has not taught me. Each of us has responsibilities before Allah that the other does not share, and you will not be able to stay with me,'

(And how can you have patience about a thing which you know not) `For I know that you will denounce me justifiably, but I have knowledge of Allah's wisdom and the hidden interests which I can see but you cannot.'

(He said) meaning, Musa said:

(If Allah wills, you will find me patient,) with whatever I see of your affairs,

(and I will not disobey you in aught.) means, `I will not go against you in anything.' At that point, Al-Khidr, upon him be peace, set a condition:

(Then, if you follow me, ask me not about anything) do not initiate any discussion of the matter,

(till I myself mention of it to you.) meaning, `until I initiate the discussion, before you ask me about it.'

Surah: 18 Ayah: 71, Ayah: 72 & Ayah: 73

فَٱنطَلَقَا حَتَّىٰ إِذَا رَكِبَا فِى ٱلسَّفِينَةِ خَرَقَهَا ۖ قَالَ أَخَرَقْتَهَا لِتُغْرِقَ أَهْلَهَا لَقَدْ جِئْتَ شَيْئًا إِمْرًا ۝

71. So they both proceeded, till, when they embarked the ship, he (Khidr) scuttled it. Mûsa (Moses) said: "Have you scuttled it in order to drown its people? Verily, you have committed a thing "Imr" (a Munkar - evil, bad, dreadful thing)."

قَالَ أَلَمْ أَقُلْ إِنَّكَ لَن تَسْتَطِيعَ مَعِىَ صَبْرًا ۝

72. He (Khidr) said: "Did I not tell you, that you would not be able to have patience with me?"

قَالَ لَا تُؤَاخِذْنِى بِمَا نَسِيتُ وَلَا تُرْهِقْنِى مِنْ أَمْرِى عُسْرًا ۝

73. (Mûsa (Moses)) said: "Call me not to account for what I forgot, and be not hard upon me for my affair (with you)."

Transliteration

71. Faintalaqa hatta itha rakiba fee alssafeenati kharaqaha qala akharaqtaha litughriqa ahlaha laqad ji/ta shay-an imran 72. Qala alam aqul innaka lan tastateeAAa maAAiya sabran 73. Qala la tu-akhithnee bima naseetu wala turhiqnee min amree AAusran

Tafsir Ibn Kathir

Damaging the Boat

Allah tells us that Musa and his companion Al-Khidr set out having come to an agreement and reached an understanding. Al-Khidr had made the condition that Musa should not ask him about anything he found distasteful until he himself initiated the discussion and offered an explanation. So they went on board the ship, as described in the Hadith quoted above -- the crew recognized Al-Khidr and let them ride on board free of charge, as an honor to Al-Khidr. When the boat took them out to sea and they were far from the shore, Al-Khidr got up and damaged the boat, pulling out one of its planks and then patching it up again. Musa, peace be upon him, could not restrain himself from denouncing him, so he said:

(Have you damaged it wherein its people will drown) The grammatical structure of the sentence in Arabic implies that this was the consequence, not the purpose, of his action.

(Verily, you have committed a thing Imr.) About `Imr', Mujahid said: "An evil thing." Qatadah said, "An astounding thing." At this point, reminding him of the previously-agreed condition, Al-Khidr said:

(Did I not tell you, that you would not be able to have patience with me) meaning, `this thing that I did deliberately is one of the things I told you not to denounce me for, because you do not know the full story, and there is a reason and purpose for it that you do not know about.'

(He said), meaning, Musa said:

(Call me not to account for what I forgot, and be not hard upon me for my affair (with you).) meaning, `do not be harsh with me.' Hence it says in the Hadith quoted above from the Messenger of Allah :

《كَانَتِ الْأُولَى مِنْ مُوسَى نِسْيَانًا》

(In the first instance, Musa asked Al-Khidr because he had forgotten his promise.)

Surah: 18 Ayah: 74 (end of Part 15), Ayah: 75 & Ayah: 76 (beginning of Part 16; included here for completing the tafsir that follows)

فَانطَلَقَا حَتَّىٰ إِذَا لَقِيَا غُلَـٰمًا فَقَتَلَهُۥ قَالَ أَقَتَلْتَ نَفْسًا زَكِيَّةًۢ بِغَيْرِ نَفْسٍ لَّقَدْ جِئْتَ شَيْـًٔا نُّكْرًا ﴿٧٤﴾

74. Then they both proceeded, till they met a boy, he (Khidr) killed him. Mûsa (Moses) said: "Have you killed an innocent person who had killed none? Verily,

you have committed a thing "Nukr" (a great Munkar - prohibited, evil, dreadful thing)!"

$$ \text{قَالَ أَلَمْ أَقُل لَّكَ إِنَّكَ لَن تَسْتَطِيعَ مَعِيَ صَبْرًا} $$

75. (Khidr) said: "Did I not tell you that you can have no patience with me?"

$$ \text{قَالَ إِن سَأَلْتُكَ عَن شَيْءٍ بَعْدَهَا فَلَا تُصَاحِبْنِي قَدْ بَلَغْتَ مِن لَّدُنِّي عُذْرًا} $$

76. (Mûsa (Moses)) said: "If I ask you anything after this, keep me not in your company, you have received an excuse from me."

Transliteration

74. Faintalaqa hatta itha laqiya ghulaman faqatalahu qala aqatalta nafsan zakiyyatan bighayri nafsin laqad ji/ta shay-an nukran 75. Qala alam aqul laka innaka lan tastateeAAa maAAiya sabran 76. Qala in saaltuka AAan shay-in baAAdaha fala tusahibnee qad balaghta min ladunnee AAuthran

Tafsir Ibn Kathir

The Story of killing the Boy

(Then they both proceeded,) means, after the first incident,

(till they met a boy, and he (Khidr) killed him.) It has been stated previously that this boy was playing with other boys in one of the towns, and that Al-Khidr deliberately singled him out. He was the finest and most handsome of them all, and Al-Khidr killed him. When Musa, peace be upon him, saw that he denounced him even more fervently than in the first case, and said hastily:

(Have you killed an innocent person) meaning, a young person who had not yet committed any sin or done anything wrong, yet you killed him

(without Nafs) with no reason for killing him.

(Verily, you have committed a thing Nukr!) meaning, something that is clearly evil.

(He said: "Did I not tell you that you can have no patience with me") Once again, Al-Khidr reiterates the condition set in the first place, so Musa says to him:

(If I ask you anything after this,) meaning, `if I object to anything else you do after this,'

(keep me not in your company, you have received an excuse from me.) `you have accepted my apology twice.' Ibn Jarir narrated from Ibn `Abbas that Ubayy bin Ka`b said: "Whenever the Prophet mentioned anyone, he would pray for himself first. One day he said:

«رَحْمَةُ اللهِ عَلَيْنَا وَعَلَى مُوسَى لَوْ لَبِثَ مَعَ صَاحِبِهِ لَأَبْصَرَ الْعَجَبَ، وَلَكِنَّهُ قَالَ:

(إِن سَأَلْتُكَ عَن شَيْءٍ بَعْدَهَا فَلاَ تُصَاحِبْنِي قَدْ بَلَغْتَ مِن لَّدُنِّي عُذْراً)»

(May the mercy of Allah be upon us and upon Musa. If he had stayed with his companion he would have seen wonders, but he said, (`If I ask you anything after this, keep me not in your company, you have received an excuse from me.'))"

www.ingramcontent.com/pod-product-compliance
Lightning Source LLC
Chambersburg PA
CBHW081108080526
44587CB00021B/3503